Seven Households

THE ARLEY ARCHIVE SERIES

The Arley Archive Series is designed to illustrate the development of the north-west of England through a detailed examination of the lives of the people living there. The core of the study is the Arley Estate in north Cheshire, a major landowner since 1200, where some unusually detailed records have survived. The first book described the residents and landowners of four townships on this estate in the mid-eighteenth century. The second volume, based on national as well as local archives, focused on north-western agriculture in the seventeenth and eighteenth centuries. Since these two volumes were written, the author has extended his research into the extensive archives of the Leicesters whose Tabley estate adjoined Arley. Two of the seven households described in this third volume are based on Arley's archives and two on those of Tabley. The other three are derived from Lancashire sources.

The fourth and final volume, *Capital and Innovation*, will be published in 2003. This will describe the lives of a large number of people who lived in the area bounded by Warrington, Knutsford, Northwich and Frodsham between 1500 and 1774. From this a picture will emerge of the development of the whole society. Using this portrait as an example of society in this region, reasons are suggested as to why the great innovations that brought about the Indu   urred in north-west England and not anywhere else in the w

D1341231

Four Cheshire Townships in the 18th Century – Arley, Appleton, Stockton Heath and Great Budworth, Charles F. Foster, 1st ed., April 1992, Arley Hall Archive Series, No.1, 88 pp., 7 maps, 5 b/w illus., 25 x 17 cm., paperback ISBN 0 9518382 0 2. This is a unique snapshot of rural life in the eighteenth century. It details the lives of the residents of 8,600 acres in the four townships – from Sir Peter Warburton of Arley Hall to Jonathan Berry, a sheep shearer. Extraordinary details of these people's incomes and occupations have survived in rare tax returns, maps, rentals and deeds in the Arley Hall archives.

'An excellent book that deserves widespread attention.' *Archives*
'Contains much fascinating detail.' *Agricultural History Review*
'This is a lovely book to look at as well as to read.' *Open University*

Cheshire Cheese and Farming in the North West in the 17th & 18th centuries, Charles F. Foster 1st ed., May 1998, Arley Hall Archive Series, No. 2, 128 pp., 4 maps, 28 b/w illus., 25 x 17 cm., paperback ISBN 0 9518382 1 0. In 1650 the first ship loaded with Cheshire cheese sailed from Chester to London. So popular did it become that within a few years several pubs in London were called *The Cheshire Cheese*. This trade led to important changes in the shape of rural life in the North-West. In the course of charting these developments Charles Foster provides fascinating details about daily life on the farms, the people who worked the land and the men who sailed the ships between London and north-western ports.

'Achieves a level of precision in understanding the operations of both the estate and its tenantry which is rare indeed.' *Economic History Review*
'As interesting and informative as the previous one.' *Agricultural History Review*
'A picture of a changing rural economy at a local level which can hardly be bettered.' *Cheshire History*

These books can be bought direct from the Arley Hall Press, Northwich, CW9 6NA. Prices including postage and packing:

	UK	Surface mail Rest of world
Vol. 1. *Four Cheshire Townships*	£6.95	£7.70
Vol. 2. *Cheshire Cheese and Farming*	£8.95	£10.00
Vol. 3. *Seven Households*, paperback	£11.95	£16.30
hardback	£19.95	£25.00

Please send orders with a cheque or credit/debit card details to Arley Hall Press at the above address or email arleyhallpress@btopenworld.com

Fax +44(0) 1565 777 465
Tel +44(0) 1565 777 231

CHARLES F. FOSTER

Seven Households

Life in Cheshire and Lancashire
1582–1774

Illustrations digitally realized
from the originals by
PAUL ATKINS

ARLEY HALL PRESS

© 2002 Charles F. Foster

First published 2002 by the Arley Hall Press, Northwich, Cheshire, CW9 6NA
(Tel: 01565 777 231 Fax 01565 777 465 email arleyhallpress@btopenworld.com)

ISBN 0 9518382 2 9 (paperback)
      0 9518382 3 7 (hardback)

Typeset in Monotype Ehrhardt by Koinonia, Bury
Printed and bound by Amadeus Press, Cleckheaton

Contents

List of figures and maps

FIGURES IN COLOUR

FIGURES IN BLACK AND WHITE

MAPS

Foreword and acknowledgements

Seven Households is the third volume in the Arley Archive Series following *Four Cheshire Townships in the 18th Century* (1992) and *Cheshire Cheese and Farming in the North West in the 17th & 18th Centuries* (1998). I intend to publish the fourth and last volume in 2003. All four volumes are parts of one large study based mainly on the archives of two old estates in north Cheshire – Arley owned by the Warburtons and Tabley, home of the Leicesters. Most of the lands of these two estates were in an area bounded by Warrington, Knutsford, Northwich and Frodsham, so much of the study describes events inside this circle. But I have not hesitated to look at other archives and secondary sources that would enable me to understand and explain what happened in the main area. Thus the second volume on Cheshire Cheese includes material from the Port Books in the Public Record Office and other ledgers in the Corporation of London Record Office. In this third volume the material on which the descriptions of four of the households is based comes from the archives of the two estates. While working on these I discovered the extraordinary quality and range of information available in household accounts. Not only do they tell us things that hardly ever appear in other documentary sources but they are really reliable. No one can believe that a man would repeatedly enter in his private ledger an incorrect description and price of what he had just bought or that he would agree to pay an incorrect invoice, whereas other sources, like legal or political papers, may involve some element of 'making a case' which makes such evidence only partly true. So I looked about for other household accounts written in the North-West to widen my understanding and found the three from Lancashire that are presented here. The Smithills accounts extend the period covered backwards by at least sixty years, while the Fell and Lathom accounts allow me to increase the range of the social groups.

Most of us know a good deal about how people lived after 1770 from the novels and pictures of the period which exist in great profusion. About life before that we are much less knowledgeable and often depend on the plays of Shakespeare, Wycherley and Congreve and one or two diarists such as Pepys and Evelyn. The seven descriptions of households in this book may help to fill this void. They tell us about the food people ate and the clothes they wore; what they made themselves and what they were able to buy. They tell us about rich families with great estates, poor ones with only a few acres and about one family of moderate wealth. It is not just a series of single pictures of these families because life in the 1580s was different in many ways to life in the 1670s or the 1750s.

The detailed portraits in this third volume are designed to provide a clearer idea of the style of life of the three main social groups who possessed capital – the major gentry, the freeholders and the three-life leaseholders – at the various epochs between 1500 and the 1770s. They are not just interesting in themselves, they also have a purpose in the overall design of my study. The fourth and last volume in the series, *Capital and Innovation,* describes the development of society in my area between 1500 and 1770. Changes in the distribution of wealth, in the way the land was owned and the occupations of the people are examined. For example freeholders multiplied and became much more independent of the major gentry. From these descriptions I aim to draw out some of the reasons why the north-west region of England – roughly the counties of Lancashire, Cheshire, Staffordshire and the West Riding of Yorkshire – saw the great innovations in spinning and steam engines that made life for people born after 1780 different to anything earlier generations had known.

Many people have helped me with this book. I am particularly grateful to my friends Colin Phillips of Manchester University and Michael Power of Liverpool University for reading the typescript and for making many valuable comments. Other kind friends, Martin Rosendaal and Robert Steele, have done the same. My elder daughter, Antonia Howatson, im-proved many of my sentences before her second baby was born and my younger daughter, Dela, read much of the script and advised me to explain more fully several passages that she thought were difficult to understand. The book would be much less attractive and interesting without the high grade images that my friend, Paul Atkins, has so kindly created. Nick Scarle has drawn some beautifully clear maps for the book.

I am also very conscious of the help I received from Dr Peter McNiven and others at the John Rylands Library in giving me such good access to the two large estate archives and also from Jonathon Pepler and the staff at the Cheshire Record Office for their help with the Tabley papers deposited there. Brian Jackson at the Lancashire Record Office kindly allowed me to photograph large sections of the Shuttleworth accounts. I would also like to thank the owners of the original pictures, maps and documents (mentioned in the list of figures and maps) for their kindness in giving me permission to reproduce them. The survey which forms Appendix 3.1 is printed with the permission of Cheshire County Council.

Finally I must thank Roger Hudson and my wife, Jane, without whose continuous encouragement and assistance the book would never have appeared.

List of abbreviations

A.R.I.	Arley Receipted Invoices
Ag. Hist. Rev.	*Agricultural History Review*
C.R.O.	Cheshire Record Office
C.L.R.O.	Corporation of London Record Office
DDK	Knowsley Estate Papers in Lancashire Record Office
DDSc	Scarisbrick Estate Papers in Lancashire Record Office
DLT	Tabley Estate Papers in Cheshire Record Office
D.N.B.	*Dictionary of National Biography*
Econ. Hist. Rev.	*Economic History Review*
H.S.L.& C.	Historic Society of Lancashire and Cheshire
L.& C.A.S.	Lancashire and Cheshire Antiquarian Society
P.R.O.	Public Record Office, Kew
Record Soc L & C	Record Society of Lancashire and Cheshire
VCH	*Victoria County History*
WCW	Will in Lancashire Record Office
WM	Warburton Muniments in John Rylands University of Manchester Library

I. Smithills Hall and its demesne lands in 1620 (see Fig 3 p. 13)

II. Burrows Hall, Cogshall, 1578.

This map of 1578 shows a Cheshire gentry house without chimneys as Smithills may have been until 1592. Burrows Hall, Cogshall (now the site of Brook Farm, Comberbach), was the principal house on a small freehold estate of about 173 acres owned by a gentry family, *Massie* of Rixton, Lancs. The large building was evidently the Hall and the three smaller ones were the barn, the stables and the cowshed. The Hall is shown as single-storey with a lantern on the ridge to let out the smoke. All houses had similar lanterns before chimneys were built. Notice the wide grassy road and the pack-horse bridge over the brook. (See Fig. 18 and pp. 44–9)

xvi

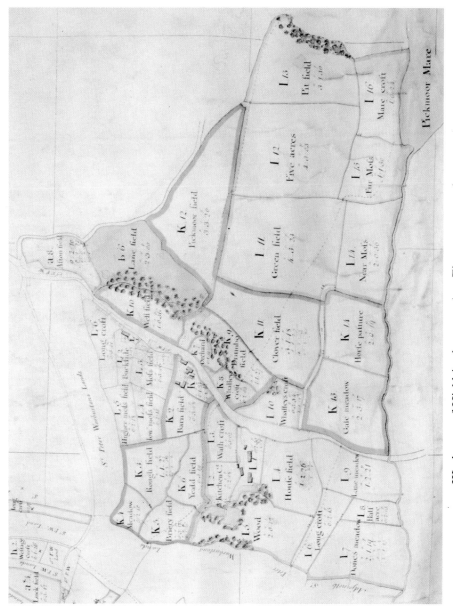

III. A map of Hield in the 1750s (see Fig. 32 p. 94 and pp. 91–5)

xvii

IV. The Millington/Watts estate in Appleton, 1765 (see Fig 36 pp. 102–3)

Introduction

This book describes the households of seven families living in the north-west of England in the 200 years before 1770. The information is derived mainly from the account books they kept and which, unusually, have survived. These are a much richer source of information than wills, inventories and parish registers, which usually constitute almost the only material available to historians. As a result it has been possible to construct a much more detailed picture of the lives of ordinary people in Cheshire and Lancashire than has been in existence up till now. Accounts are boring to read as well as difficult to understand so I have tried to present readable stories from the vast amount of information they contain.

Four of the seven stories come from the archives preserved by the Warburton family at Arley and the Leicester family at Tabley (see Map 1). These two huge archives have been the core of my research over the last 12 years – material which has not previously been studied by any historian. The fifth story is derived from the Shuttleworth papers in the Lancashire Record Office which were last described in the 1850s. The other two stories, of the Fells and Richard Latham, are new analyses of previously published account books. With the help of information derived from other sources I have tried to bring these families alive. I look at their origins and sketch the fate of their descendants. Their loves, their children and their deaths are described as well as their jobs and incomes. All families experience their own dramas and these seven had their share of successes and bankruptcies, illnesses and early deaths.

The seven families belonged to several different groups in society. The Leicesters and the Warburtons were old major gentry families who had owned thousands of acres since the twelfth and thirteenth centuries. Around a hundred families of this kind owned most of the land in Cheshire in the sixteenth century. They dominated the rest of society and ran the government of the county. There is also a vignette of an unmarried member of one of these gentry families – George Dockwra, the nephew of Sir George Warburton, 3rd Bt; he is shown as a middle-aged

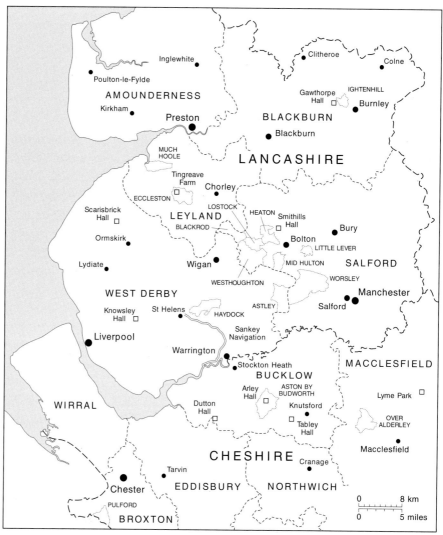

Map 1. This map shows the area in which six of the seven households lived and most of the other places mentioned in the text. It also shows the Hundreds into which the counties used to be divided. The townships of Bucklow Hundred are shown in Map 2.

man living on a small fixed income in the country. The other four families profited in various ways from the great redistribution of wealth that occurred between 1540 and 1640. During those 100 years the value of land increased about twenty-fold. Many of the families occupying small farms in Cheshire and Lancashire acquired property rights in their land around 1540 and thus enjoyed a great increase in their wealth. The Shuttleworths and the Fells became copyholders with rights nearly as large as freeholders. The Jacksons and Lathams held their farms by the privileged tenure called three-life leasehold, which gave them about half the value of the freehold.[1] One effect of this new wealth was that all these four families were able to afford to educate their children well. The Shuttleworths and the Fells, with their more valuable lands, had sufficient money to pay for their clever sons to become barristers, in which profession they made considerable fortunes. The Shuttleworths created a new position for themselves as major gentry.

Thomas Jackson and Richard Latham were brought up on small three-life leasehold farms of less than 20 acres. These were farms which had originally been occupied by serfs and their leases still contained the old badges of serfdom – the boon works and the heriots.[2] Some historians have referred to this group as peasants; however these two men were not born on the bottom rung of society. They each inherited from their fathers assets worth more than £50. Neither they nor any of their immediate relations was ever a full-time manual farm worker. Richard Latham was not successful, but he brought up a large family and handed his property on to them. Thomas Jackson made more than £1,000. In his unusual story we see three generations of his family. Some of his grandchildren were accepted as gentlemen while others are last seen in great poverty. As is well known history is almost entirely about the rich and famous. The rare quality of these archives is demonstrated by the extraordinary details provided of the descent into poverty of some of Thomas Jackson's children and grandchildren and of some of the great-grandchildren of Sir George Warburton, 1st Bt. Socially midway between the major gentry and the three-life leaseholders were the Fells of Swarthmoor Hall. Each member of this family had some freehold property and business interests. When all are put together, these seven stories begin to form a portrait of society. If some of the protagonists were to meet we might almost hear their conversations and gauge their opinions of each other.

The accounts of the gentry households at Smithills, Tabley and Arley together cover nearly 200 years from 1582 to 1774 and so provide a history of the development of life in country houses. Major gentry households

---

1 See Foster, 2003, Ch. 3, for a much fuller discussion of these tenures and how they came to exist.
2 See examples in Chs 3 and 5.

slowly evolved from their sixteenth-century style as small courts with attendant minor gentry and farm workers, all living together in the big house, to the kind of arrangements with which we are all familiar from the novels of Jane Austen. The old documents also record many of the problems these families had with shortages of male heirs or too many younger sons, with settlements and portions for daughters.

From all this a picture emerges of the culture of the gentry, a principal feature of which was that all the wealth was kept together in the hands of the head of the family. He lived in the big house and owned the estate, leaving all his relations dependent on him for money. They could probably only be provided with a niche in life, whether it was a marriage or a secure job, through his influence and with his approval. The family's position and standing therefore had to be maintained: unseemly behaviour by minor members was rebuked. Younger sons were not given sufficient money to enable them to marry but were encouraged to remain on the estate. If the eldest son should die or should fail to produce a male heir, the younger son was then expected to marry and step into his shoes.

The culture of the Fell, the Jackson and the Latham families was very different and I have called it business culture. Every father divided his wealth among all his children. Girls got a good share – sometimes even more than the boys. The younger sons were encouraged to leave home and become apprenticed in an occupation. When they were trained they were given their portion and expected to make their own way in the world. The girls were expected to earn their livings until they married and possibly again after that.

Most of the account books describe farming operations, the animals kept and the crops grown. They all tell us that the farm work was usually done by young people employed by the owner of the farm, who himself did not do much, if any, farm work. This information suggests we need to be cautious in thinking that the main occupation of most country dwellers was farming.

Changes were made in the way the big estates managed their demesne[3] lands as the structure of the economy developed. These large estates slowly became less self-sufficient and relied more on the market to provide their needs. The smaller farms became more commercial and crops were produced not only to supply the family's needs but also in order to provide

3 The land farmed by the Lord of the Manor to support his own household.

a surplus which could be sold at a profit. All the property owners were employers, so the account books also provide evidence of wages paid to farm workers. In the sixteenth century these workers were often fed, housed, and clothed by their employers and they received money only once a year. By the middle of the eighteenth century these arrangements had been replaced by the modern system of a weekly cash wage to people who provided their own clothes, food and housing. The workers were free of the social restrictions which had been imposed on them when they were living in their employers' houses and were therefore able to marry. However, as landless wage earners, they were in the grip of market forces so that their earnings often left them more miserably poor than their ancestors had been.

Before 1600 the production of textiles was a major activity in all households. The account books provide a wealth of information about cloth and clothing, and the slow rise in the standard of living can be observed in the better quality of the clothes worn. For example, around 1600 the fibre most cultivated was hemp. It was widely used for clothing and household textiles like sheets. This coarse fibre slowly gave way to flax, which was finer and softer, and by the mid-eighteenth century hemp was used only for nets and ropes. Textile production was the part of the household controlled by the women. The way it was managed in the early period in different houses and the slow progress towards the practice of buying textiles in shops is examined in some detail.

The three big estates were so rich that their purchases included almost everything that was on offer in their vicinity. Their accounts therefore provide evidence of most of the goods and services available. The information forms a sort of map of the structure of the local economy. It tells us about the occupations of other people in the area and the technology in use. For example, the Smithills household in the 1580s satisfied most of their needs locally. Only a few items like wine, iron and spices were brought from far away. The estate was virtually self-sufficient in food and textiles, while other goods and services were almost all provided by people living within a few miles. The countryside seems to have contained a surprisingly large number of skilled men. There is evidence of around 40 different occupations being pursued by people living in the country around this estate. In the later Tabley and Arley accounts, we can see from the new and improved products purchased that the technology in use in the area was being continually improved.

All the account books enable us to follow the slow development of the market economy. From the largely self-sufficient world of the 1580s we move to households where more and more was bought in the market for money and a growing number of people were engaged in providing goods and services that other people wanted to buy. Their earnings provided them in turn with money to buy whatever they needed. We see the vigour with which this society strove to improve its technology as we watch the Jackson family investing in the new framework knitting machines in the 1660s, the technical marvels of their time. The Jackson brothers were sadly not among the successful entrepreneurs in this important new industry and two of them went bankrupt. However, the coastal trading business started by the Fells in the 1670s seems to have been more successful. We see a number of people joining together as partners to finance these larger undertakings. These two examples illustrate how families possessing small amounts of capital and a strong interest in commerce were able to transform the economy of the north-west in the century after 1650.

All these seven stories provide information about both the income and the capital which the families owned. This allows the reader to see where each family stood in relation to others in the whole society and to see the huge changes in wealth that occurred. Richard Shuttleworth, whose father probably owned less than £50 when Richard was born in 1541, became a senior judge and was probably worth more than £5,000 when he died in 1599. The Fell family, who were probably no richer than the Shuttleworths in the 1540s, owned property worth perhaps £7,000 by the 1670s. Thomas Jackson had only about £50 when he married in 1650. In the course of his life he was able to give away to his children a total of at least £1,200 either on their marriages or when they had run into debt. At his own death in 1708 he probably had only enough left to provide for a decent burial. All these three men owed much of their great gains to the Law. Other families who made money in business have not left us account books. For example, the ancestors of Thomas Hough, 1653–1721, were three-life leaseholders of a 36-acre farm and in 1545 had assets worth only £3 or £4. Thomas's grandfather died in 1642, worth around £140, and Thomas himself died on the same farm in 1721, leaving his children some £2,500 that he had made in business.[4] Perhaps, as these examples

4 Foster, 2003, App. 3.1 and Ch. 8.

suggest, it was easier to make money in the Law before the Civil War whereas after 1650 many fortunes were made in business.

Although banks were not established in the north-west until the late eighteenth century, all the basic banking services were available from families who owned property and had a reputation for integrity. Six of my families provided these services. Examples appear of how they kept money safe, paid interest on deposits, made loans at interest and also borrowed money at interest themselves. The stories also show how money could be transferred from Cheshire to London.

The Jackson story provides a number of examples of schooling and apprenticeships. These illustrate how it was possible for people with only a small amount of capital, like our Thomas Jackson's father, to educate a son to enter a professional career. In a similar way the Shuttleworth story shows Sir Richard's parents educating their two elder children for the Law and the priesthood in the 1540s and 1550s when their income is unlikely to have been more than £20 or £30 p.a. The Lathams, who were the poorest of our families, were also able to educate their children and the account of their family life shows that it could have been the platform from which their son, if he had lived, might have become a successful entrepreneur.

The stories are arranged in chronological order so that they illustrate the development, through the centuries, of social and economic life in the two counties and contribute to an understanding of how the vigorous market economy, which is described in the final chapter, came into existence, and how it naturally led on to the Industrial Revolution.

I

The Shuttleworths of Smithills and Gawthorpe 1582–1621

I. INTRODUCTION

The Shuttleworth account books provide a detailed picture of life in an Elizabethan country house in Lancashire.[1] Indeed, they do more than this – they also describe the way of life of a whole community. However, this picture only emerges from an analysis of hundreds of entries. The description of the community around Smithills is therefore based on much detailed analysis. For example, by using the evidence provided by the tithes[2] that the Shuttleworths collected, we get an indication of the crops grown in a number of complete townships. The evidence suggests that each family was usually growing its own grain supplies. It also shows that this did not occupy a major part of their working time. The section on textiles suggests that the community was making almost all the textiles it used. The women probably played a major part in organizing the production of the textiles each family needed and this task probably occupied the largest part of these women's working lives.

Rich families living in large houses required a great many different supplies and services. In many parts of Europe it is known that, at this period, these were provided by craftsmen and traders living in towns, but in Lancashire this does not appear to have been the case. The Shuttleworths had little contact with Manchester, Preston, Wigan or Warrington, which were the only towns in the area. The people who tanned their leather, made their ropes and forged their nails all lived in the country around them. There were so many of these people – coopers, builders, blacksmiths, and so on – in the rural areas that the evidence suggests that such trades were the principal occupations of the tenants living on small farms in the country. It has been usual for historians to describe country people as farmers with bye-occupations. In Lancashire, it seems that this description

---

1 See Appendix 1.1 for a description of the account books and the volumes of extracts published by the Chetham Society in the 1850s.

2 Tithes were the tenth part of every crop originally given to support the Church. See Foster, 1998, pp. 68–9 for examples.

should be reversed. Many people appear to have been principally crafts-men and traders who did a little farming if they had time, and otherwise employed the few specialist farmers among them to do their farmwork. The two holders of small farms whose account books we examine in this book both usually employed others (see Chapters 3 and 5 below, Jackson and Latham).

2. THE FAMILY

The Shuttleworth family had lived at Gawthorpe between Padiham and Burnley since the early fifteenth century. They were tenants of the Duchy of Lancaster which was part of the royal estate. They were not freeholders, but like most Duchy tenants were 'tenants at will'.[3] who paid a full market rent. When Hugh Shuttleworth married Ann Grimshaw in 1540, his father gave them some land and they inherited the rest of his 170½ acres when he died in 1557 (see Appendix 1.2 for more details). The Crown, unlike almost all the neighbouring Lancashire and Cheshire gentry, did not adopt a system of written three-life leases in the 1540s. It continued to transfer the tenancies in the Manor Court 'by copy of Court roll' and did not attempt to increase the rents or the entry fines[4] in the period after 1530 when market rents were rising so strongly. The tenants ceased to be called 'tenants at will' and became 'copyholders'. With this highly privileged form of tenure the tenants grew steadily richer as their rent became, every decade, a smaller proportion of the full market rent.[5]

Hugh and Ann were therefore able to bring up their children in comparative affluence. Their eldest son Richard, born in 1541, was sent to Gray's Inn in London and became a barrister. He was successful and by 1582 he had acquired a substantial property at Forcett in Yorkshire. When the accounts begin in September 1582 Richard had recently married Margery, widow of Robert Barton, who had died in 1580. Margery was a daughter of Sir Peter Legh of Lyme, Cheshire, and Haydock, Lancashire. This marriage brought Richard Shuttleworth into the society of the major

---

3 See Foster, 2003, Ch. 3 (ii), for a fuller discussion.
4 Payments made by each new tenant on entry.
5 The events at the Crown's Lordship of Bromfield and Yale (Salop/Denbigh) in 1562 seem to have formed a precedent for other Crown Lordships. Tenants there were given new 40-year leases on the old terms. These leases were inheritable and renewable on the same terms. They were effectively grants of the freehold title. See Palmer, 1910, pp. 204–11, Hoyle, 1992, pp. 202–3 and 255, and Foster, 2003, Ch. 3 (iii).

gentry. Richard continued to be successful in his legal practice and bought more land almost every year until he died. In 1584 he was promoted to the senior legal position of Sergeant and in 1589 he was knighted on his appointment as Chief Justice of the Palatinate Court in Chester.

The Smithills estate, which had been Robert Barton's family land, was retained by his widow Margery after his death. She probably did this on legal advice offered by Richard Shuttleworth and after they were married it became his estate. In 1581, in order to recover the property, the Barton family began a lawsuit which was finally brought to an end by a compromise in 1596. Sir Richard agreed to give the estate back to the Bartons on his death.[6] This, fortunately for the Bartons, occurred only three years later in 1599.

Hugh and Ann's second son Lawrence, born 1545, was sent to university and became a priest. His elder brother Richard seems to have provided the money to buy for him his appointment as Rector of Wichford, Warwickshire, a job he took up in 1582.[7] He never married.

The third brother Thomas, born in 1546, must have had a good education. He came to Smithills in 1582 to manage the farm and estate on behalf of his elder brother. Up to 1593 he kept the account books which are the source of this chapter. By 1586 his elder brother Richard had been married for five years but had no children. Richard must have realized that there might be no heir to inherit the substantial fortune he was making at the Bar so he seems to have encouraged Thomas to marry and probably also made the marriage possible by undertaking to settle part of his Forcett lands on the bride as her jointure. In September 1586 Thomas married Anne, the daughter of a neighbour, Richard Lever of Little Lever. She bore him three sons and three daughters in quick succession in the seven years before he died at the end of 1593. Throughout their married life they lived at Smithills. During this time Sir Richard was usually at the courts in London or Chester, so they often had the house to themselves. For nearly two years, however, they had to nurse his wife, Margery, who injured her leg in an accident in 1590, never managed to get the wound to heal and eventually died in April 1592.

After Thomas's death, Anne and the children continued to live at Smithills until she remarried in 1596. Her eldest son, born in 1587 and appropriately named Richard, became recognized as his uncle's heir. To

6 Harland, 1856, pp. 282–91.
7 Harland, 1856, p. 293.

Fig. 1. Gawthorpe Hall, built between 1600 and 1605 – a painting of the south front in the eighteenth century. This was a novel type of house in Lancashire in 1600. Designed in London, probably by Robert Smythson, its use of internal chimneys enabled the house to be four storeys high with four main rooms on each floor. The flues from the fireplaces were formed in the walls of the central staircase tower which rose above the main roof of the house. Compare this to Smithills Hall (Figs 17, 19, 20), Burrows Hall (Fig. 18) and Arley Hall (Fig. 48).

fill the gap at Smithills left by Thomas's death, his brother Lawrence took over some of the management of the estate, spending less time at his Wichford Rectory as a result. From 1593 onwards, parts of the accounts are in his handwriting. Hugh Shuttleworth, the father of the three brothers, Richard, Lawrence and Thomas, lived well into his seventies on the old family farm at Gawthorpe. When he died in 1597 the farm descended to Sir Richard. Before Sir Richard died, only two years later, he put his whole estate in trust for Thomas's children, so Lawrence was only a life tenant.

Now that the estate had grown substantial as a result of Sir Richard's purchases it must have been felt that a grander, modern house would be more in keeping with their new status. Presumably Sir Richard and Lawrence had discussed the type of house it should be. Building work on the new Gawthorpe Hall started in February 1600. Enough of this fine Elizabethan house survives in the care of the National Trust to give an idea of the splendid style in which the Shuttleworths were to live in the

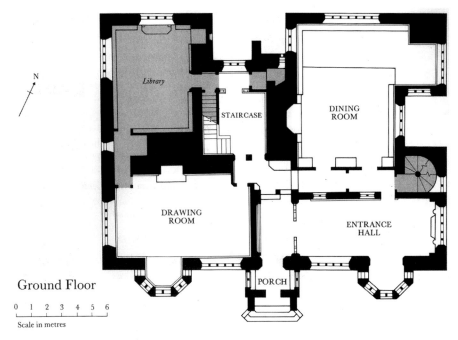

N

Library

STAIRCASE

DINING
ROOM

DRAWING
ROOM

ENTRANCE
HALL

Ground Floor

PORCH

0 1 2 3 4 5 6
Scale in metres

Fig. 2. Plan of the ground floor of Gawthorpe Hall today. Alterations to the partitions have been made since 1850, but the division into four large spaces and a staircase is original.

seventeenth century. When Lawrence died in 1608, Thomas's eldest son Richard, then aged 21, inherited the estate. Thus, in the course of about two generations a new major gentry family had been created in Lanca-shire. It was the combined work of the three brothers – Richard made the money, Lawrence built the house, and Thomas produced the children to inherit it.

3. THE ESTATE

Sir Richard Shuttleworth owned the Smithills estate from 1582 to 1599. Smithills Hall was a substantial complex of buildings (see Figs 3 and 17–22) which is now open to the public. Several of the buildings used by the Shuttleworths remain to give an impression of their establishment. On the north side there was a deep wooded ravine with a stream at the bottom. On the south side, there were gardens and orchards. Around the house were fields encircled by a deep wooded valley. At the lowest point the stream turned a mill to grind their corn. In Fig. 3 the area of each

12

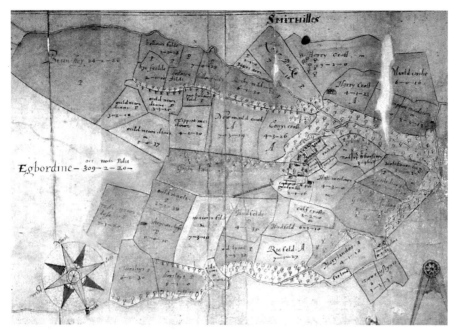

Fig. 3. Smithills Hall and its demesne lands surveyed and drawn by 'William Senior, Professor of the Mathamatiques A.D. 1620'. See map in colour p. xv.

field is given in Cheshire acres.[8] Its use is indicated by a letter such as 'A' for arable, etc, so that we can see how the farm was arranged:

	Statute acres
Gardens and orchards	6
Arable to be ploughed to grow corn	82
Meadow to be cut for hay to feed the animals in winter	95
Pasture to feed the animals in summer	258
	441
Egburden, rough pasture	655
	1,096

Smithills Hall is situated about 500 ft above sea level, much higher than most of the Lancashire/Cheshire plain, which is usually below 200 ft. The land is therefore more suitable for animals than for grain. The Egburden, a long, wide, grassy slope stretching up to the moors at 1,300 ft is still exclusively reserved for pasture. So it is not surprising that only 82 of the 1000 acres at Smithills was used to grow grain. Fortunately, the

8 Appendix 1.3, Table F.

Estate had three other manors where there were demesne lands as well as tenants. The nearest was Lostock, only two to three miles away. The other two farms, one at Tingreave (now Ingrave) in Eccleston, and the other in Much Hoole, were between 12 and 18 miles away. The land at Lostock was at about 350 ft, but the Tingreave and Hoole lands were under 50 ft. If the water could be drained off the land in these last two places they were among the best Grade One agricultural lands in Lancashire. Unfortunately, there is nothing in the accounts about the size of these three farms, but from items of expenditure on the farming (Section 5, below), one might estimate them to be between 100 and 300 acres each. The accounts provide little information about the tenants on these manors and elsewhere. There appear to have been about 50 tenants on Smithills lands paying the usual modest 'old rents', but I have found nothing about their leases or the size of their farms except the map of the tenant farms near Smithills (Fig. 4).

4. THE STAFF AND THEIR PAY

It has been a commonplace among historians for a long time that wage earners suffered a serious decline in their standard of living in the sixteenth century because the price of food rose about six-and-a-half times in the century after 1540, while wages only doubled or trebled. The Shuttleworth accounts provide an unusually detailed picture of what happened in south Lancashire. We see that the permanent staff employed at Smithills Hall remained as well off as they had ever been, because they were fed and clothed by the estate. Short-term workers were also protected because they were fed at the Hall as part of their wages. The tenant farmers were likewise unaffected because they grew their own food with their own labour. It was only a new class of landless wage earners, who did not live and eat with their employers, who became poorer than anyone had been in 1500.

In 1587, the Shuttleworths employed about 14 full-time men and three women. The highest paid were:

	£	s	d	
Peter Stones	2	5	8	p.a
Henry Harte	2	3	4	p.a.
Peter Aston	2	2	8	p.a.
Robert Aspeden	2	0	0	p.a.
John Hindley	1	13	4	p.a.
William Hewood	1	12	0	p.a.

14

We are not told each man's job, but the following five roles emerge in various contexts: butler and brewer, cook, miller, shepherd, and gardener. It is likely that five of them did these jobs. We know much more about Robert Aspeden. One of the families living near the Shuttleworths at Gawthorpe was called Aspeden and Robert may have been a member of this family; he was certainly a man whom Richard Shuttleworth trusted. He was usually sent to supervise the gathering of the tithes the estate owned and to superintend their threshing. He accompanied the young lawyers when they went to hold manor courts. He collected rents. Unlike most of the employees who stayed only a few years, he served the Shuttleworths all their time at Smithills. By 1598 he seems to have acquired a lease of all the tithes the Shuttleworths had had in earlier years. He was still doing the same work gathering these tithes, but he was no longer an employee. He had become a contractor and his pay was no longer an annual wage, but the difference between the real value of the tithes he gathered and the amount he had to pay the Shuttleworths each year as set out in the lease.

The other eight servants appear to have been farm workers. Two earned £1 6s 8d p.a., one made £1 3s 4d, and three were paid £1 0s 0d a year. William Ducworth, who was the farm worker resident at Tingreave, Eccleston, earned £1 6s 8d and was clearly a fully trained competent adult, as he looked after the farm and animals. This suggests that £1 6s 8d to £1 3s 4d was the range of pay for adult farm workers, depending on competence. The other five were probably not yet adults. Thomas Longworth, who earned 16s 0d in 1587, and Adam Turner, who got 12s 0d, were definitely boys, though we don't know their ages. Thomas Longworth's rate was raised to 18s 0d in 1588, to 21s 0d in 1590, and to £1 3s 0d in 1591. If this analysis is correct, five out of the eight farm workers were youths and we shall see the same pattern at the Fells' farm in the 1670s. These archives do not tell us where they came from or how old they were but in the much fuller material available at Arley in the mid-eighteenth century we find that some were the children of neighbouring country families who seem to have been able to earn wages for farm work from the age of eleven.[9]

9 See 1) Foster, 1998, p. 77, for Mark Winstanley, who worked on the Arley farm aged eleven; 2) below, Ch. 7, (vii), for the two Hulme boys, aged 12 and 14, who were not living at home; and 3) WM Box 24, Folder 2, for John Hind of Aston who went to work for Jonathon Vernon, aged eleven. See Foster, 1992, pp. 26–7, for the Hind family.

By 1590 the male staff had increased in numbers to 17. There was a kitchen-boy by then, but whether this was a new job or whether one of the boys had always been kitchen-boy we don't know. There were also three women. Cecily Moss was the dairymaid at 18s 0d a year. Ann Wilding gave many years service at 12s 0d p.a.; Elizabeth Ainsworth, who left in June 1590, had been paid £1 10s 0d p.a. No other woman ever earned so much.

All these people were unmarried and lived at Smithills where, in addition to their food, they were also given clothing. We will examine this subject in more detail pp. 26–41 below. For now we will note that most and perhaps all of the men received 'liveries'. These suits were not made locally but were sent down from London. In April 1597 the cost was £27 10s 0d. In 1618 livery suits made in London cost £2 per man, so perhaps £27 10s 0d in 1597 bought liveries for 16 or 17 men. The women were given wool which they presumably spun and made into clothing of their own choice. Working for other people in the sixteenth century seems not to have been the purely economic contract to which we are now accustomed. The Shuttleworths also rewarded their servants for long service. We have seen that Robert Aspeden had acquired a lease of the tithes before Sir Richard died, which was probably Sir Richard's way of giving him a good income for the rest of his life, in recognition of his many years' service. When Ann Wilding left to get married in 1593, Sir Richard gave her £3 6s 8d. This was more than the money she had been paid for her previous five years' work.

When considering wage rates in the late sixteenth century one must recognize the fact that board and lodging represented a very high proportion of the total wage. William Ducworth, one of the farm workers, did not usually live at Smithills. Like all servants, he was unmarried, so he was boarded with Henry Dicconson, one of the estate's tenants in Eccleston. In March 1586, Dicconson was charging the estate 16s 8d a quarter (1s 3½d per week, or 2.2d a day) for 'tabling' William Ducworth. So we can work out his yearly board at £3 6s 8d. With his wage of £1 6s 8d, this makes the total cost of employing him £4 13s 4d p.a. For 285 days of work a year (Sundays and 27 other holidays probably made up the balance), this works out at approximately 4d a day.[10] This figure of 4d a

10 5 and 6 Edw. 6 c. 111 (1552) declared all Sundays and 27 Saints' and other days to be holidays.

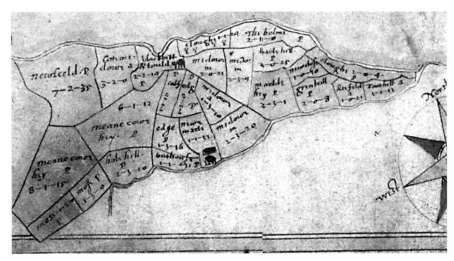

Fig. 4. Two tenant farms west of Smithills surveyed by W. Senior, 1620. The field areas are in Cheshire acres. Each field was fully enclosed and the only 'common' land was the rough pasture on the moor.

day may perhaps be taken as the basic lowest daily rate for a farm worker in the early 1580s in this area. However, wages were also affected by the price of food and the scarcity of labour – for example, at harvest-time. The price of grain rose sharply in the summer and autumn of 1586. Tenant families 'tabling' transient workers therefore raised their rates. Two threshers who went to Hoole for one week cost the estate 4.3d per day in July 1586. Henry Dicconson was charging 3.5d per day for William Ducworth who was a long-term lodger by early 1587 – a 56% increase. In May 1587 the estate contracted with another tenant to board Ducworth for a year at £4 13s 4d (3d a day), a 40% increase over the 1586 rate. At this rate, Ducworth cost the estate a little over 5d a day. Sometimes, as in December 1591 at Heaton, the meals supplied are described as meat meals. As these 22 meals only cost 28d it makes it seem likely that a meat meal a day was part of the usual diet.[11]

In addition to the permanent staff, the estate hired other workers by the day, especially on the outlying properties. At Smithills in winter, they got rates similar to the annual rates of the permanent staff, but they had to be paid more in the summer. Richard Longworth who had been on the permanent staff in 1587 at £1 p.a., worked for six days in December 1589

11 Emmison, 1961, discusses the diet at Ingatestone Hall, Essex, in 1548-52 (pp. 123–59), and gives menus (pp. 306–16). These suggest that meat or fish were served twice a day.

at 1d a day, equivalent to about £1 3s 9d p.a. In April 1590 he worked for six weeks at 1½d a day (£1 15s 7½d p.a.), which was the summer rate. These temporary workers enjoyed all the same meals when working at Smithills as the permanent staff. When working by the day at outlying farms, people might be 'tabled' by the estate or they might be 'at their own table'. Giles Janion threshed for 16 days at Hoole in July 1586 and was paid 2¼d a day. He stayed with Robert Stones's wife, who charged the estate 4¼d a day for his table, so he cost a total of 6½d a day. The rates paid to workers 'at their own table' had to keep pace with these total costs. In June 1586 four men cleaned a watercourse in Lostock and were paid 6½d a day each at their own table. Rates were highest for harvest work. That same summer Giles Janion went from Hoole to Smithills. There he did 10 days mowing at 4½d a day. His meals in the big house must have been worth at least 4d a day, so he cost a total of 8½d a day on this work.

Rates of pay seem to have risen slightly as the years went by. In December 1590, Roger Kenyon, a new cook, was paid £2 10s 0d a year. This was more than anyone had been paid in 1587. It may have been because of this general rise that George Dowson was paid 8d a day 'at his own table' for loading dung in August 1590, or perhaps it was because it kept him from highly-paid harvest work. He was content with 6½d a day in September. He had received only 3d a day when he was boarded with Mrs. Stones in Hoole in July.

So we find quite a range of rates of pay. Low money wages were paid to permanent staff who enjoyed year-round work with food and clothing. Temporary workers got the same low pay in winter but when there was a lot of work to be done in the summer, and particularly at harvest time, they had to be paid more. The price of labour in the country was highly responsive to market forces; scarcity drove the prices up, a surplus supply depressed them.

The main produce of north-western farms was cattle whose price had approximately trebled between the 1510s and the 1580s.[12] The surprising thing therefore about these rates of pay is that they differed so little from the maximum rates laid down in the Act of 1514 (6 Hen. 8 c. 3).[13] These rates included:

12 Thirsk, 1967, p. 860.
13 The Black Death, *c.* 1350, led to a shortage of labour and higher wages. A number of Acts, including this one, sought to limit wage rises. See p. 77, note 20 for a 1663 example.

	£	s	d	
A Shepherd with diet and clothing	1	5	0	p.a.
A Common servant in husbandry with diet and clothing	1	0	8	p.a.
A Woman servant with diet and clothing	1	4	0	p.a.

DAILY RATES	with food	without food
Labourers in winter	1d	3d
Labourers in summer	2d	4d

We know that the rates paid in the north-west were similar to this because Sir William Brereton paid a number of farm workers in Cheshire 4d a day in 1531.[14] He also paid 1s a week (1.7d per day) for board, or tabling, workers sent to distant manors in the same year. This suggests that tenant farmers were not conscious of a great surge in the price of food before the 1580s. We have seen (p. 16 above) that Dicconson only charged the Shuttleworths 1s 3½d a week for William Ducworth's tabling in 1586.[15]

Market rents went up from 7d or 8d to 6s an acre between the 1520s and the 1580s, which was an increase of nine or ten times.[16] In this period wages seem to have barely doubled from £1 to £2 a year (with food and clothing) or from 4d to 8d a day without. We shall see later (pp. 76–7)[17] that for most of the seventeenth century and on up to the 1760s the standard rate of pay for a labourer in this area was in the region of 8d a day in winter and 10d a day in summer. Market rents had reached 10s to 12s an acre by the 1640s, and never went down again. So the 'Great Tudor inflation' in the north-west meant an increase in rents of up to 20 times while wages only doubled or trebled.

The effects of these changes on the living standards of some workers was considerable, while others were not much affected. The farm workers living in Smithills will have enjoyed meals and clothing at least equal in quality to those they had had at home. The food at Smithills is likely to have been better than that provided by Mrs Stones in Hoole. Sir Richard Shuttleworth's honour was involved in the food served in his Hall. Furthermore, the workers living at Smithills were entirely insulated from

14 Ives, 1976, pp. 231–2, 247. See also Youngs, D., 1999, pp. 145–60, where around 1500 the most senior living-in farm-worker earned the low rate of 14s a year. However 2d per day, evidently with food, was paid for harvest work. This rare small archive lacks information about the cost of board or tabling but there cannot be much doubt that all workers were receiving meals and that most of those who 'lived-in' were youths.
15 See note in Appendix 1.3, Table E.2.
16 See Foster, 2003, Ch. 3.
17 Also Foster, 1992, p. 10.

changes in the price of grain. The three-life leaseholder families from which many of these workers probably came were also partly insulated from the market price of grain. We will see that they normally grew just enough grain for their own needs (see pp. 25–6 below). This fact probably explains why the cost of tabling visiting workers had only risen from the 1s a week paid by Sir William Brereton in 1531 to the 1s 3½d a week charged by the Dicconsons in early 1586. In these 55 years national grain prices had doubled or tripled,[18] but the north-west was not part of the national grain market, as we shall see on pp. 24–5 below.

When the bad harvest of 1586 forced tenant farmers to buy in the market the price of 'tabling' rose sharply. For those who always had to buy their food, like poor people living in towns, changes in the price of grain were more important. It is clear from this analysis that workers who were not fed by their employer and those who were not living on the family's farm suffered a substantial decline in their living standards between 1530 and 1630. National statistics show that their standard of life approximately halved.[19]

5. FARMING

The main purpose of the farming operations appears to have been to provide food for the household at Smithills, where the land was mostly pasture supporting a flock of sheep with a shepherd. How large the flock was we never learn. There were sheep also at Lostock, Eccleston, and Hoole. In May 1594, 27 sheep were clipped (shorn) at Eccleston at a cost of 6d. In June that year, clipping all the sheep at Smithills cost 3s 4d, so if the same rates applied there would have been about 180 at Smithills. The lambs with them would not, of course, have been shorn.

The accounts rarely mention the purchase of sheep so the initial stock must have been bought before the account books begin. Cattle, however, were bought in all the early years. In February 1583, 21 animals were acquired, and in most subsequent years between 10 and 20 animals were bought. Thomas Shuttleworth, accompanied by two or three farm workers, went around the local fairs each spring. Sometimes they bought a few head not far away at Bury, Wigan, or Salford. Their favourite fairs were further north at Blackburn, Burnley, Colne, Inglewhite, and Preston.

18 Hoskins, 1964; Harrison, 1971.
19 Thirsk, 1967, pp. 595–9.

They paid toll at the fairs and then drove their cattle home. Oxen usually cost £3 to £4 each, steers £2 10s, and 'twinters'[20] around £2. Cows were rarely bought, but heifers often were at £1 5s to £1 12s. The Shuttleworths probably built up a herd similar in shape to those described in the Warburton of Arley inventories of 1575 and 1626 (see Appendix 1.3).[21]

The Shuttleworth cattle were not all at Smithills. In 1593, the farrier at Lostock bled 50 beasts. Draught oxen were always kept at Eccleston so that William Ducworth could do the ploughing there and at Hoole. There must also have been cows at Tingreave because in 1594 a new calf house was built there. They probably suckled their own calves as it was too far to carry milk to Smithills and there was no dairymaid to make butter and cheese. As well as pulling ploughs the draught oxen also probably drew the carts and wagons around the farms. The fat oxen were being prepared for the table. At Smithills the cows provided milk, butter, and cheese, and the rest of the cattle were building up and maintaining the herd.

As well as sheep and cattle, there were pigs; 130 hogs were bought in 1583. Their progeny must have kept the pigsties full because only a few more were ever purchased. No doubt there were also chickens, geese, ducks, and turkeys at Smithills.

We know that there was a slaughterhouse at Smithills because a rope to tether the animals there was bought in January 1594. From the sales of hides and skins we can get an approximate idea of the number of animals that provided food in the Hall each year. Between 10 and 15 cow and ox hides were sold each year to the tanner, Adam Platt of Westhoughton, usually at around 18s each.[22] The glovers or curriers bought between 10 and 20 sheepskins at around 1s each. Calf- and lambskins were much less valuable so their numbers are less certain. Veal and lamb must have been regularly eaten in the Hall, as the calves of milking cows were not usually reared.

The only demesne farm on which the Shuttleworths did not keep cattle was at Hoole. As a result, they were able to lease 46½ statute acres of meadow there to John Stones at 6s 9d an acre. This example suggests that rents were similar across the south Lancashire and Cheshire plain at

20 Two-year-old animals.
21 The 1626 inventory of Peter Warburton provides an unusually detailed description of the contents of a gentry house, so it is used here several times to amplify the account of the Smithills farm.
22 See p. 51 below.

this period.[23] A few sheep and cattle were sold each year. The sheep sold are often described as 'no mutton fit for my mistress table',[24] and one of the steers sold we are told had a broken leg.[25] It seems likely therefore that the purpose of sales was usually to improve the quality and to keep the age-range of the herds and flocks in good order, rather than to earn an income.

Animal products formed one important part of the home-grown food eaten at Smithills. The crops they grew formed the other. Of the 82 acres of arable land at Smithills itself, we know little. The grain cultivation there was almost all done by the permanent farm workers and does not appear in the accounts. Help with the harvest and the hay was sometimes provided by temporary workers.

At Lostock, crops were regularly grown by temporary staff. This farm was only two or three miles from Smithills. It is not clear who looked after the animals that lived there and drew the plough, as no cost ever appears in the accounts. Perhaps one of the tenant farmers did the job in lieu of rent or perhaps a man walked over each day from Smithills. Certain it is that every year Lostock men ploughed, sowed, harvested, and threshed between 25 and 33 acres on piecework rates. The details of this work in each of the eight years 1586 to 1593 is shown in Table B of Appendix 1.3, and the piecework rates for the principal activities are shown in Table C in this appendix (see pp. 60–1). It would seem likely that the fields on which these crops were grown were the best quality level land in the township and that these fields were reserved for arable. Each year part of these fields seems to have been ploughed only once, then harrowed to make a seed bed, sown and harrowed again to cover the seed. The crop was almost always oats yielding in seven out of the eight years between 18 and 31 bushels per acre. In only four years was a little barley grown. In spring 1591 the 2.2 acres being prepared for barley were ploughed twice. These oat yields are surprisingly good when compared with those achieved in the townships around Arley Hall in the mid-eighteenth century which averaged 27.3 bushels.[26] The Lostock yields seem to have benefited from some dung, and possibly every other year was fallow. In the year 1586 the crops were disastrous. The weather must

23 See Foster, 2003, Ch. 2, Table 2 where the Leicesters of Tabley were letting land at 6s 1d an acre in 1584.
24 February 1596.
25 October 1594.
26 Foster, 1998, pp. 102–3.

have been unfriendly as the oats yield was only nine bushels per acre. This brought down the average yield for the whole eight years to 23.8 bushels. The average yield on the small barley crops at 18.2 bushels compares with the Arley township's yield of 22.4 bushels.

It is interesting to observe in Table C the modest number of man-days that seem to have been involved in growing oats in the sixteenth century. Around three man-days were needed to plough and harrow an acre. Four or five days, of which three were probably woman-days, were enough to shear the corn, bind it in sheaves, stook it to dry and load it on carts to take it to the barn. Threshing the average crop of 24 bushels an acre probably took less than three days. So for about 11 days' work, a man obtained 24 bushels weighing about 1,100 lbs. This would feed two adults for a year. It is interesting too, when comparing Table C with the eighteenth-century figures for Arley, to notice that the higher yields obtained in the later period were partly the result of more cultivation. Two ploughings instead of one and more attention to drainage were among the improvements introduced. The contrast between the sixteenth and the eighteenth centuries is probably greater than it seems because on specialist dairy farms in the later period the best land was used for grass, not corn, as dairy products were more lucrative.

When we examine the farming done at Eccleston and Hoole, we see why the Smithills estate owned these farms. These low-lying lands were ideal for growing their wheat and barley, but because the work on these lands was mostly done by William Ducworth and permanent staff sent from Smithills, we have less information about it. Temporary local workers were occasionally used and their pay gives us a few clues. The area normally ploughed on these two farms seems to have been 25 to 30 acres – perhaps about half on each farm. Wheat and barley were probably grown most years. Beans and oats were also grown and so were hemp and flax.

It seems likely from this analysis that at Smithills, the highest of the four farms, little was grown except oats. With pre-1660 technology this was the only reliable crop in the upland areas of north-west England. Apparently all these crops were not enough for the establishment at Smithills, because the family had also bought the tithes of four neighbouring townships.

It was the practice of many ecclesiastical owners of tithes in the north-west to sell their rights to local landowners. The Shuttleworths or Bartons of this period had bought the tithes of Heaton, Middle Hulton, and probably half the tithes of Blackrod and Bolton. The tithes were evidently gathered in the fields by the estate staff, who were often supervised by Robert Aspeden. The corn was taken to a local barn, sometimes owned by the estate, sometimes rented, where it was threshed during the winter by the estate staff. Sometimes a local woman was paid to winnow it on piecework. When that happened the accounts have details of the crops. These are set out in Table D in Appendix 1.3. This confirms that almost all the grain grown in the area at this period was oats. Less than 10% was barley and there were only tiny amounts of rye and wheat. Table D also shows that Smithills received around 600 bushels of oats a year from the three townships of Bolton, Blackrod, and Heaton. No details of the Middle Hulton tithes have survived but the indication from the length of time spent threshing there is that they were similar in quantity to Heaton. So the four townships contributed about 900 bushels of oats to Smithills and perhaps 100 bushels of barley.

The total amount of grain available to the Smithills household must therefore have been between 2,000 and 3,000 bushels. Was a part of this grown for sale? The answer to this important question seems to be no, although in some years some was sold. We have seen earlier (and in Table B) that 1586 was a disastrous summer for grain crops in this area. Lostock only harvested about 200 bushels instead of its usual 600-800. The yield on the four acres of barley grown there was only 3.6 bushels an acre – the same as had been sown as seed.

An examination of the sales of grain by the estate in 1586–7 and the contrast with the earlier 1580-5 period reveals much of interest. Appendix 1.3, Table E.1, shows the prices of grain in the English national market in this period, and Table E.2 shows corresponding prices from the Shuttleworth accounts. Comparing the two sets of figures shows that the grain market in the north-west was separate from the national market. For example, in oats, which we have seen was the major north-western crop, the national average price for 1580–4 was 10d a bushel. The Shuttleworth price was 1s 2d a bushel, 40% more. In 1586 the national price rose to 1s 1½d, but in south Lancashire it was over double this at 2s to 2s 5d. In wheat, which we have seen was rarely grown in the north-west at this time, the contrast was even more striking. A national average of 2s 6d a bushel in 1580-4 compares with 4s 5d and 6s 4d in Lancashire. In 1586 when the national price rose to 5s 8½d, in Lancashire it climbed to between 9s 3d and 13s 6d.

The reasons for this are not hard to find. The main national market was created by ships on the east and south coasts carrying grain to London – from Newcastle upon Tyne to Exeter. In 1585–6 more than 48,000 tons arrived in London,[27] in more than 1,000 shiploads. Virtually no ships arrived in the north-west from London or from the south and east coasts,[28] because nothing produced in the north-west required sea carriage to London. The only products of the north-west that Londoners bought were sheep, cattle and textiles. The animals walked and the textiles were sufficiently valuable (say £50 a ton) to afford road transport. Wheat at 2s 6d a bushel cost approximately £4 per ton. Road transport, without a return load, cost about 1s per ton mile. The nearest areas to south Lancashire which produced surplus grain were south Yorkshire and Lincolnshire, about 100 miles away over the Pennines. It would have cost around £5 per ton to move their grain to Lancashire, so the north-west was dependent on its home-grown grain supplies.

In the period 1582–93, the Shuttleworth accounts show that only in 1586–7 did the estate make significant sales of grain, and it is interesting to see who the purchasers were. Sales for that year are set out in Table E.3 in Appendix 1.3. Barley was a minor crop in the area, but 54 families each bought small amounts, presumably for beer, the average sale being about three or four bushels. Some sales were as little as one-eighth of a bushel. The purchasers seem to have been mostly families of tenants or employees. Many employees had the same surnames as tenant families but we don't know how they were related, if at all. Similar quantities of wheat were sold to 36 people. These customers seem to have been neighbours rather than tenants. Seventy-two bushels of oatmeal was sold to 11 people. Much the largest quantity of grain sold was the 869.5 bushels of oats. They were bought by only seven men, of whom four bought over 90%: William Rigby bought 442 bushels for £54; Thomas and Richard Ainsworth bought 270 bushels for £28 4s 0d; John Sindall bought 72 bushels for £7 6s 8d; Adam Godbere bought 27 bushels for £2 14s 0d.

One possibility is that these seven men were businessmen or carriers who bought the grain to resell it elsewhere. John Sindall was probably the tenant of that name in Blackrod. One James Sindall, as we shall see, was a wool dealer who bought large quantities of wool from the estate. The Ainsworths bought their supplies in April, May and June, as did John

27 Fisher, 1935, p. 47.
28 Woodward, 1970, pp. 68–133.

Sindall and Adam Godbere. Rigby bought his in August at Hoole, but he may have bespoken it earlier. Godbere was one of only three people in Hulton who paid tax in the Subsidy of 1600, so he was a comparatively rich man.[29] The amounts of money involved in these transactions and the foresight displayed in anticipating the poor crops so early strengthens the likelihood of a business connection. A strong possibility is that these large purchases were bought for resale to upland communities who grew no grain. The Sindalls, as wool dealers, would have had friends in these areas.

The absence of small sales of oats suggests that most families had enough of their own produce for their needs, even though prices had doubled. Appendix 1.3, Table E.3, shows that the estate sold £212 worth of grain at the high prices caused by the failure of the crops in the summer of 1586. Was this a shrewd commercial move by the Shuttleworths? The evidence of the tiny sales in the other 11 years 1582–93 argues against such an interpretation. It is also likely that the deterioration of grain kept for long periods in barns in the damp north-west would have led to greater financial loss than the profits made by occasional high price sales. It seems more likely that the important consideration for these large estates was to have adequate supplies at all times for their large households and many visiting workers. They accepted that they had to be the supplier of last resort in times of need. It is likely that there was no one in the sixteenth century but the big estates who had enough land to fulfil this role.[30] So the picture that seems to emerge is that the north-west lacked substantial grain markets. The evidence is consistent with a world in which each family was growing its own food, but we don't have enough evidence in this study to be sure of this.[31]

6. TEXTILES

There is a wealth of information about textiles in the Shuttleworth accounts. The estate manager/accountant, however, was not in control of the textiles as he was of the farming. The lady of the house, originally Mrs Richard Shuttleworth, seems to have been in charge. She had her own money which did not come from the accountant, but perhaps direct from her

29 Tait, 1924, p. 81.
30 See Foster, 2003, Ch. 3 (ii), for the structure of land-holding in 1545.
31 This suggestion is supported by evidence of the small amount of grain shipped from Chester 1576–98. In the six years for which Port Books survive, only 94 quarters oats, 574 barley, and 458 wheat were shipped. Woodward, 1970, p. 67.

husband or from the trustees of her marriage settlement. There is little information in the early years. More details appear only after June 1590 when, as Lady Shuttleworth, she was taken ill. Even then the coverage is not comprehensive. The accounts provide examples of what was made at home and what was bought rather than a complete list of everything the family did. Before 1589, when Richard Shuttleworth was appointed Judge in Chester and was knighted, he and his wife spent much time in London where he worked in the Courts. They bought their own clothes there, and later they bought them in Chester, so these never appear in the accounts. The servants' liveries were also bought in London and perhaps much else.

After Lady Shuttleworth's death in March 1592, Mrs Thomas Shuttleworth became the lady of the house. Her husband died in December 1593 and she remarried in 1596. Her six children were left at Smithills in the care of their uncles and it is in this period that their new clothes are described in the accounts. After 1600 the family returned to Gawthorpe, and there are some interesting examples of clothes bought for young men growing up in the household.

We have seen that the estate had several flocks of sheep. The only occasion in the early years when anything was made from the wool of these sheep was in 1587 when two lots of blankets were produced. The second and larger batch is described as follows:

	s	d
Spinning 4 stone 4 pounds of wool at 2s a stone	8	8
Adam Oldham of Manchester for dyeing two pounds of yarn blue	1	0
Alexander Cartell for weaving two pieces at $^3/_4$d a yard being 44 yards	2	9
Peter Unsworth for walking (fulling) them	1	4
John Cramton (Crompton) for shearing and frysing them	4	8
	18	5

In November 1589 when the price of wool reached 10s a stone, the estate sold 15 stone for £7 10s 0d. Between then and July 1590, a further 238 stone were sold. It all went to James Sindall at 10s a stone, realizing £126 10s 0d for the estate. This was not an enormous reward for eight years' shepherding. Perhaps other uses were made of the wool of which we are ignorant.

There is much more in the accounts about hemp and flax. These two fibres were a significant part of the lowland economy in Lancashire and

Cheshire. Indeed, they were an important part of medieval European technology. They were both grown on the estate at Hoole. Hemp (*cannabis sativa*) is a tall slender plant six feet or more high with a stem diameter of about ¼ inch (see Fig. 5). Flax (*linum usitatissimum*) is more delicate. It is under three feet high with a stem diameter of ⅛ inch and has a charming blue flower. In both plants the useful fibres are around the stem and run from the top to the root. It seems to have been the practice to sow a bushel of hemp seed (costing 4s to 7s) on perhaps a third of an acre each year. Linseed (at a similar price) was also often sown to grow into flax. In September 1587 it took 14 people (probably women) one day to 'dress' the hemp at Hoole. They were each paid 1d but their 'table' cost 4s (3½d each). After 1591 when Sir Richard Shuttleworth bought the tithes at Hoole from the Earl of Derby, we get more reliable descriptions. In 1592:

		£	s	d
April:	Hempseed to be sown at Hoole		1	2
May:	10 loads dung to hemp ground in Hoole		3	1
June:	Weed flax			7
July:	Pulling and rippling flax at Hoole		2	6
Aug-Sept:	Pulling hemp and laying in the water			
	(hemp of your own growing)		1	8
	Spreading abroad the line[32] and hemp when			
	it was taken out of the water		2	0
	7 loads of turf to dry the said hemp and line			
	to make it fit for braking		2	11
	62 days work about braking and swingling hemp			
	and line at Hoole, part of the tithe hemp			
	(men's work at 4d per day)	1	0	8

(See Figures 6–11 and their captions to understand the technical processes involved in producing the two fibres.)

In the swingled or scutched condition, the two fibres look very similar except that hemp is coarse and stiff compared with the finer, softer and more flexible flax. A good crop of hemp was about 45 stone an acre, whereas flax usually yielded about 19 stone an acre. In these accounts hemp fibre was usually about 3s to 3s 6d a stone (January–April 1590); flax was about double at 6s to 7s a stone (October 1610).

When swingled or scutched the hemp and flax fibre was transported to Smithills. The next process was heckling, which would have been done

32 'Line' is an old word for flax from which we derive 'linseed' and 'linen'.

Fig. 5. The author in a field of hemp in 1996. This was a resin-free variety grown under licence from MAFF, now DEFRA.

by the male servants on wet winter days (Fig. 12). Neither heckles nor heckling is ever mentioned in these accounts. Heckling thinned the long fibres and broke off short fibres and knotty bits called hards or hurds. The long fibres were called tear and the short tow. The more the fibre was heckled the finer it became, so fine hemp and coarse flax were similar. The tear was spun directly. The hards – the large bits broken off by the heckling – could be picked apart and the fibres added to the tow. In the sixteenth century the word hard was often used instead of tow, so we find 'cloth of hards' or 'harden (hurden) sheets'. The tow seems to have been 'carded' like wool or cotton before spinning.

| April 1593 | A pair of cards to card flax on | 6d |
| June 1590 | Spinning sack tow | 8d |

The women servants probably did spinning when they had nothing better to do. This was evidently not often enough as other women came in to spin (Figs 13 and 14).

| November 1592 | Margery Cockett for spinning 6 weeks at Smithills | 3s |

Six pence a week seems to have been a good rate of pay. No doubt the good food, warmth and company in the big house made it a fairly attractive way of spending part of the winter for women without other responsibilities. In July 1593 three women spinners were paid for 36 weeks' work (12 weeks each) at 4d a week – 12s.

Figs 6–15. These ten scenes of flax-working are details from engravings made by William Hincks in Northern Ireland in 1783. The completed drawings are beautifully executed but are unfortunately too large to be reproduced here.

Fig. 6. [Above] Pulling the flax, stooking it to dry and loading it to take to the 'retting' pool.

Fig. 7. [Right] 'Ripling' or saving the seed and then laying the flax in the water until the woody stems begin to rot.

Fig. 8. Taking the flax out of the water.

Fig. 9. Spreading the
flax to dry

Fig. 10. Drying and 'braking'. The woman in the open tent is drying the bundles of flax over a peat (turf) fire. The man with the hammer is 'beetling' the bundles to start breaking up the woody stems, and the man with the 'brake' (on four legs) is making the woody fragments as small as he can.

Fig. 8. Scutching or swingling. The woman in the left foreground is completing the braking process with a small beetle (mallet). The woman with the wooden sword is 'scutching' (or 'swingling') the broken pieces of woody core away from the bundle of fibres, and the woman beyond her is checking the bundles of fibres.

32

Fig. 12. This man is 'heckling' (or 'hackling') the flax to divide it up into the long thin fibres that remain in his hands, the 'tear', and the short fibres that break off and form the white cloud on the floor, the 'tow'. The three heckles – coarse, medium and fine – were used in turn to produce the required grade of fibre for spinning.

Figs 13/14. Two views of spinning on a treadle operated wheel.

Fig. 15. [Left] Winding or reeling the spun yarn into measured hanks for the weaver.

Fig. 16. [Right] The hemp in this heckle, photographed in Bridport Museum, Dorset, is virtually indistinguishable from the flax in Hincks's drawings, but the heckle is larger and stronger to suit the coarser hemp fibre.

After it was spun the yarn was wound into measured lengths ready for weaving (Fig. 15):

August 1592   Winding yarn at Smithills   16d

An idea of the variety of yarn produced appears in Peter Warburton's inventory in 1626. There was in stock at Arley in one room:

805 slippings of teere of hemp
440 slippings of ribbings (weft made of tow?)
35 slippings of candlewick
20 slippings of canvas yarn
TOTAL: 1,300   £32 10s 0d
75 dozens of flax and some huerdes (hards)   £3   0s 0d

In other rooms were:

34

395 fine slippings of yarn
315 slippings of a coarser sort
     with certain clewes (balls of yarn) of the same
TOTAL: 710   £20   os   od
24   slippings of linen yarn   12s   od

The first group of 1,300 slippings seems to have been valued at exactly 6d each, as were the last 24 slippings of linen yarn. The 710 slippings work out at 6.7d each, but perhaps the clewes were the extra value. The dozens of flax seem to be valued at 9d each and the hards at 3s 9d. Whether the 'dozens' of flax are the same as the 12 leas or cuts which made one hank in later times, and whether 'slippings' and 'dozens' are the same we don't know, but the prices suggest they probably were (see Appendix 1.4 for yarn measures). Certainly the yarn needed to be measured before it was given to the weaver so that the owner knew how much cloth the weaver should provide.

A variety of cloth could be woven from the different grades of yarn. It seems that hemp and flax cloth were normally woven on a loom worked by a single person, so it was rarely more than a yard wide. Some articles were more easily and cheaply made from narrow widths. For example, many sacks were best made from 24-inch-wide material so that only the sides had to be sewn up. So cloth seems to have been made in widths from 18 to 36 inches.

Widths are never given in the accounts. Thomas Pendlebury was the usual weaver but others, including John Morre's wife, did some. In October and November 1591 Pendlebury wove 120 yards of hemp cloth for 6s. This is 0.6d per yard. Later evidence suggests that three yards a day may have been a weaver's output on coarse cloth, so his pay may have worked out to between 1½d and 2d a day. We have seen that such a rate for an adult implies that he was getting meals at Smithills worth 3d or 4d a day. He may even have stayed in the house. There was a weaver's room at Arley in 1626.

Prices for weaving hemp cloth, often called canvas, varied between a halfpenny and a penny a yard. Flax cost more. In January 1597 weaving 38 yards of flaxen cloth cost 4s 3d or 1.34d a yard. In most years between 100 and 200 yards of standard hemp or flax was woven. Weaving fine linen for Sir Richard Shuttleworth's shirts was more expensive. In October 1594 38 yards cost 19s or 6d a yard, but this price may be partly because the work was not done at Smithills but in the weaver's own home.

These large rolls of ordinary cloth were kept in stock and used as required. A memorandum of 1602 gives an idea of what went on in these large houses:

> Delivered to Elizabeth (the seamstress) 33 yards canvas, teere of hemp, to make 3 pair sheets for the workmen.

This works out at 5½ yards a sheet. If the cloth was 3 ft wide, this would produce a sheet with a seam down the middle of 6 ft wide by 7 ft 6 in. long. The memorandum continued:

> Delivered to her 48 yards canvas to be sheets of hemp huerdes (hards) and she made it 5 pair and one sheet.
> Delivered to her 50 yards canvas of flax huerdes and she made 5 pair sheets and 2 shirts for Watmough.

Tear (teere) was, of course, stronger than tow because of the greater length of the fibres. The warp normally had to be of tear to stand being stretched on the loom, but tow was quite satisfactory for the weft or the 'shoot', as it was sometimes called because it was woven with the shuttle.

Despite these stocks of yarn and cloth, it was still often necessary to buy to meet urgent needs. The list of items that follows shows some of the uses plain cloth was put to. The difference in the prices per yard probably reflects both quality and width. It was almost all bought from local people.

		s	d	per yard
Oct 1584	4 yds canvas to wrap a package to London	1	6	4.5d
Nov 1586	5 yds canvas bought in Warrington for a little towell (twill?) sheet	1	3	3d
Nov 1568	20 yds great canvas to be a great towell (twill?) sheet	7	0	4.2d
Nov 1568	16 yds twill to be sacks	6	8	5d
July 1587	20 yds housewife cloth for shirts for brother	33	6	1s 8d
Feb 1589	4 yds canvas for horse collars	1	8	5d
Oct 1589	3 yds canvas for covering a gelding	1	9	7d
June 1594	3 yds canvas to line saddles	1	9	7d
Oct 1600	1 yd canvas to be 3 towels for workmen		7	

These prices, and many more like them in the accounts, suggest that 7d a yard was a common price for the type of 'canvas' made in the Shuttleworth house and used as sheets above. In October 1589 the Shuttleworths bought a quarter pack and one pound of Irish yarn in Manchester for £4

14s 9d. If this was linen (flax) yarn and weighed 101 lbs, then the yarn cost 11¼d lb. The only occasion high quality linens appear in the accounts is in August 1593 when Mrs Morte, a local gentlewoman, supplied a tablecloth, a cupboard cloth and a towel of damask for £2 13s 4d.

An interesting possibility is that all this linen and hemp cloth was used or worn 'in the brown'. The first mention of bleaching does not occur until:

April 1612 William Wood's wife for ashes and bowking
       44 hasps (slippings) of yarn   7s 10d.

'Bowking' was the common word used in the seventeenth and eighteenth centuries to describe boiling yarn in an alkaline solution to bleach it. Hasps were the same as slippings. In 1602 Elizabeth, the seamstress, was given '27 hasps or slippings of line yarn'. In August 1592 two-and-a-half mettes of fern ashes were bought for 1s 8d, but whether this was for bleaching or for other washing purposes or for making soap is not stated. A bushel of ashes was bought in London in 1608 for 2s 4d. In September 1612 Crosse's wife was paid 6d a day (and her table) for eight days burning fern ashes. In April 1618 Mrs Shuttleworth was reimbursed 12s 4d for getting 37 score of linen yarn whitened at 4d a score.[33] This all suggests that bleaching may not have been a common practice in the countryside in Lancashire in the early seventeenth century. On the other hand, it may never appear in the accounts because it was just done by the servants with ashes they had made.

Other types of cloth were either bought from or made by local people:

		s	d	per yard
Nov 1590	2 yds bolting cloth (for sieving flour)	1	8	10d
Nov 1590	3 yds coarser bolting cloth	1	6	6d
Jan 1595	Giles Ainsworth spinning and 'rolyvinge' 38 yds haircloth	11	0	
Jan 1605	34 yds haircloth for the kiln, to dry on	33	0	1s

Cloth was not the only use of hemp and flax. These fibres could be twisted directly into anything from thread to rope. Thread (for sewing), which normally consisted of two or three spun yarns twisted together to make 2 ply or 3 ply, was still made at home:

33 Score = 20; so 37 score = 740 leas or cuts = 61.6 dozens or hanks. See Appendix 1.4.

May 1589 A woman of Hoole spinning thread for my Mistress, 6 days   6d

A thicker thread, more a twine, was presumably made for this net to catch fish in a pool behind a dam:

		s	d
May 1595	2 stone of hemp to make a net to draw the dam	5	4
Aug 1595	Ann Tonge of Rivington knitting a net to draw the dam	2	6
Feb 1596	Cords for the fishnet to draw the dam	2	2

As there is no payment for making the twine, this was probably spun and the strands twisted at Smithills. Making cords and ropes was evidently a job that the ordinary farm worker could not do. They were among a group of products made of hemp that were manufactured by local specialists, as the following entries show:

		s	d
Sept 1584	12 yds of girth-web	1	6
Apr 1587	3 hemp traces	3	2
Aug 1587	50 yds hempen ropes to hang cheeseboards	4	8
Feb 1588	A dozen halters	1	0
Apr 1591	A gavel rope 8 yds long for tying sheaves of corn	2	8
Mar 1601	2 hemp 'temes' (plough ropes?)	1	0
Mar 1601	4 headstalls for horsecollars for the cart horses	1	2
Mar 1601	4 hempen reins for the horsecollars		8

These entries suggest that at this period the harness of oxen and working horses was largely based on hemp. The cheeseboards were presumably for storing cheeses and they were to be suspended from the roof timbers on ropes knotted under each shelf. Other uses for hemp cords and ropes mentioned elsewhere in these accounts have now completely vanished. Bed cords – stretched between the timber frame to support the mattress – are now unknown as are nets to catch game birds. Clock ropes are still in use among antiquarians.

In September 1596, for the first time the accounts include entries about Mrs Thomas Shuttleworth's children's clothing. She remarried that summer and left her six children, three boys and three girls, to the care of their two uncles, their schoolmaster James Yate and the other servants at Smithills. The eldest, Richard, was nearly ten and the youngest was probably four.

The following entries probably do not cover all the children's clothes. They are merely illustrations. For example, their shirts and shifts will have been made from the stock rolls of linen:

		s	d
Sept 1596	Five pairs of children's shoes	4	8
	The wife of Giles Morrice for blending and spinning 5½ stones of wool for children's clothes and blankets in the house	13	9
	For colouring part of the wool and weaving all	3	8
	For walking (fulling) and dressing the cloth	4	10
Jan 1597	Colouring and dressing a piece of cloth to be the children's clothing	5	4
June 1597	7½ yds of canvas at 1s 2d a yd, to be the children's doublets	8	9
	Silk, buttons, and pompillion for the doublets	3	4
	For knitting every boy a pair of hose	2	6
	3 pairs of shoes for the wenches	1	10
	Making 3 doublets, 3 jerkings, and 3 pairs of breeches for the boys; for six pair of linen and woollen stockings; for three gowns and 3 petticoats [for the girls]	4	8
Feb 1598	¾ yd linen cloth for the boys falling bands	2	0
Sept 1598	2 yds green fustian to be the little wenches aprons and inkle to be apron strings	3	5
Nov 1598	1¼ yds green [cloth] at 3s 8d yd to be breeches for the boys	8	0
	4¾ yds 'garc' frieze for their jerkins	9	2

In December 1598 John Woodruffe, a lawyer who had worked for Sir Richard since 1588, was paid £8 12s 6d for last year's board of the children, which shows that the family home at Smithills had broken up. By 1600, with Sir Richard's death, the land reverted to the Barton family and the Shuttleworths left Smithills.

The next account book was written by Abraham Colthurst and Edward Sherborne who were at Gawthorpe looking after the estate and preparing for the building of the new hall. The accounts give details of the clothing they provided for Tom, their cowboy:

		s	d
Jan 1601	Making a pair of stockings for cowboy		2
	A pair of clogs for cowboy		6
Feb 1601	2 calfskins and 2 sheepskins for cowboy's doublet and breeches	4	0
	Coarse canvas for lining the same	1	8
Mar 1601	A pair of shoes for Tom cowboy	1	8

		s	d
	Making the cowboy's clothes 6d, thread 3d,		
	buttons 1d		10
June 1601	4 yds canvas for Tom cowboy's two shirts	2	6
	Making his two shirts		2
Jan 1602	Cloth for a pair of stockings for the cowboy	1	5
	Making		2

In August 1602, another boy came to Gawthorpe, perhaps to assist the two managers:

		s	d
Aug 1602	3⅝ yds of green cloth at 1s 10d yd for a jerkin		
	a pair of breeches and a pair of stockings		
	for John Watmough	6	7
Sept 1602	Tailor making John Watmough's jerkin, breeches,		
	and stockings 8d, thread 3d		11

We saw John Watmough's shirts being made by Elizabeth earlier on p. 36.

Similarly in 1610, two boys were living at Gawthorpe. They were perhaps in their early teens and waiting to be placed as apprentices. They may have been cousins to the Shuttleworths.

		s	d
April 1610	5 yds of canvas cloth at 8d for shirts for John Leigh	3	4
May 1610	Making two shirts		5
	5 yds of canvas for shirts for Lawrence Shuttleworth		
	at 9d yd	3	9
April 1611	5 yds fustian at 2s for doublets for Leigh and		
	L. Shuttleworth	10	0
	4¾ yds blue cloth at 2s 4d for breeches for them	11	6
	3 yds linen cloth for linings to the doublets	2	6
	For bearing lining		11
	2½ yds of cloth to line the breeches	2	0
	5 dozen of buttons and threads to the buttonholes		9
	Black and white thread		6
	A sheep skin for pockets		4
May 1611	2 lb of wool for their clothes	1	0
	Tho. Smalley for making doublets and breeches for		
	making them on his own table	4	0
	2 hats and bands for them	2	2
	A girdle for John Leigh		4

These extracts provide examples of the clothing of ordinary people at this period. Cheap woollen cloth and blankets were processed entirely by local people. The cloth was suitable for the children even of the rich; Sir Richard Shuttleworth's grandchildren were still being clothed in local cloth in 1621 at Gawthorpe. By this time new-fangled comforts like curtains and carpets were also being made of this cloth, but for those concerned with status and fashion there seems to have been a preference for cloth from the main manufacturing districts: kersey and frieze for the young people, bays and minikins for their elders. It seems that the most likely reason for this was the better range of colours and finishes that were available. The colours of the more expensive cloths were usually specified in these accounts. New types of cloth like fustian displaced the old canvas for doublets. Both white jean fustian and white holmes fustian are mentioned after 1610.[34]

Working clothes were not always of wool. For those working with animals like Tom the cowboy, leather was often preferred. The linen lining could presumably be removed for washing. Whereas shirts were usually made by women, woollen clothes seem to have normally been cut and sewn by male tailors. Tailors also made stockings of cloth which were standard, until knitted hose or stockings like those the children had in 1597 came into fashion. Style was given to the outfits of the better off by a few luxury touches even when they were still young – silk, buttons and falling bands for the Shuttleworth boys, hats and girdles for John Leigh and Lawrence Shuttleworth before they went to be indentured. The gentry, as we know from many portraits, had very elaborate costumes at this time.

7. SUPPLIES AND SERVICES

The accounts of a large establishment like Smithills Estate tell us much about the whole local economy, since they bought or used most things that were available. More than this, they tell us about the jobs of many people who do not otherwise appear in history. This section aims to give some idea of the range of jobs people had in south Lancashire in the late

34 Jeans – a cloth originally made in Genoa and named after the town. Holmes in the same way derived its name from Ulm in south Germany. A similar cloth known to the English as denim got its name from Nimes in the south of France. All these fustians had a warp of linen and a weft of cotton.

sixteenth century. Over 40 occupations are mentioned in this section. The boundaries of 'trades' were probably not well defined in the Lancashire countryside because there were no Guilds such as existed in towns, so some men may have had more than one skill.

Only about five types of goods used at Smithills were not available locally. Almost every year they bought three of them on the docks in Chester or Liverpool. They were wine, iron, and pitch or tar. For example, in June 1586 they bought:

	£	s	d
18 gallons sack @ 2s 8d gallon and a cask for it	2	7	10
2 hogsheads wine; 1 white, 1 claret	8	5	0
½ ton Spanish iron (25 bars)	7	13	4
24 lb pitch		3	6
Richard Urmeston and Nicholas Grimshaw's expenses in Chester		5	6
James Houlden and Roger Barrs carriage to Smithills		17	0

The other two items were spices and saltfish. Spices like pepper, mace and cloves, and dried fruits like raisins and prunes came into London from the East Indies and the Mediterranean. In the early years at Smithills the Shuttleworths usually bought most of what they needed in London. When Sir Richard became Judge in Chester, other ways were found. In August 1591 £8 was sent down to London with Lawrence Fogge, the carrier, to buy spices. In August 1593 Cuthbert Hesketh bought £2 18s 6d worth in York when he was there on business. It was possible to buy such things in Lancashire but they were more expensive and usually only available in small quantities. In a similar manner saltfish were cheaper and easier to buy near the main long-distance fishing ports. The fish the Shuttleworths bought at 'Sturbridge' in September 1589 had probably been caught by the Bristol fleet and carried up the Severn to Stourbridge, Worcestershire:

	£	s	d
8 couple ling	1	6	8
15 couple cod and one fish		12	0
15 couple stockfish and one fish		10	0
Carriage of 8 couple ling and 4 couple cod from Sturbridge		10	0

The fish, the spices, and the wine were the luxuries of gentry tables in the north-west. The pitch was for marking the sheep.

The buying of the iron seems more unusual to later generations. It formed the stock of the smith's workshops at Smithills and the other demesne farms. Smiths were hired when needed. They rarely charged for iron as they used the estate's own supply. A typical entry was:

Feb 1587   Arthur Bradley, smith, 12 days   4s 0d

His rate of pay at 4d a day implies he had his meals at Smithills. When he came for a week or two like this he probably stayed in the house. The Arley inventory of 1626 included a 'smith's chamber'.

Smiths were employed in every township in which the estate farmed. Often when ploughing started, a smith had to be called in. Sometimes the workmen summoned were called ploughwrights. Whether ploughwrights just repaired the wooden parts of the plough and smiths the metal parts we don't know. In the four years from the spring of 1586 to the spring of 1590 16 or 17 different smiths or ploughwrights were employed. This suggests that there were a lot of such craftsmen in the country and that the design of ploughs left much to be desired. This may be a reason why fields were kept in arable and only ploughed once a year. The later practice of ploughing up some old grassland each year might have been more than Lancashire ploughs could manage in the 1580s.

These smiths will have repaired more than just the ploughs. They were responsible for making all the iron parts around the farm and the house such as parts on carts, harnesses, hinges, casements, handles, fire-irons and so on. It may be that the smiths who were employed to make or repair edge tools were specialists. The estate bought small amounts of steel, usually 20 gads for 1s. Axes, scythes, garden shears, a rake, a spade, and a hook were all supplied or repaired. Screw and nut assemblies for cheese presses may have been an even more specialized area. One Thomas Marche is called cutler in the accounts. Presumably he supplied, and perhaps sharpened, knives. He had a contract to appear half yearly to 'dress' the armour in the late 1580s during the Armada scare. He also repaired guns and calivers. Locks were often bought for various purposes – for a barn door, a gate, or a chest. Sometimes they were just called stocklocks. They were usually repaired by smiths, who also made keys. They were probably manufactured nearby on the coalfield. A variety of nails such as horse nails, ox nails, axle tree clout and doubly spikenes were bought nearly every month. The main supplier was William Hurst of Hulton, but whether he was a merchant buying from the actual makers or was making them himself with his own staff does not appear. The makers probably lived at Hilton (in modern Hulton) where there was a coal mine.[35]

The millwrights solved all the problems of making corn mills work, and possessed an expertise in both metal and woodworking. One called Robert Kingsley chose a suitable tree, cut it down and made a new cogwheel. Another cast a new brass step for a mill looked after by Thomas Ducworth. Wheelwrights were in a similar multi-skilled trade. One Peter Greenhough made wooden wheels, ringed with iron, and wheelbarrows.

The tinker's is a craft now completely disgraced, but then it was important. Cooking pots in most houses were made of brass, and since tinkers were skilled in brazing and soldering, they were often called in to make repairs. Thomas Munson, tinker, even soldered the cracks in the lead gutters at Smithills in December 1588. Leadwork was properly the work of a plumber, but Humphrey France, the plumber who worked at Smithills in these years, came from Wigan, which was ten miles away. He did a small repair with 48 lbs of lead in 1586 and a much larger job in 1593. Then 476 lb of new lead was bought for £1 13s 6d and he recast some gutters. Plumbers often did glazing too because the diamond-shaped 'quarrels' of glass were set in lead, but at Smithills the glazier seems not to have been the plumber from Wigan.

The fuel used at Smithills in the 1580s, as in much of Lancashire, was turf or peat, as wood was too scarce. At least 200 or 300 'wain' loads were consumed each year. Local teenagers, both boys and girls, dug it, stacked it to dry and loaded it on wains. The wains and draught animals were provided by local farmers at $1\frac{1}{2}$d a load. The teenagers drove them up to Smithills. They got paid around a penny each day and presumably had meals at the Hall. It usually took more than 100 teenager days a summer. In the 1580s, the house also used a little 'cannel' coal.[36] In 1586, seven loads were bought for 5s 3d (9d each). By 1590, eight loads only cost 4s (6d each). 12 shillings worth of coal was bought at Hilton (Hulton) in 1588, but no more was bought till 1593 when 60 horse loads were bought at Mr Bolton's pit for 7s 6d and nine wain loads from Stanley Gate for 6s 4d. From then on coal was bought each year while the family was at

35 May 1595.
36 An unusual coal that burns with a bright flame.

44

Fig. 17. The Great Hall at Smithills, looking towards the doors to the kitchen and the buttery. The logs indicate where the fire was placed originally. Notice the head of the window on the left is only just below where the roof begins to rise. Beyond the window can be seen the speer truss which divided the Hall from the entrance passage with its great door. The family, the resident servants and all the visiting workers probably ate together here in the 1580s and 1590s.

Smithills. In 1594, 240 horseloads were bought from Mr Bolton's pit at 1½d each for £1 9s 9d. As well as Mr Bolton's pit, the Hilton pit provided 15 wain loads at 1s each in 1595 and 32 loads in 1596.[37] In 1597 the pit at Stanley gate got the lion's share of the business – 38 loads for 34s 8d. The estate or their tenants seem to have provided the carriage.

The great increase in coal burning which began in 1593 suggests that new fireplaces with chimneys were built at that time, and indeed we find in the accounts that considerable building works were carried out in 1592, as described below. Wood and peat could be burned in fireplaces in the centre of rooms and the smoke allowed to escape through vents in a lantern on the roof. Coal smoke was too unpleasant and necessitated a chimney. (See Figs 17–22).

Building work was an important occupation. The peculiarity of it at Smithills, to a twenty-first-century person, was that most of the materials were already on the site. John March got slate in the Egburden for 15 days in 1589. All the stone for the walling done in 1592 was gathered nearby, and trees were felled when carpenters needed wood. The major item that had to be brought in was lime for mortar and the white limewash with which all the buildings were finished. In 1589 they bought 106 bushels of limestones (at 3d each) and six loads of coal for the lime kiln and set up their own kiln. In October of that year, they discovered that they could buy lime already burnt from Clitheroe. It cost 1s 3d a horseload, compared with 6d a load (of two bushels) for the unburnt, but it was evidently worth it as they bought 63 loads for £3 18s 9d. In 1590, repairs were made at the mill. In 1591 materials were gathered for the major works planned for 1592: 408 loads of 'limestones' from Clitheroe at 1s 1d, and 1,500 bricks. This was unslaked or 'quick' lime which had to be mixed with water in a pit to be ready for use the next summer – a process called 'breeding lime' in the accounts. 427 more loads were bought in 1592. It was all delivered by a dozen or more men who seem to have been from the Clitheroe area.

The accounts do not say what works the builders carried out in 1592.

37 We shall see on p. 51 that horseloads were normally about 150 to 160 lbs. There are eight 1½d in 1s, so a 'wain' load was probably 8 x 150 = 1,200 to 1,300 lbs, approximately (just over half a ton). Presumably turf 'wains' were the same. We will see on p. 210 that at Arley in the 1750s 'carts' which had only two wheels carried about one ton of stone and wagons, which had four wheels, carried up to two tons. There was, no doubt, a continuous improvement in these vehicles in the 150 years, and the words used to describe them changed their meanings too.

Fig. 18. This map of 1578 shows a Cheshire gentry house without chimneys as Smithills may have been until 1592. Burrows Hall, Cogshall (now the site of Brook Farm, Comberbach), was the principal house on a small freehold estate of about 173 acres owned by a gentry family, *Massie* of Rixton, Lancs. The large building was evidently the Hall and the three smaller ones were the barn, the stables and the cowshed. The Hall is shown as single-storey with a lantern on the ridge to let out the smoke. All houses had similar lanterns before chimneys were built. Notice the wide grassy road and the pack-horse bridge over the brook. See map in colour p. xvi.

Fig. 19. The south elevation of the Great Hall at Smithills. The window to the right of the large door is the one shown in Fig. 17. The building of chimneys enabled people to insert second storeys in these old high rooms. It can be seen that the wall above this window has been raised and a new, flatter, pitched roof made over the Great Hall so as to allow first-floor rooms to be constructed over the kitchen to the left of the door. In a similar way the range of building to the right may have been converted to two storeys by the insertion of a floor behind the white quatrefoil timbering. These changes were part of the building revolution brought about by the invention and use of chimneys. The other part was the construction of multi-storey brick or stone houses like Gawthorpe Hall – Fig. 1 above.

Six or seven wallers with assistant labourers were employed from May to July. Slaters and thatchers worked on the roofs. It is possible that this work included building new hearths and chimneys using the bricks that had been bought which would resist the heat of the new coal fires (see Fig. 20). In the summer of 1594, Oliver Ashley, the whitelimer came. Hair was bought from the tanner to bind the lime slurry. Four-and-a-half bushels of leather patches (presumably offcuts) were bought in Manchester

Fig. 20. Part of the west elevation at Smithills. The hearth and chimney on the left may be one of those built in 1592. The single flue above the large hearth suggests that it may have been built before the first floor was inserted. Similar chimneys were built outside the walls at Arley Hall, see Fig. 48.

to boil up to make size to seal powdery parts of the old walls before the whitewash was applied. As well as the wallers who laid roughstones, the estate employed a skilled mason who could shape stones. The only other building craftsmen to work at Smithills were the pavers Roger Yate and Ellis Geste, who worked with a helper for $2\frac{1}{2}$ weeks in 1589. Their materials were cobblestones from the fields and sand. Almost all these building craftsmen were paid 4d a day when they worked at Smithills. With their meals in the Hall worth 3d or 4d a day, their total cost to the employer was 7d or 8d a day. Only Robert Kingsley, one of the millwrights, charged more than 4d. He and his man cost $10\frac{1}{2}$d a day in October 1587.

A good number of occupations have now been mentioned – in textiles, in fuel, in building, as well as smiths and wrights of various kinds. A

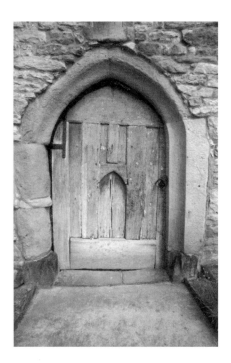

Fig. 21. [Left] The entrance door of the Great Hall with its small wicker door to reduce draughts when people went in and out in winter.

Fig. 22. [Right] The stone window beside the door of the Great Hall.

surprisingly large group of miscellaneous employments remain to be touched on. We have seen goods brought to Smithills from the docks at Chester, from 'Sturbridge' and from the hills near Clitheroe. This by no means exhausts the range of the carrying trade revealed in these accounts. A number of men seem to have been regular carriers to and from London. John Page in August 1589 charged £2 17s 9d for bringing 10½ hundredweights (cwts) from London to Smithills. This works out at 5s 6d a cwt or 6d a ton mile. There was a significant two-way trade to London in this period. Textiles went south and luxuries were carried north. The established view of historians is that 1s a ton mile was the rate for a journey out and the return empty. This was reduced to 6d a ton mile if loaded in both directions.[38] A week earlier, in July, the Shuttleworths had

38 Willan, 1976, pp. 6–7, lists the prices but fails to discuss the pricing of 'return loads'. The full cost of a two-way trip was divided between the two journeys in accordance with market forces, e.g., it could be 50–50 or it could be 80–20. These accounts confirm these rates.

been charged 8s a pack for seven other packs from London. If this was also at the rate of 5s 6d a cwt, these packs weighed about 160 lbs each. This was probably the approximate weight of a horseload in this period. That there was in existence a tariff for carriage to London based on weight is indicated by another item. In May 1587 Lawrence Fogge charged 1s for taking six puddings weighing a total of 16 lbs. This was only one of a number of instances when choice eatables like 'three cheeses' and 'a woodcock pie' were sent to London. There seem also to have been regular carriers who would carry small packages to other towns like Chester and Manchester.

Part of the reason for the importance of the carrying trade in the north-west was that it was prime livestock country. By far the best agricultural product in the area was, as it still is, grass, so there was no problem in keeping and feeding horses for use in carting. A number of other non-agricultural trades were also dependent on the presence of large numbers of livestock, foremost among them being tanning. Adam Platt of Westhoughton was the tanner to whom the Shuttleworths almost always sold their ox and cow hides. He probably had a good business as is suggested by the fact that he was one of only nine people who paid tax in that township in 1600[39] The hides were tanned into leather with the tannic acid from oak bark. This process produced a hard, tough leather fit for the soles of shoes. Sheep and calf skins also had a commercial value, though for different purposes, and they were prepared in a different way. These hides were 'tawed', or dressed for use by steeping them in a solution of alum and salt, after which they were oiled. This created a soft, pliable leather for clothes such as breeches and gloves.

These two basic leather trades gave rise to further occupations creating the end-products. The shoemakers were probably the most numerous, but glove-making was also important. Parchment was probably a minor product. An old trade that seems to have been growing strongly in this period was saddlery. As the basic leather-making processes were improved and cheapened, leather came to replace hemp in the harnesses for horses and oxen. At the same time horses started to replace oxen as the principal draught animals so another craft that must have been growing in importance was the making of horse-collars. Oxen did not wear collars; they were normally used in pairs attached to a yoke. The Smithills accounts record purchases from all these different craftsmen.

39 Tait, 1924, pp. 30 and 81.

Yet another group dependent on livestock were the veterinary experts. This seems to have been a part-time occupation for some people who acquired a reputation for this work. Horses' health was looked after by farriers. The Shuttleworths' favourite farrier was Robert Markland who seems to have been the same man who was one of the principal shop-keepers in Wigan, and in this guise he supplied a hundredweight of iron in June 1586.[40] In February 1587 a cow apparently dislocated its shoulder; this was 'put in' by Humphrey Marsh, who evidently had a reputation as a bonesetter. John Bouteman, the horseleech, was paid 2s for cures in May 1588.

One other major craft remains to be mentioned. Richard Kerslay, the cooper,[41] was a frequent visitor to Smithills. He always came when a new consignment of wine arrived, but he also had to attend to the beer barrels and all the other pitchers, firkins, vats, and so on that were in use around the house and farm. His materials, both wooden staves and iron hoops, seem to have been produced on the estate. The other occupations that appear in the accounts were those that many families would have done for themselves. The estate regularly employed people to lay bait to kill rats and mice. Less often it employed men to fish in the pools and streams. This was probably done with nets like the one described under 'Textiles' (p. 38). Other people made baskets, wiskets, sieves, wooden spoons, and other implements that were purchased. During the Armada crisis, the family bought two 'steel coats', made of canvas covered with about 1,500 small steel plates and fabricated by a specialist called Abram Asherwood.

Two common products that many people probably bought were made at home in Smithills. Beer was usually made by the brewer on the staff. Occasionally one had to be hired. They malted their own barley in their own kiln. A few pounds of hops were bought in a town. It seems that the usual practice was to make a small quantity of the first strong brew of ale for the use of the family and their guests. A much larger quantity of weak beer known as 'small beer' was made in the second brew. This was the common drink of the whole household for every meal.[42] At Smithills they also made their own soap and candles, using the tallow from their own cattle. To make soap it was boiled with an alkaline water made with wood or fern ashes. This was not the practice at Gawthorpe where they regularly

40 Bagley, 1958, pp. 48–68.
41 A man who made casks and barrels.
42 Harland, 1856, p. 217.

bought soap and employed candlemakers. Finally I must mention an item that was bought regularly each year by both houses – salt. The salt industry is the subject of Chapter 7 in my forthcoming *Capital and Innovation*.[43] The analysis there includes information from these accounts.

8. THE HOUSEHOLD (AT SMITHILLS) AND THE YOUNG MEN IN ATTENDANCE

In the years up to 1589 when Richard Shuttleworth was working in London, he and his wife visited Smithills twice a year. Often it was in March/April and August/September. Evidence of these visits appear in the accounts because Richard checked his brother Thomas's bookkeeping and signed his approval in the account book. These were also the periods when luxury foods were bought. In the spring, fresh fish was most important because only fish was eaten in Lent. Herring, salmon, smelts, pike, eels, bream, freshwater trout, mussels and cockles were purchased, all caught on the coast or in the rivers and ponds nearby. In the autumn the principal addition to the ordinary diet were chickens and wild fowl. The latter came in amazing variety and size from sparrows and larks to the more usual game birds like woodcock and partridge. When Thomas and Ann Shuttleworth were on their own at Smithills, their diet was confined to the produce of the estate or, if there were luxuries, they bought them with their own money.

After Sir Richard's appointment as Judge in Chester in the summer of 1589, they were more frequently at Smithills, though it seems that they stayed in Chester in term time. In June 1590, Lady Shuttleworth hurt her leg while they were at Shrewsbury. She had treatment from a surgeon and returned to Smithills where she received prescriptions from an apothecary. For several weeks she was attended by a beggar in whose advice she put her trust. However, none of these remedies were successful and she slowly declined, dying in March 1592. As she got worse during this long illness, it seems she increasingly had to be tempted to eat by being offered delicacies. Richard Stones, who had always been the main provider of wild fowl, was kept so busy that he was taken onto the permanent staff. He was then paid a salary rather than a fee for each parcel he obtained.

---

43 Foster, 2003.

The neighbouring gentry had often sent presents to Smithills when the Shuttleworths were in residence. During Lady Shuttleworth's illness, they were even more attentive. Those with parks like the Earl of Derby sent stags or bucks. Small freeholders sent fish or fruit.

The owner's prolonged presence in the house being unexpected, supplies of other quality foods ran low. White bread and pots of ale were bought. Wheat was bought in Preston. As her illness progressed, she had to be more frequently distracted by troupes of travelling players. Her last Christmas was enlivened with troupes from Rochdale, Blackburn, and Cheshire as well as one from Garstang, complete with a piper.

The other people often in the house were the young men attached to Sir Richard. Seven men's names appear several times in the accounts in the Smithills period. Cuthbert Hesketh is called cousin. Richard Urmestone's father sent presents to the Hall. Nicholas Grimshaw and John Woodruffe may have been relations and neighbours from the Gawthorpe area. We can infer that they were the social superiors of the ordinary servants. They helped Sir Richard with managing his estate, his legal business, and sometimes just assisted with the running of the household. One is tempted to assume that they were young men learning about the Law and landed estates, but we are never given a clue about their ages. Their wages seem not to have been greatly different from those of the better paid servants. Christopher Smith got £2 a year in 1590. Edward Shireburn's rate was £3 6s 8d per annum in 1601, when he was managing the house at Gawthorpe. We saw earlier that Robert Aspeden, who was paid £2 a year, occupied a special position of trust among the other servants. He was always paid by Thomas Shuttleworth. On only two occasions were any of these young managers paid by Thomas, so they must have had money direct from Sir Richard. This marked their close relationship with him.

Their duties were varied. Cuthbert Hesketh must have been knowledgeable in the Law. He received money to progress Sir Richard's lawsuits in 1592 and '93. He took possession for Sir Richard of newly acquired lands at Heblethwaite in July 1592 and at Inskipp in December 1595. In 1589 Richard Urmestone was accompanied by Robert Aspeden when he went to keep the manor court at Barbon. The next year he went with Nicholas Grimshaw. Christopher Smith helped arrange for two stags to be killed at Lyme and taken down to London in 1583. The previous year he had fulfilled the estate's obligation to provide a light horseman at the parade before Lord Strange in Preston. In 1592 John Woodruffe and Abraham Coulthurst accompanied Sir Richard on the circuit to Welshpool. In February 1591 John Woodruffe supported Thomas Shuttleworth on a visit to Forcett. The relative position of these men in the household may have been defined on these occasions.

One or two of the men in this group were probably in attendance on Sir Richard wherever he went. Whether they were always living at one or the other of his establishments when not on an expedition we don't know. Equally, we don't learn from these accounts whether they had other jobs or business and so were only in effect part-time with Sir Richard. They seem to have formed a miniature court around him which was, no doubt, modelled on the much grander court surrounding noblemen like the Earl of Derby whose entourage contained between 115 and 140 people in the 1580s.[44] He, in turn, had derived the style of his household from that of the Queen at Westminster.

9. SIR RICHARD SHUTTLEWORTH'S INCOME AND WEALTH

Finally, before leaving the Shuttleworths it is desirable to say something about Sir Richard's financial affairs. The estate that his brother Lawrence inherited in 1599 consisted of the ancestral Gawthorpe lands and the properties purchased by Sir Richard. These had been bought with his earnings from the Law over the previous 30 years. The Smithills estate had been returned to the Barton family. We have much less evidence than is desirable about this land, but it appears to have been producing an income of about £500 p.a. around 1600.[45] The value of property in the century 1550–1650 was very much dependent on the legal position. Without a full knowledge of this, which is seldom available to historians, estimates of value are speculative. An example in the Shuttleworth estate is provided by the Forcett lands. In the 1580s the rents there appear to have been about £30 a year. By 1590 they seem to have increased to £47 13s 8d for half a year, i.e., £95 7s 4d a year. By 1605 they seem to have become £131 8s 4d a half year, i.e., £262 16s 8d a year. As well as spending money buying land, Sir Richard appears to have been lending money to people throughout the last 17 years of his life. Mostly these loans seem to

44 Girouard, 1979, p. 82, and Raines, 1853.
45 Annual receipts and payments shown in the accounts in the early 1600s seem to run around this figure.

have been sums under £50. In the accounts, amounts were continually being paid at Sir Richard's order. Equally sums were often received and sometimes it was noted that the debtor's bond had been delivered to him. We never get a clue as to the rate of interest charged, so we don't know how important a part of Sir Richard's income the proceeds of money-lending were.

We can give some estimates of the value of the family's Gawthorpe lands in Sir Richard's lifetime. When he was born in 1541 the family had, as we have seen, 170½ statute acres at Gawthorpe. The annual value of these upland acres was probably about 4d an acre in 1507. The Duchy of Lancaster could not get more than 4d a statute acre for land in the area when it raised the rents in 1505–7.[46] The family's gross landed income would have been about £2 16s 10d p.a. so that after paying their rent to the Duchy of Lancaster of £1 15s 1d, their net income was £1 1s 9d. The value of upland acres in south Lancashire increased rapidly in the sixteenth century. Helped by improvements in communications, like the rebuilding of Warrington bridge in 1495, the area became part of the market economy. Hill land had traditionally been cheap because it was difficult to grow grain there, but sheep and cattle flourished in the hills nearly as well as in the plain. As it became possible to sell animals and to buy grain, the value of upland acres improved. As well as the growing profitability of their farm, the Shuttleworths enjoyed an improvement in their property rights. In the 1560s 'copyhold' tenure received greater legal recognition so that they became virtually freeholders of their 170-acre farm. These great accessions of wealth no doubt played some part in the Herald's decision to recognize the family in the Visitation of 1567.[47] By 1600 the annual value of the ancestral Gawthorpe lands was probably about 6s an acre. The gross income from them would have risen to £51 3s 0d. After paying the Duchy rent of £1 15s 1d, they would have had £49 7s 11d left.[48] If the rental income of the whole estate in 1600 was £500 p.a., Sir Richard's purchases were mainly responsible for the increase. They were bringing in about £450 per annum.

46 Farrer, 1912, Vol. 2, p. 373 describes 60 acres let for 33s 4d. This is 6.6d a Lancashire acre which equals 4d a statute acre.

47 Ormerod, 1851, p. 19. Compare this with the recognition of the Millingtons on their 70-acre freehold in Appleton in the Visitation of 1580, Ch. 3, p. 101–3 below.

48 Upland acres were worth about half as much as plains land. See Foster, 2003, Ch. 3, (iii).

APPENDIX 1.1

The Shuttleworth Account Books

The account books kept by the Shuttleworth family have been known for a long time. In 1856-8, the Chetham Society published four volumes about them edited by John Harland (Volumes 35, 41, 43, 46). There are nine account books, and they cover the period September 1582 to October 1621. Up until 1600, they are concerned with the family's life at Smithills near Bolton (see Map 1). After that, they cover the building of Gawthorpe Hall and the life lived there. Mr Harland printed extracts from these account books to create a compendious dictionary of prices. He gives one or more examples of every type of entry. These extracts from the accounts only fill 258 of the 1,171 pages contained in the four volumes. The rest is explanatory material. There are notes on the family, and other lists of prices. More than two volumes consist of notes about the items in the accounts and the words used to describe them. This is excellent and interesting scholarship. I have used his work liberally in this chapter. However, no picture emerges about many aspects of life at Smithills. For example, it remains unclear how many people were employed in the household or how much land was being farmed. There are many examples of payments to the staff, but the cost of their total annual remuneration is not worked out.

My study has been mostly based on the first 400 pages of Volume 2 of the original accounts. This covers the period from March 1586 to August 1594. The number of entries on these pages is probably between 6,000 and 8,000. The receipts and expenses follow a similar pattern in each year. The picture of the way of life at Smithills that emerges is therefore amply supported by evidence. The first volume of the accounts shows the establishment at Smithills being built up. The third volume, which covers the family's last six years at Smithills, adds little new information on most topics. On some subjects I have drawn examples from the whole 39 years covered in the account books.

The Shuttleworth family's land at Gawthorpe

W. Farrer translated *The Court Rolls of the Honour of Clitheroe* and published them in 3 volumes 1897–1913. These books allow one to trace the Shuttleworth family. The references are to Farrer's volumes.

1. Ughtred Shuttleworth attended a Court in 1425 (Vol. 2, p. 7). He was a tenant in Padiham in 1443 (Vol. 1, p. 506). His relationship to those who follow is uncertain.

2. Lawrence Shuttleworth attended the Court between 1496 and 1529 (Vol. 2, pp. 10–86). In the Rental of Tenants at Will in 1527, he held property as follows (Vol. 2, pp. 379–81):

Township	Rent p.a.		
	s	d	
Ightenhill	8	6	'Old Fines'
Padiham	3	9	'Old Fines'
Padiham	6	6½	New Fines Copthurst Hey
	18	9½	

3. Nicholas Shuttleworth attended the Court between 1522 and 1557. His property comprised the above which he inherited from Lawrence together with (Vol. 2, pp. 277–8, pp. 386–8):

Township	Rent p.a.		
	s	d	
Padiham	12	0	
		12	
	2	6	Goldfield
		10	2 ox gang
	16	4	

He therefore paid total rents of £1 15s 1½d.

4. Hugh Shuttleworth (*c.* 1520–97) was the eldest son of Nicholas and inherited all his property (Vol. 2, pp. 154–5, pp. 277–8). The total rent payable was £1 15s 1d. Farrer suggests that all these rents were at the

rate of 4d per Lancashire acres (Vol. 2, pp. 398–9). This means that the total acres Hugh inherited was $105\frac{1}{4}$ Lancashire acres, which equals $170\frac{1}{2}$ statute acres. In addition to this enclosed land, all the tenants had rights in common to the extensive grazing on the hills. These lands were not divided among the tenants until 1594.

Gawthorpe is on the banks of the river Calder at about 300 ft above sea level. The land rises up to the moors on both sides of the narrow valley.

APPENDIX 1.3

Farming

Table A. Cattle herds from Warburton of Arley inventories

	1575				1626			
	No.	Each			No.	Each		
		£	s	d		£	s	d
Draught oxen	28	1	11	8	32	5	10	0
Fat Oxen	13	3	6	8	14	5	15	0
3 yr old Steers	—	—			8	4	10	0
Twinter Steers & Heffers	40	1	10	0	21	3	10	0
Sterks	40	1	3	4	25	1	13	4
Calves	26		9	6	35	1	2	6
Cows	59	1	11	10	64	3	8	4
Bulls	3	1	17	10	14	3	15	0
TOTALS:	209				213			

These inventories also illustrate the rise in the value of cattle between the two dates.

Table B. Grain crops at Lostock

	1586	1587	1588	1589	1590	1591	1592	1593
Ploughed, statute acres	25.3	27.5	27.5	30.1	25.3	28.6	25.3	33.8
Sheared, statute acres	21.1	23.2	21.1	24.6	25.3	26.4	25.3	31.2
Threshed – oats, in bushels	189.0	657.0	663.0	555.0	672.0	828.0	724.5	757.5
Threshed – barley, in bushels	15.0	60.0	–	–	–	90.0	–	42.0
Yield oats per acre	9.0	28.3	24.1	18.4	26.6	31.4	28.6	24.3
Yield barley per acre (Notes 1, 2)	3.6	14.0	–	–	–	39.1	–	16.2

Average yield of oats over 8 years: 23.8 bushels per acre

Average yield of barley over 4 years: 18.2 bushels per acre

Notes

1 The difference between the amount of land ploughed and the quantity sheared is probably because a member of the permanent staff such as Robert Aspeden was present to supervise the work and himself sheared part of the crop. The part this person sheared in 1586 and 1581 was the part planted with barley because we know the acreage sown with barley and the piecework shearers are described as shearing only oats. I have therefore assumed that the staff member sheared the barley in 1587 and 1593.

2 Barley acreage   1586: 4.2 acres
   1587: unknown, probably 4.3
   1591: 2.3 acres
   1593: unknown, probably 2.6.

Table C. Piecework rates of pay for farm work at Lostock

These were the usual rates paid for farming operations on Smithills estate 1586–94. The worker was always 'at his own table', i.e., not getting food and drink. The original Cheshire acres, sieves and bushels (see Table F below) have been converted here to statute acres and Winchester bushels. To recapture the original figures, one can convert back to the old measures. Thus there are 2.1157 statute acres in a Cheshire acre, so 7.1d x 2.1157 = 15d or 1s 3d, which was the rate paid for holding the plough for a Cheshire acre. These rates are for the supply of Labour only; the estate's oxen and equipment were always used. By using the rates of pay discussed in the previous section, one can get an idea of the length of time these jobs took. Thus 'holding the plough' for spring sown crops was usually done in March and April when an adult rate of between 4d and 6d a day might have been appropriate. So they probably ploughed less than an acre per day. A detailed description of the technology of north-western farming is to be found in my *Cheshire Cheese and Farming*, Part 3, II–V, pp. 50–75 . Ploughing seems to have always been done with oxen, except in April 1589, when Oliver Moors was paid 1s 8d for holding a horse plough at Lostock for four days.

Operation	Rate per statute acre
Holding the plough	7.1d
Driving the plough	6.6d
Harrowing	2.8d
Shearing oats	18.9d
Shearing barley and wheat	up to 24.6d
Mowing hay	7.6d–8.5d
'Tenting' hay	8.5d
Threshing oats	9 bushels for 4d
Threshing barley	5 bushels for 4d

Notes

1 In addition to these 'standard' works, temporary workers were often employed on ditching and other drainage works.
2 'Tenting' hay at piece rates at Smithills was the only work done there for which food was not provided, presumably because the worker came and went according to the weather.
3 When Henry Davidson mowed at Smithills in August 1587, he was only paid 4.3d an acre because he worked alongside the permanent staff for whom food and drink were provided. In August 1588 he mowed again at Smithills at 5d a day – a similar rate if he did just over an acre a day.

Table D. Tithes gathered by Smithills estate in Winchester bushels

Crop	Township	Oats	Barley	Wheat	Rye	Beans	Cost of winnow	Cost of winnow, in other years
1589	Blackrod	144	20	–	–	2	10d	1s; 1s; 1s 2d
1589	Bolton	144	20	½	2	–	1s	1s; 1s 4d; 1s
1590	Bolton	90	14	1	5	–	1s	1s; 1s 4d; 1s
1590	Heaton	333	13	–	1	–	1s 10d	3s 7d in 1591
1592	Bolton	162	25	2	5	–	1s 6d	–

Notes

1. The figures for Blackrod and Bolton are probably only half the tithe of these townships, as in November 1592 the payment for these tithes says 'the moitie of the tithe corn'. However, the figures for 1590 are described as 'all the tithe, corn there'.

Table E Grain prices and sales 1580–87

Table E.1. English national market price per bushel

	Wheat	Barley	Oats
Average 1580–4 (5 years)	2s 6d	1s 6d	10d
1585	3s 10½d	1s 10¾d	1s 1¼d
1586	5s 8½d	1s 9d	1s 1½d

Source: Rogers, *A History of Agriculture and Prices*, Vol. 4, 5, 1882–7.

Table E.2. Prices from Shuttleworth accounts (purchases or sales) per bushel

Calendar Year	Wheat	Barley	Oats	Oatmeal
1582	–	2s 6d to 2s 9d	–	–
1583	6s 4d	2s 4d	1s 2d	2s 4d
1584	4s 5d	2s 1d	1s 2d	2s
1585	–	–	–	2s 4d
1585 June–July	6s 4d to 7s 6d	3s 4d to 4s 8d	2s to 2s 5d	4s 4d
1585 Aug.–Dec.	9s 3d to 9s 9d	3s 4d to 4s 8d	2s to 2s 5d	4s 4d
1587 July–Sept.	11s to 13s 6d	5s 4d to 7s	–	–

Table E.3. Shuttleworth grain sales April 1586–September 1587

	Bushels	£ s d	No. of Buyers
Wheat	124	56 5 6	36
Barley	172	41 14 10	54
Oats	896½	98 9 7	7
Oatmeal	72	15 12 0	11
	TOTAL:	212 1 11	

Table F. Measures

1. *Square measures*

   A Cheshire acre was based on an 8-yard rod, pole, or perch, so:

   1 square pole = 64 square yards

   1 acre or 160 square poles = 10,240 square yards

   A Lancashire acre was based on a 7-yard rod, pole, or perch, so:

   1 square pole = 49 square yards

   1 acre or 160 square poles = 7,840 square yards

A statute acre was based on a $5\frac{1}{2}$-yard rod, pole, or perch, so:

  1 square pole = $30\frac{1}{4}$ square yards
  1 acre or 160 square poles = 4,840 square yards
1 Hectare = 2.4711 statute acres

N.B. Acres are always statute acres in the text of this book.

2. *Grain measures*
a) **mett(e)** All grains were sometimes measured in the Shuttleworth accounts in
mettes. 'Mette' is an old word for a measure. At Arley Hall in the 1750s and '60s,
grain was usually sold by 'measures.' J. Harland, Shuttleworth Accounts, Chetham
Society, Vol. 46, p. 791, quotes Ray 'a mett or strike = 1 bushel', and agrees that
this is the meaning of mette in these accounts. This was a Winchester bushel.

b) **bushel** The reason the words mette or measure were used was because in
Cheshire and Lancashire, barley was traditionally measured in bushels. These
bushels contained 5 mettes. For example, 20 May 1587 'received for a mette of
barley 6s 0d', and same date 'received for a bushel of barley £1 6s 8d'. The five
mettes in the bushel fetched 5s 4d each. These large five mette bushels continued
to be used into the middle of the eighteenth century. Harrop's *Manchester
Mercury* reported grain prices regularly. On 10 March 1752, the price of wheat
was given as 24 shillings and this was stated to be for a 'load of 20 Winchester
pecks', i.e., at 4 pecks to a Winchester bushel = 5 Winchester bushels. On 5
March 1754, the price of barley was given as 15s to 19s and this was stated to be
for 20 pecks. At Arley Hall the price wheat sold for in March 1752 was 5s a
measure. Also at Arley Hall, the price paid for barley in March 1754 was 3s 4d a
measure, and the price paid for oats in February 1754 was 1s 10d a measure.

c) **sieve** Oats were usually measured in the Shuttleworth accounts in sieves.
For example, '1st Sept 1586 received from William Rigby for $15\frac{1}{2}$ sieves of oats
at twenty-two shillings £17 1s 0d'. The piecework rate for threshing oats was 4d
a sieve or less. We know people could thresh nine or more bushels per day.[1] This
suggested there were nine bushels in a sieve. The price quoted in Harrop's
Manchester Mercury on 5 March 1754 was 14s–17s, and this was stated to be for
'36 pecks' = 9 bushels.

NB The old measures have always been converted to Winchester bushels just
called 'bushels' in the text of this book.

1 Foster, 1998, p. 56.

APPENDIX 1.4.

Measurements of hemp and linen yarn

Very little seems to be known about English linen manufacture. The main
eighteenth century centres of production were Ireland and Scotland.
Both their systems of measurement used a wheel with a 90-inch (2½ yard)
circumference.[2] These measures were established by Parliament in Scotland and Ireland:

1 thread	= 90 inches	
120 threads	= 1 cut (Scottish) or 1 lea (Irish) = 300 yards	
12 leas	= 1 hank in both Scottish and Irish	
4 hanks	= 1 spindle or spangle	

It seems likely therefore that the English system was similar. Hasps and
slippings are probably to be equated with cuts and leas. 'Dozens' were 12
leas or 1 hank. I have found only two examples of yarn measures in these
accounts: (1) in March 1617 a woman was paid 9d for spinning 30 leas of
canvas yarn, and (2) in February 1618, 7 score of linen yarn were bought
at 1s 10d a score for a total of 12s 10d. The variety of yarns that could be
spun and the character of the cloth that could be made from each
together with the costs of each yarn and cloth make a large subject. No
textile historian has so far attempted it.

2 Horner, 1920, p182.

II

Sir Peter Leicester of Tabley
1613–78

1. FAMILY LIFE

The archive left by Peter Leicester, the famous Cheshire historian, is one of the principal sources used in my research. It provides material for a more rounded portrait of the man than the surviving legal documents allow of any of his ancestors. He was born in 1613, the eldest son of Peter and Elizabeth, daughter of Sir Randle Mainwaring of Peover. Like so many Cheshire gentry he went to Brasenose College, Oxford,[1] from 1631–3. In addition, he acquired some legal knowledge at Gray's Inn to which he was admitted on 20 August 1632. In a more unusual move his father made over the whole estate to him in December 1636, reserving only for himself and his wife a rent charge of £200 a year. Peter's parents appear to have continued to live at Tabley where his mother died, aged 54, in 1641 and his father in 1647, aged 59.

The result of this was that young Peter had full control of the estate in the difficult period leading up to the Civil War. His sympathies were Royalist. He appears to have been involved in a number of schemes to raise money in this period but whether this was for himself or other Royalists or the cause in general is not clear in the surviving papers.[2] He was certainly not free from these entanglements for many years. He appears to have joined the Royalists with a group of his tenants. He certainly participated in the defence of Chester. In November 1642 he married Elizabeth, youngest daughter of Gilbert, Lord Gerard and Eleanor, sole daughter and heiress of Thomas Dutton of Dutton, Cheshire. Her mother had married Robert Needham, Lord Kilmorey, as her second husband and seems to have been living with him and all her children at Dutton Hall at the time of the marriage. See Appendix 2.4 for genealogy. Both Lord Kilmorey and Elizabeth's brother Dutton, Lord Gerard, were Royalists,

---

1 This college was founded in 1509 by William Smith of the parish of Prescot, Lancashire and Richard Sutton of the parish of Prestbury, Cheshire.
2 DLT/D395, for example.

Fig. 23. Sir Peter Leicester, 1st Bt, 1613–78.

so they were not in a position to pay her portion of £3,000, or perhaps even the interest on it, in cash.

Peter Leicester appears to have started his married life at Dutton Hall. In his account book he noted that his wife owed £30 for the diet of her maid and herself before marriage and that he owed £70 for the diet of his man, his footboy and himself together with his wife and her maid for the

Fig. 24. The entrance to Dutton Hall – detail of a watercolour by Piers Egerton-Warburton, *c.* 1880. This Hall was built in 1539 and in Sir Peter's time was surrounded by 1,400 acres of demesne lands – the largest demesne in Cheshire. The Great Hall was so much admired that it was carefully taken down and re-erected in East Grinstead, Sussex *c.* 1933.

Fig. 25. John, 1st Lord Byron of Newstead, Notts, Governor of Chester during the Civil War, an ancestor of the nineteenth-century poet, died in France, 1652.

year to Christmas 1643.[3] There must have been journeying between Dutton and Chester, because their first two sons were both born in Chester – Robert on 11 September 1643 and Byron on 26 November 1644. The latter was

3 DLT/B52, Peter Leicester's notebook which is the source of much of the financial information set out here.

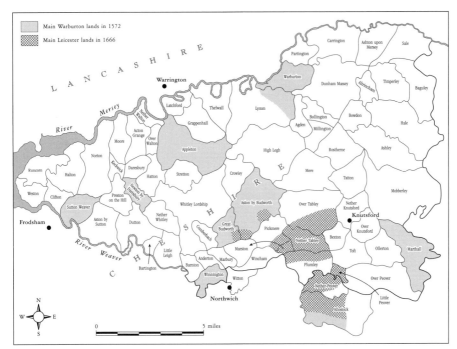

Map 2. The Bucklow Hundred of Cheshire showing the main estates of the Leicesters and the Warburtons. On the southern edge are Witton, Nether Peover and Allostock in Northwich Hundred and Winnington in Eddisbury Hundred. The hatching shows the approximate proportion of each township owned, not the actual areas. See Foster, 2003, App. 2.3–2.4, for more details of the two estates.

named after his father's general, Lord Byron. Peter Leicester's admiration for his commanding officer and his wife no doubt also accounts for the magnificent portraits of Lord Byron by William Dobson, and of his wife Eleanor, by Peter Lely, which are still in Tabley House. Separated from his estate, which was in Parliament-controlled country, it must have been difficult to provide for the expenses of his military life. In order to keep going during the war he sold £69 worth of silver in August 1644 and a further £38 worth in September 1645.

After the war the Leicesters returned to Tabley where the rest of their children were born. In 1647 Peter compounded for the estate and paid a fine under the Oxford Articles of £747 10s[4] This fine was equal to Peter's income for one year from the estate. The total estate income was around

4 Committee for Compounding, p. 1286.

Fig. 26. Eleanor Needham, 1627–63, was married to Lord Byron from 1644 to 1652. A half sister of Lady Leicester, she had earlier been married, aged 11, to Peter Warburton, heir of Arley. He died of smallpox at Christ Church, Oxford, aged 19. Sir Peter Leicester described her as 'a person of such comely carriage and presence, handsomeness, sweet disposition, honour and general repute in the world, that she has scarce left her equal behind'. By contrast, John Evelyn told Pepys that she was 'the King's seventeenth whore abroad, [who] did not leave him till she had got him to give her an order for £4000 worth of plate to be made for her; but by delays, thanks be to God, she died before she had it' – Latham and Matthews.

£1,000 p.a.[5] (see Map 2) but deductions were allowed for annuities, so that after paying £200 to his father and (say) £20 to each of his three brothers, Peter's fine was probably an accurate statement of his income.

Peter Leicester was still substantially in debt. To help find the money to redeem the estate he sold timber from Springwood for £890 in 1648.[6] Despite paying off £2,300 of debts between May 1647 and November 1648 there were still long lists of creditors.[7] Perhaps it was in order to economise that the family spent the year up till November 1649 at Dutton Hall. Such economy measures and the sale of a further £410 of timber from Flittowwood in 1656 seems to have got the family more or less clear of debt by the end of that year.[8] Political incidents which occurred in 1655 may have encouraged Peter Leicester to lead a quiet life. In March 1655 he and George Warburton of Arley were called to Warrington by the authorities to answer questions about a mysterious visitor who had called at Tabley and Arley. Their denials that they had ever met this person were not accepted, so in April they were escorted by a trooper up to London. They never saw the Protector or his Council, but in May they gave bonds of £2,000 each against plotting and were released. In June 1655 Peter Leicester was among a number of Cheshire gentry taken up by Colonel Lilburne in Chester and made to sign more bonds against plotting.[9]

Another factor which may have persuaded Peter Leicester to pursue the quiet study of history rather than the passions of politics may have been the nature of his estate. He had land in a number of townships,[10] but the only one of which he owned both the manor and all the land was Nether Tabley. The ownership of manors was important in the seventeenth century because in principle the Lord of the Manor owned the 'waste' (i.e., the uncultivated land) of the manor. The estate was involved in many disputes that revolved around the ownership of manors. In 1559, 1578 and 1590 there had been lawsuits at Over Alderley. Peter Leicester was to have another one in 1658–9,[11] and he had a dispute with the Daniel family of Over Tabley in 1668–70.[12] In order to establish the fact that Hield was a group

5 See Foster, 2003, ch 2, (ii), where the Leicester estate is described in detail.
6 DLT/D408.
7 DLT/B54.
8 DLT/D26.
9 DLT/B38.
10 Foster, 2003, Ch. 2 (ii).
11 DLT/D172, D31/32.
12 DLT/D394.

of farms on his manor of Aston by Budworth George Warburton built a cottage in the wide road there. This action outraged Peter Leicester who believed that he owned a Manor at Hield and that the road, as part of the 'waste', therefore belonged to him (see Fig. 32). However, on this occasion, he decided against having a row with his friend and neighbour.

Peter's interest in history may have started with his personal concerns; it spread to encompass the whole Hundred of Bucklow and from it he created a pioneering book[13] which was admired by contemporary historians such as William Dugdale. This book has been the foundation of local history in the area ever since. With the return of Charles II in 1660 Peter Leicester was made a baronet and took up active life again as a magistrate. In this role, and also as treasurer of the County Militia, he played a leading part in county government.

A continual problem for landed gentry families was the succession – it was vital to have a male heir. Moreover, it was useful to have a younger son in reserve in case the elder son died. It was convenient if the younger son knew the estate and the local community so that he could take over efficiently if needed, and consequently they were often kept on the estate, living on small allowances. Peter Leicester had three younger brothers. The eldest, Philip, born in 1618, became the Royalist Collector in Oxford in 1641 and was made a Fellow of Brasenose in 1643. After the war he returned to Tabley where he lived quietly until one day in July 1653 he ran out of the front door of the Hall, jumped into the pool and drowned himself.[14] His brother Thomas, born in 1620, was at Gray's Inn in 1647 but died unmarried in 1652. The youngest brother Adam, born 1625, went as an army officer to Ireland, probably after 1660. He married there but had no children, and died in 1672.[15] The frustration of these younger sons kept without their own capital but within the ambit of gentility was seldom shown so starkly as in the suicide of Philip Leicester, but it was often present in these gentry families.

Sir Peter's own children chanced to present few problems. His eldest and only surviving son, Robert, was married aged 23 in 1667 to Meriel, five years his senior and the only daughter and heiress of Francis Watson of Church Aston, near Newport, Shropshire. They had four children, Robert, Francis, Peter and Meriel. Robert, a brilliant child who 'knew

13 A History of Bucklow Hundred, usually known as *Cheshire Antiquities*.
14 DLT/D440.
15 DLT/B20.

72

Fig. 27. Sir Robert Leicester, 2nd Bt, 1643–84. Captain and Treasurer of the County Militia.

Latin aged 5', died in 1676, Peter died in 1685 but Francis and Meriel survived into adult life.

Sir Peter's eldest daughter, Eleanor, married Ralph, son and heir of George Leycester of Toft. His second daughter, Elizabeth, married Samuel Birch. The youngest daughter, Byron, was provided with a portion of

73

£1,000. After her father's death she married John Venables of Agden and received a 'jointure' of £100 p.a. in her marriage settlement. A jointure of one-tenth of the portion was the standard terms of the period.[16]

Like his own father, Sir Peter Leicester made room for his son. He, his wife, his daughter Byron and their estate manager, Thomas Jackson, seem to have gone to live in one of Sir Peter's daughter Eleanor's houses. She and her husband, Ralph Leycester, inherited the Toft estate from his father in 1671. They appear to have invited her parents to rent their manor house in Mobberley in 1672. The reason for this may have been because Sir Peter and his son Robert had decided to rebuild the front of Tabley Hall. The newly married young Robert and Meriel Leicester stayed at Tabley to manage the builders.

Sir Peter was a cultivated man with wide intellectual interests. His library included books on the full range of knowledge in his day, from Greek to astrology and from religion to medicine, but music was evidently his main recreation. While in Chester Castle he found a set of seven viols that had been on their way to Ireland when the war started. They had been destined for Sir George Radcliffe, a friend of the Earl of Strafford.[17] He persuaded Lord Byron, the Governor of Chester, to let him borrow them and wrote a long justification of his actions which survives. In his will he made the seven viols, his virginals, psittyrne, gittyrne, lute and violin as well as all his books into family heirlooms, which could not be sold.

2. THE ACCOUNT BOOKS – FARMING

From 1642, when he was preparing to go off to join the war, till his death in 1678, Peter made notes about the finances of the estate and about his expenses, which survive in two small books.[18] They are not such detailed and complete accounts as those made in the Shuttleworth household. However, they provide sufficient evidence for us to see some of the changes in the way affairs were managed in gentry houses between the beginning and the middle of the seventeenth century. One reason for these changes was the great increase in the goods and services that were

---

16 A jointure was an annuity paid to a woman who was left a widow.
17 The Earl of Strafford, lord lieutenant of Ireland, was attainted and executed in 1641. Sir George Radcliffe, his right hand man, was imprisoned in the Tower of London 1640–2 and after supporting Charles I in the Civil War died abroad in 1657.
18 DLT/B52, B54.

Fig. 28. The new front of Tabley Hall built in the 1670s. This was a new brick façade to the old timber-framed hall. Watercolour by Piers Egerton-Warburton *c* 1880.

on the market. For example, lime, bricks and coal became both cheaper and more readily available. This in turn encouraged people to improve their houses. I have divided the information in the same way as in the previous chapter on Smithills. I start with farming and the staff, then go on to textiles and end with other goods and services.

The first entries in the earliest notebook describe the corn grown on the demesne and that collected as tithes in Nether Tabley in the autumn of 1641 and sold in 1642 (see Appendix 2.1). If we subtract the amount likely to have been collected as tithe we are left with about 1,500 bushels grown on the demesne and worth about £170. This was a substantial amount of grain and was probably the produce of some 80 acres. This suggests that until 1641 a large household may have been maintained at Tabley complete with farm servants living in and perhaps meals provided for visiting workers. If it was so, this was certainly to be the last of the old style of living in Tabley Hall, for some years at least. During the war from 1642 to the end of 1646, the whole demesne was let as grassland, probably on annual leases.

In early 1647 Peter Leicester went back to live at Tabley with his wife and their children. Several of his brothers may also have returned with them as 18 servants were hired for the year to 12 January 1648 (see Appendix 2.2). However, this grand style lasted less than two years. In November 1648, Peter, Elizabeth and the three children, along with four servants, went to live with her mother at Dutton Hall for a year. The reason for this was probably to save money to pay off debts. Peter and his wife paid £20 each for their diet at Dutton. The four servants and three children at £10 each cost another £70 making a total bill of £110. These figures illustrate that the ordinary expenses of gentry living – their food and their servants – were not large. This £110 was only just over a tenth of the estate's gross income of £1,000 p.a.

The family returned to Tabley at the end of 1649, but it was not until 1651 that their arrangements for managing the household and farm took the shape they were to have for the next 16 years. In the years 1648 to 1650, various arrangements were made with people to do the farming work. Sometimes they were paid by the day and sometimes for the job. The following examples probably illustrate the manner in which a lot of farming was done in the middle of the seventeenth century:

		£	s	d
Dec 1648	Peter Beaumont, 4 days (at 8d a day)		2	8
Dec 1648	Dic Leigh (who was employed at £3 10s 0d p.a. in 1647) 8 days (at 9d a day)		6	0
Mar 1649	Peter Beaumont – threshing 100 bushels barley and 40 bushels wheat		13	4
Mar 1649	Hen Hayes holding plough 10½ days (9d day)		7	10
	Sam's brother driving plow 10½ days (8d day)		7	0

At other times, local farmers were employed to plough with their own draught animals:

		£	s	d
Dec 1648	Tho Newall 1 day plowing		2	8
Aug 1650	Matt Key 4 days ploughing		12	0

Sometimes work was let at a rate:

		£	s	d
Sept 1650	Reaping wheat at 5s Cheshire acre (2s 4d statute acre)		2	10	0
	Hired reapers at 9d day		2	0	0

76

These examples show how the typical payment to workers had become a cash wage. The provision of food was not mentioned as it was assumed by this period that wages were without food. The change may have been due to social dislocations during the war, such as the absence of many gentry from their homes.[19] The rates of agricultural wages seem to have been 8d or 9d a day with little regard to summer or winter or harvest.[20]

From 1651 there was a return to employing agricultural workers who lived in the Hall and were paid an annual salary. The list of staff in 1651 in Appendix 2.2 shows that there were probably four or five farm workers on the staff. These people appear to have done almost all the agricultural work. In the accounts the only regular annual farming expenses were £10–£15 p.a. for help with mowing the hay and reaping the corn. Occasionally people were hired to do some ditching or harrowing, but these were evidently exceptional requirements. There were only a few items recording the purchase of grain, so the permanent staff usually grew sufficient for the household and their animals.

In November 1650, perhaps in preparation for resuming his own farming operations, Peter Leicester bought three cart horses for £24 7s 6d. In June 1651 he bought four oxen for £32 10s 0d. This does not make it clear whether horses had superseded oxen as the principal draught animals.[21] Both may have been in use or the oxen may have been for fattening for meat. Certainly animals bought to provide meat occur in the accounts. For example:

		£	s	d
Mar 1660	5 cows to feed	13	8	6
May 1660	20 sheep to feed	7	13	4

19 See Foster, 2003, Ch. 5 (iii) and (iv), b, for the appearance of 'inmates' or 'strangers' (i.e., families without a lease direct from the owner) in rural townships from 1647 onwards.

20 Among the Tabley papers is a copy of the Rates of Wages set by the Justices of the Peace at Middlewich, 8 April 1663. In this, a Common Labourer should get 8d a day in summer and 6d in winter. A master mason, millwright, or bricklayer was to get 1s 0d in summer and 10d in winter. A master carpenter, plowright, etc., was only to have 10d in summer and 8d in winter, and their servants and journeymen only the same as common labourers. Sir Peter Leicester was an energetic magistrate, but evidently the market was superior to the Law. See also the rates paid to craftsmen by Sir Peter (below, p. 83).

21 In the pre-1646 wills and inventories examined in Foster, 2003, Ch. 4 (v), it is noticeable that only a few freeholders and leaseholders had oxen. Virtually all inventories include horses and most include immature cattle. The only 'draught' horses mentioned were owned by Peter Warburton, 1625, heir to Arley. One yoke of bullocks appears in Anthony Maisterson of Winnington's inventory in 1616.

The total number of cattle kept at Tabley is never made clear. Two lists of 1668-9 show '10 cows now being milked'.[22] A herd like this, cared for by the dairymaid and producing milk, butter and cream, is likely to have been a permanent feature of the domestic economy. The second list has four cows 'turned out to feed', six calves 'worth £3 12s 0d', and four young and two old oxen. So perhaps a dozen animals being brought on for meat or to replace dairy cows represents the usual pattern of their stock. Some sheep seem to have been kept. 19 wethers (neutered males) were bought for £7 6s 8d in 1652 and shearing sheep cost a few shillings each year. Though this evidence is incomplete one can say with some confidence that the practice of keeping a large herd to supply the Hall, which we saw still being followed at Arley in 1626,[23] was not part of the Leicesters' arrangements from 1651 to 1678. Meat was provided partly by the butcher, from whom frequent purchases were made, and partly by fattening a few animals at Tabley.

One advantage of the reduced scale of farming at Tabley was that a considerable part of the demesne was available for letting. At 11s p.a. per acre, this was the estate's most valuable land, and letting it made a significant contribution to their cash income. If they were able to let 400–500 acres it would have brought in around £250 p.a. Perhaps the reason Thomas Jackson was able to value each field of the demesne in the 1666 survey[24] was that many of them were in fact let each year. The estate needed cash income to pay the interest on its debts, debts which may have arisen because of the building work that Sir Peter and his son, Robert, carried out (see below) or perhaps from providing dowries for the daughters. Some 35 creditors were listed by Thomas Jackson in 1671.[25] They had lent a total of over £3,000. The interest at 6% was costing £180.

After the death of Sir Peter in 1678 the Tabley household continued in the same style for another six years until the unexpected death of Sir Robert at the early age of 40 in 1684. After this the family only consisted of his widow, her son Sir Francis, the heir, aged ten, and his younger sister Meriel. The establishment was reduced. All the demesne at Tabley except the house, the garden and the woods was let. In 1695 it brought in a total of £350.[26]

22 DLT/B52.
23 See Appendix 1.3 above.
24 See Foster, 2003, Appendix 2.1.
25 Memorandum Book of TJ. DLT/ 5224, Temp. Box 29.
26 DLT/B55.

Three large farms were carved out of this demesne. The rest was let as individual fields to the adjoining tenants.[27]

3. TEXTILES, SUPPLIES AND SERVICES

There seems to have been less change in this area than in farming. Hemp is not mentioned in these accounts. However, flax was grown. Linseed was bought in 1651 and flax was pulled and spun. Breakers and swinglers were paid 11s 9d and 12s 4d in 1649. Richard Newall was paid 5s twice in 1652 for weaving linen cloth. In 1654 he was paid 15s. Henry Buttering was another linen weaver employed. Christian was paid 7s 6d for weaving napkins in 1654 and Jane got 4s for the same work in 1655. The spinning and weaving of linen cloth continued to appear in Sir Peter's notebook into the 1670s.

Wool from their own sheep seems also to have been used. Christian seems to have led a team of women who carded and spun wool between 1652 and 1655. In 1654 Peter Hewett was paid £2 for weaving 120 yards of woollen cloth. He was paid a further £2 in 1655. Dyeing seems also to have been a service available locally. Richard Key was paid 7s 6d for dyeing a piece of cloth red in 1652 and more dyeing was done in 1653.

Again this evidence is less detailed than one would like. There cannot be much doubt, however, that the textile working skills found at Smithills and Arley in the earlier period were still in existence in this area in the middle of the seventeenth century.

Tabley Hall was situated on the old Roman road from Chester to Manchester, always referred to by Sir Peter Leicester as 'the Street' (see Map 3). A spur off this road called Mawkins Lane led past the Hall to Knutsford two miles away. The Tabley estate ran right up to Knutsford and indeed included the White Lyon Inn there. Knutsford was the principal town in the area until the second half of the eighteenth century, so Tabley was peculiarly well placed to purchase whatever goods were being transported and traded in the middle of the seventeenth century.

Taking advantage of its ideal position on a main road leading to a town Sir Peter's ancestors had established a mill at Tabley about 1409.[28] Sir Peter's father had built new mills of freestone under the Hall in 1630.

---

27 Compare this with a similar division at Arley, see Foster, 1998, p. 16.
28 DLT/B20.

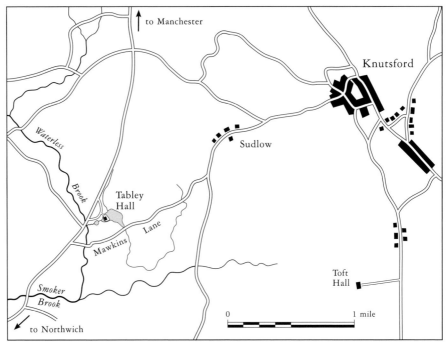

Map 3. Tabley Hall and Knutsford in the seventeenth century based on Burdett's map of 1777 and sundry topographical notes by Sir Peter Leicester. The present road layout was created when the Park was laid out at the end of the eighteenth century.

Cleverly exploiting the lie of the land he had converted the pool surrounding the island on which the Hall stood to the Mill Pool. He probably diverted a second brook into this pool to keep it full. There is enough difference in height between the level of water in the pool and that in the brook to the south for there to have been installed an early example of an overshot wheel. The mill must have had substantial business from outside the estate because its profits were estimated at £40 p.a. in the 1666 survey. (See Appendix 2.3 for details of milling in 1642 and 1732–40.) The knowledge of the grain market which this mill provided may have encouraged the Leicesters to buy more grain. Increasing purchases were recorded, as much as five or ten pounds worth in a year. It is possible that they ceased making their own malt since no kiln is referred to in these notebooks whereas the 'maltman' appears regularly in the notes. Annual purchases ranged between £5 and £15. All this gives the impression that the estate was usually growing just about enough grain for the family's needs and

Fig. 29. Elizabeth, Lady Leicester, 1620–78, in a fine silk dress, no doubt made for her in London.

that they were confident that the market would be able to supply any extra that they might require.

Some things were still bought in London. Sir Peter and his wife both had London tailors. The more expensive items sold by mercers were also bought there. The scale of this expenditure on luxury clothes and other

Fig. 30. Tabley Hall and Chapel, as built by Sir Peter Leicester and his son Robert, seen across the lake. From an engraving commissioned by G. Ormerod, *c.* 1815.

textiles can be roughly gauged from the payments and debts mentioned. Edmund Griffith, mercer, of London, was paid £64 before November 1648. Mr Dethiche, Mrs Leicester's tailor, was owed £30 in March 1649 and £58 10s 0d in 1652. Peter's own tailor, Mr Gilberts, was only owed £31 3s 0d in March but £103 in November 1655. Although some groceries, spices and mercery were still bought in London, Henry Antrobus, mercer, and Peter Swinton, stationer, in Knutsford and other shops in Chester were also patronized. Candles and soap were bought from Nathaniel Dewsbury in Great Budworth.

Some new kinds of expense were incurred. In 1657 Peter Leicester bought a coach in London. It was fitted out with fabric linings and fringes by the mercer in Knutsford. The coach required six coach horses so with the half-dozen riding horses that the household needed there was a total of a dozen horses for the family. These horses in turn required quite elaborate harness and saddlery. Another novelty which had not been available at Smithills was better quality medical assistance. Sir Peter appears to have paid £209 for his son's 'cure' in London in 1655. Some innovations were to increase the comforts of home life. Rafe Tarleton, a pewterer of Wigan, was paid 12s for two 'close stool pans'[29] in July 1670. Another improvement was the introduction of wine bottles. 36 dozen cost £4 10s 0d

29 Presumably chamber-pots.

in May 1679. There were also changes in the provision of fuel. Some peat was still being used, for example,

'July 1649 Getting and tending 40 loads of tierves £1 1s 8d.'

However, coal seems to have become the main fuel in this period. In October 1651 two Aston by Budworth tenants, Ralph Griffith and Robert Key, were paid £2 for carting six loads of coal, 6s 8d a cartload. The same price occurs again in later years. This may not include the money paid for the coal at the pit and it does not tell us how much was on the cart. In 1678 Thomas Jackson recorded that Sir Robert bought 42½ tons at a cost of £24 15s 8d which works out at 11s 8d a ton. In 1681 he bought nearly 40 tons at exactly 10s a ton.[30]

The main expense of gentry life seems to have been the maintenance of old buildings and the erection of new ones. Payments to craftsmen for repair work on buildings were frequently recorded. The men were usually employed on a contract at a fixed price, although sometimes they were paid by the day. Adam Wilkinson received 1s a day for repairing the mill in 1649 but William Dale charged 1s 4d a day in 1679. Other craftsmen were usually paid something between these two extremes. A joiner received 1s 2d a day in 1679. These figures show that the pay of craftsmen had maintained the margin over that of farm labourers we found at Smithills in the 1580s.[31] The two big new projects which the Leicesters undertook in this period were building a chapel at Tabley and building a new front on the Hall. The chapel was built by local craftsmen between 1674 and 1678 entirely at Sir Peter's expense and cost about £800. Sir Peter and his son Robert shared the expenses of the new brick front on the Hall (see Figs 28 and 30). The costs of this are not easy to disentangle but they may well have been much more than the cost of the chapel.

We have seen earlier that Sir Peter provided a £1,000 dowry for his daughter, Byron. So this dowry and his building projects were his largest expenditures. The other major expenses of their way of life were their clothes, their coach and their trips to London. In comparison with these their ordinary life in the country was relatively inexpensive.

---

30 DLT/B55. See also Chapter 7 for the coal prices paid at Arley, 1750–70.
31 See pp. 16–19 and 49.

Corn grown on the demesne at Nether Tabley
plus *the tithes gathered in N. Tabley.*
Reaped in 1641. Sold in 1642.[1]

	Bushels	Approx. prices		Total value		
		s	d	£	s	d
Barley	538	2	8	76	16	6
Oats	1020	1	5	72	5	9
Wheat	162	5	0	40	12	2
Beans	25	2	8	3	5	3
Peas	19	1	11	1	16	11
Wheat and rye	7	4	8	1	12	8
Totals:	1771			196	9	3
Deduct likely value of tithes (see Note 2):				26	0	0
Total:				170	9	3

The grain harvested on demesne land probably totalled about 1,500 bushels.

Notes

1. The original is in Lancashire/Cheshire bushels which contained five 'measures' each. Each 'measure' was approximately equal to a Winchester bushel (see Appendix 1.3 F). The approximate price per bushel is calculated from the total values given in the original.

2. The probable value of the tithe has been estimated at about £26 from eighteenth century figures in the archives of Christ Church, Oxford.[2] We know these figures are reasonable from the details of actual tithe values 1749-65 in the Arley Hall archives.[3] The Leicesters were actually paying the Christ Church tithe farmer £12 p.a. in the 1650s and 1660s.[4] It cost 11s 7d to thresh the tithe in 1679, when ten bushels of oats were threshed for 6d. They paid £23 in 1733 and £28 in 1761. See also Appendix 2.5 in Foster, 2003.

1 DLT/B52.
2 Christ Church Great Budworth tithes rentals 1726, 1733, 1751-61.
3 Foster, 1998, Appendices 10 and 11.
4 DLT/B54 and B55 give this figure in a number of years.

The staff at Tabley

Year ending 12 January 1648	£	s	d	Year 1651	£	s	d
Mrs. Mosley	4	0	0	Mrs Ferrars (Mrs Leicester's			
Besse Jackson	2	0	0	maid and housekeeper?)	4	10	0
Anne Dennis	2	0	0	Christian Starkey (children?)	2	0	0
Kate Proby	1	10	0	Mary Leigh (general?)	1	10	0
Besse Key	1	10	0				
Anne Faulkner	1	10	0	Dairy woman	1	10	0
Mary Bennett	1	10	0	Mary Bennett (laundry?)	1	10	0
John Cragge	5	0	0	John Pickerne (butler or			
Thomas Gandy	3	0	0	underservant?)	2	0	0
John Pickerne	2	0	0	Sam Widder (groom)	3	0	0
Sam Widder	3	0	0				
James Foxley	4	0	0	Ray Rylands (undercook)	2	0	0
Dic Leigh	3	10	0	Cook	4	0	0
John Houghton (cook)	2	0	0	Miller finds himself at	8	0	0
Will Cragge (miller)	3	0	0	John Dale (cowman)	3	12	0
Robin Wright	2	0	0	'Tasker' (agricultural worker?)	2	0	0
Ned Walker (kitchen-boy)	clothes only			Rob Davy (ag. worker?)	2	6	8
Tom Pierson	1	5	0	Rob Hough (ag. worker?)	4	10	0
Tom Burrows	1	5	0	Rafe Wilkinson (ag. worker?)	4	0	0
William Curbishley (cowman				Ned Steele (gardener)	4	0	0
and field waiter)	2	6	8	Thomas Jackson (part-time			
				estate manager)	4	0	0

Source: B54 for lists. Various clues in the accounts suggest the duties.

See also Appendix 5.2 in Foster, 2003.

APPENDIX 2.3

The profits of Tabley Mill 1642–1740

A. 12 January to 19 August 1642

	Measures	£	s	d
Breadcorn	96	15	16	1
Wheat and rye	2½		12	0
Shullings	6	1	5	8
Malt	8½	1	13	0
		19	6	9

Source: DLT/B52

B. February 1732 to February 1740

	1732/3 meas.	1733/4 meas.	1734/5 meas.	1735/6 meas.	1736/7 meas.	1737/8 meas.	1738/9 meas.	1739/40 meas.
Corn to house	81	147	207	160	155	148	117	148
Corn sold	26	52		17		16	26	31
Wheat to house	5	6	42	4	22	7	1	2
Wheat sold	20	24		10		56	43	19
Shullings to house	7	5	15	9	10	4	5	5
Shullings sold	10	13		–		3	7	8
	£ s d	£ s d		£ s d		£ s d	£ s d	£ s d
Value to house	23 17 10	20 14 0		22 11 9				
Value sold	9 12 10	15 2 1		8 9 10		14 8 4	15 6 7	14 7 1

Source: DLT/D153. Several lists consolidated.

For 'Measures' see Appendix 1.3 F.

Notes

1. The practice at mills was to take a part of the grain as toll for grinding. The 'measures' or bushels shown here are the toll.
2. The price of breadcorn in 1642 was 3s 3½d a measure. Wheat and rye was 4s 10d. In 1732 a sample price of 'corn' was 2s 6d, and a sample price of wheat was 4s. Corn or breadcorn was therefore barley or some mixture which was mostly barley. See Appendix 2.1 for grain prices in 1642.

APPENDIX 2.4

Leicester of Tabley and Dutton of Dutton genealogy

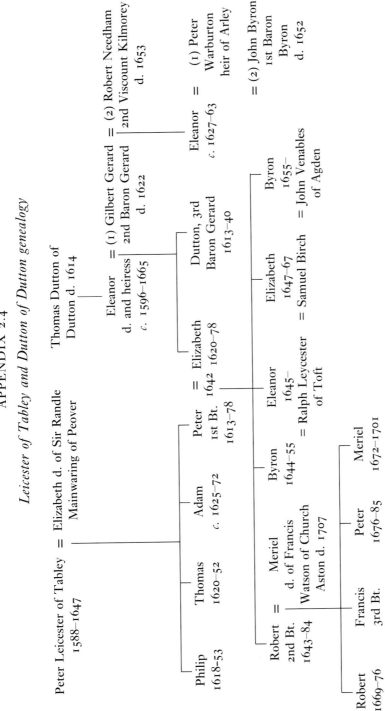

Many other children not mentioned in the text omitted for clarity

Souce: Ormerod 1882, GEC Peerage

87

III

Thomas Jackson of Hield,
Aston by Budworth, 1622–1707

1. INTRODUCTION

In this story we leave the world of the major gentry, their estates and their households. Thomas Jackson's family property was a three-life lease of a 15-acre farm at Hield in Aston by Budworth. Very little is known about such people in the seventeenth century. This highly unusual account of a family over three generations has survived because Thomas Jackson became the manager of the Tabley estate. His jottings on his life, his farm, his income and his children are scattered through various notebooks among the estate papers. It will come as a surprise to many readers to discover that a large estate's tenant on such a small farm could be an educated man. Some historians have referred to the occupiers of such farms as 'peasants'. This description is clearly inappropriate for Thomas Jackson or his children and grandchildren. Whether the family was typical of such tenants in the north Cheshire countryside we do not know. More information on the subject emerges in my *Capital and Innovation.*[1]

The story that unfolds in these pages presents extraordinary contrasts between gentility and abject poverty. Thomas Jackson himself had a successful career. He became one of the most respected solicitors and land surveyors in north Cheshire. As manager of the Tabley estate he was no doubt on good terms with all the local gentry. He married the daughter of an old established minor gentry family. He gave a handsome dowry to his only daughter when she married into a similar gentry family. In his maturity he was undoubtedly accepted as a gentleman.

However, two of his three sons and his son-in-law all went bankrupt. We see two of them escaping from their creditors by fleeing to Ireland, while one joined the Marines. Their families were left in poverty and the old solicitor had to pay some of their most pressing debts. He kept the families going with little gifts of cash and clothes and he paid for the boys to be apprenticed in London. Four of his grandsons became variously a

---

1 Foster, 2003, Chs 4 and 5.

silk dyer, an apothecary, a working goldsmith and a barber. All the granddaughters whom we hear about went out as domestic servants. One son re-established himself after the crisis in the 1680s. He became a senior official in the Post Office with a salary and perquisites that would not have disgraced a gentleman. His second son got a scholarship to Cambridge and spent his life as a rector in Northamptonshire. The unusual details that have survived about these people's lives open a new window on the social life of seventeenth-century England.

2. THE FAMILY, 1620–55

Our Thomas Jackson's father, also called Thomas Jackson, probably bought the lease of the Hield farm from the Kirkman family when he got married around 1620. George Kirkman had bought the lease about 1585. His widow was the tenant between 1600 and 1604 while in 1610 the lease was owned by John Kirkman who was presumably his son.[2] Our Thomas Jackson was born in October 1622. Following the common practice his father waited till his son had survived the dangerous early years of childhood before he renewed the lease with the Tabley estate in February 1629, paying £26 for it.[3] The three lives in this lease were himself, his wife Anne and their son Thomas. The rent payable was 10s per annum. There were also ancient boon works to do. These required them to give the Leicesters one hen and work two days at reaping and one day filling muck. In lieu of the boons they could give the Leicesters 1s 2d in cash.[4] There was also a 'heriot' due at the death of each life. This was usually the best beast or other chattel on the farm. As well as their son, Thomas, his parents had two daughters, Anne and Mary.

In a tattered notebook, among lists of Sir Robert Leicester's debts, Thomas Jackson wrote the following:[5]

I was borne October 17 1622. I went to Northwich schoole at Whitsontyde 1634 and went from there to serve Mr. Daniel of Daresburye at Whitsontyde 1639 and came from Mr. Daniel at Michaelmas 1640. I came to London to serve Mr. Daniel of [Over] Tabley November 11 1640 and from thence I came to Ashley to serve Mr. Richard Brereton October 1642. I came to Tabley to serve Mr. Leicester May 3 1649.

2 DLT/5524/2/2.
3 For the background to these leases see Foster, 2003, Ch. 3 (ii), and Appendix 3.6.
4 DLT/B17 and B84.
5 DLT 5224, Temp. Box 29. I refer to this as 'The Memorandum Book of Thomas Jackson'.

Fig. 31. The old school in Great Budworth, built *c.* 1620.

This bald description of his education needs some explanation. He will have gone to a local school at the age of seven or eight. This was probably the school in Great Budworth which had been built with money left by Richard Worrall in his will of 1611 and of which John Key may still have been the master.[6] As well as the basic 'primary' subjects Jackson will have started to learn Latin there under John Key. No doubt because he demonstrated ability his parents paid for him to go on to the 'secondary' school in Northwich aged 12.[7] There he must have become proficient in Latin before he left, aged 17, so that he was able to learn the Law with his early employers. Most legal documents including Manor Court Rolls were in Latin until the Commonwealth period. He would also have studied sufficient mathematics in Northwich to enable him to learn land surveying from one or more of these early masters.

Among Jackson's earliest surveys of the Leicester's estate is the one of the Hield showing his family's tenement (reproduced in Appendix 3.1. Fig. 32 is a map of Hield in 1750s). His other principal role at Tabley was

6 Foster, 2003, Ch. 4 (v), Ch. 5 (ii), Ch. 8 (ii) and Chapter 5 (iv) below for the cost of schools.
7 Now Sir John Deane's School, see Cox, 1975.

as Steward of the Manor Courts. He presided at his first Court in November 1650 and his last in 1704.[8]

At Tabley Thomas Jackson lived in the Hall and it was there that he met Christian Starkey. She had started work for the Leicesters at the beginning of 1649 on a salary of £2 p.a. On 29 December 1650 they were married. She was the daughter of George Starkey of Stretton, gentleman.[9] This may have been a new connection with the minor gentry for Thomas, or he may have been related to one of the other Jacksons in the area who owned property.[10] The newly married couple continued to live in Tabley Hall where Christian had four children: Thomas, born 10 November 1651; Penelope, born 1 December 1652; Peter, born 17 January 1654, and Charles, born 25 November 1655. Although she was not salaried by the Leicesters she continued to organize textile work for them. She was the Christian we met under 'Textiles', on p. 79 above, who herself spun woollen yarn and organized others to card and spin wool and linen yarn. She was paid piecework for this work and so she appeared in the accounts.

3. THE FARM AND THE HOUSE

It is likely that Thomas inherited the Hield farm when his mother died in September 1650. It may well have been because he owned the farm that Christian and her parents agreed to the marriage. Whatever the truth was, on 7 April 1653 he surrendered the lease of 1629 made to his father in which his own life was now the only one left 'in being'. Peter Leicester, without charge, perhaps as a wedding present to them both, gave him a new lease in which he and Christian were the two lives. On 2 February 1654 he surrendered this lease and paid £8 for a new one which included his son Thomas as the third life. The first notes 'touching my estate' were probably written in April 1654 as they record:

	£	s	d
My house set to Lawrence Steele for one year now coming	9	5	0
One cow hyred to L Steele for this next year wh(ich) will end 1 May 1655		10	0
One cow hyred to Sam Widder for a yeare from thence to be payd at Martlemas		10	0

8 DLT/B17.

9 According to the Parish Register. He was probably the fourth son of Richard and Christian of Nether Hall. See Armitage and Reynolds, 1909, p. 225.

10 See Foster, 2003, Appendix 3.4 for example.

	£	s	d
3 cowes hyred to my M^{rs} for this yeare	1	16	0
2 cowes more hyred to Sam	1	0	0
One cow more hired to L Steele		10	0
One cow hyred to John Leycester		10	0
The higher field set to Wm Whalley	1	10	0
The Worralls field set to John Whalley	1	6	8
One cow hired to Arthur Key		10	0
Unkle Minshull by Bond	30	0	0
and for interest due at Candlemas 54	1	16	0
Cousin Varnon by Bond	4	0	0
	53	3	8

In his survey of 1649 for the Leicesters (Appendix 3.1), Thomas Jackson had estimated the value of the farm at £9 10s 0d p.a. That it did let five years later at a figure so close to his estimate is a confirmation of the quality of these estimates. But as a good surveyor Jackson was interested in every clue about the full market value. He notes in his book four instances of how L. Steele in 1654 and 1655 had sublet some of Jackson's fields to others for more than Jackson had charged him.

Two other features of this account are notable. Cows were a capital asset that could be hired, so that buying a cow and hiring it out was an alternative (for a man with money) to lending the money at interest. The other feature to note is that the Higher field and Worrall's field were not part of Thomas Jackson's lease from the Leicesters (See Appendix 3.1). They were parts of the leases of Ralph Whalley and John Jackson, respectively. The Thomas Jacksons had acquired a lease of these fields for a period of years from R. Whalley and J. Jackson and so were able to rent these fields by the year to the highest bidder. The next year Thomas continued letting the main holding to L. Steele at £9 5s 0d, but the Higher field was let to John Whalley for £1 12s 0d, and Worrall's field to John Jackson for £1 6s 8d. Early in 1656 he bought the Loont Field or Sandy Field from Ralph Whalley and had it added to his main Leicester lease.

On 1 May 1656, Christian and her children moved from Tabley into the farm at Hield. Some of the cows were presumably then kept on the grassland so they had milk and butter in the house. The arable fields were evidently let 'at halves' because Thomas notes in September 1656:

The moity of ye Pease in ye Loontfield to my part was 18 thrave within a sheafe. In ye higher field I had 32 thraves of oates within six sheaves.[11]

Thomas noted the crops he grew and the fields in which they were grown in most years up to 1669 and they are shown in Appendix 3.2. Further notes describe the area 'mucked' each year. He slowly worked around the whole farm, mucking each field in turn. The only exception was the large 'Tanny Flat' (eight acres) which he marled in 1666 at a cost of £34 18s 6d. From the figures in Appendix 3.2, it can be seen that he usually had about four acres in arable each year. Once ploughed up, fields seem to have remained under crops each year till the amount of the crop declined. Then the field was returned to grass and a new field was ploughed up. Under this system a 'good' field could be cropped for many years. The higher field seems to have borne a crop every year for at least nine years from 1656 to 1664. Worrall's field, on the other hand, was returned to grass after only three years. The crops grown were principally barley and oats with only occasionally peas and beans. The average of his share over the 12 years was 43.5 thrave of barley and 21.75 thrave of oats a year. As he didn't grow both each year, it would seem that he was not relying on these crops to provision his household. He rarely planted the same crop in any field two years running, and it seems to have been such farming considerations that determined what crops he grew each year. He evidently had confidence that he could always swap one crop for another with someone else or buy what he needed.

It seems likely that Thomas Jackson continued the system of farming the arable 'at halves', although the word moiety is not present after 1658. He also paid cash for farming work. He records in 1656,

I payd for plowing the Higher Field twice over 15s 0d.

A little undated note (followed by an entry made in 1686) reads:

To Ralph Griffith, this was for John Griffith
For plowing the higher field   2s   0d
For sowing and harrowing it   3s   0d
For ploughing the hemp ground   2s   0d

11 'At halves' meant that the man who did all the work got half the crop and the landlord got the other half. 'Moiety' is a half. 'Loontfield' was a field divided in loonts or strips. A 'thrave' usually meant 24 sheaves. The grain was taken to the barn in sheaves and threshed later.

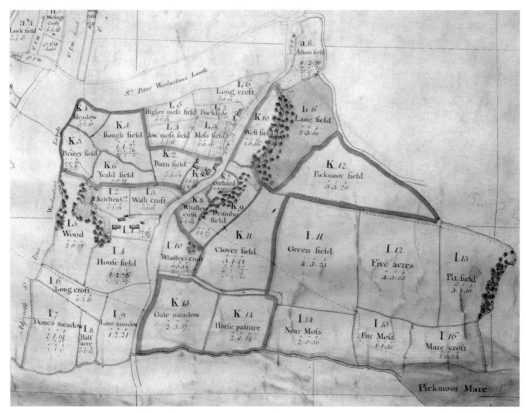

Fig. 32. This Leicester estate map of Hield in the 1750s may be compared with the survey of 1649 in Appendix 3.1. Because all the three-life leaseholder families had changed, all the field names in 1750 were different, but many of the field boundaries were the same. John Jackson probably had L1–6 and K3. Thomas Jackson may have originally had K1, 2, 5, 6 and 12 – the Tanny Flat – to which he gained access off the Pickmere road. The Whalleys and Kirkman probably had K7, 8, 9, 10, part 11 and L10, where the stream running through the woodland and the mill pools can be identified. Israel Leicester's Hield House and the Rack-ground were the remainder. K1–14 in the map represented Thomas Jackson's holding at its largest. His son sold it to Mrs Robinson around 1706 and her descendants were still there in the 1750s, as described in my *Four Cheshire Townships*, pp. 59–60. The Leicesters' adjoining land in Great Budworth appears in the top left-hand corner. The two cottages, built in the wide road by the Warburtons in order to show that they owned the manor, are also marked. See map in colour p. xvii.

Ralph Griffith had married his sister Anne in October 1649. The Griffiths owned another three-life leasehold in Aston. John was probably their younger son.

It seems unlikely that Thomas ever did any farming work himself when he was adult, but he may have done some as a schoolboy. His wife and children possibly did some work with the cows, the hemp and flax crops and in the garden. It seems likely that Christian had a teenage girl to help her in the house and with the children. Little is said about animals. He had a 'team', of horses or oxen, which helped with the marling. He was credited with £2 18s 2d for their efforts in that work. This team may have been used by the man who worked the arable and at other times it may have been hired out. He apparently kept a pig or two as he repaired the fence at the pigsty in July 1673 (Appendix 3.3). No doubt they also had hens, ducks, geese, and a few sheep like other country dwellers.

Thomas also noted the improvements he made to the house and farm-yard. These are set out in Appendix 3.3. The house seems to have consisted of two rooms on the ground floor, the 'house' and the 'parlour', and one or two chambers over them. He built on a new kitchen perhaps with a chamber over it. He rebuilt the parlour chimney. He also built a new 'house of office', what later generations called a privy or a toilet. He put in new floors and windows and whitewashed the place with lime and hair. He made new farm buildings. He dug a well and installed a pump in it. Finally in 1676–7 he made 10,000 bricks and built one side wall of his house in brickwork. This was presumably what we would call the front wall of his house. In short, in the course of 20 years, he had rebuilt or improved almost everything on the property that he inherited. The same spirit activated him on the rest of his estate. He cleaned out old ditches or made new ones, and laid several 'throughs', probably culverts under farm gateways. He put up new farm gates and provided for future timber needs by planting some poplars in the Tanny Flat.

4. THOMAS JACKSON'S OCCUPATION AND INCOME

Thomas's salary from the Leicesters was £4 a year. The only additional money he received from them was 2s 6d twice a year for collecting the rents in the Aston, Budworth and Northwich area. He originally lived in Tabley Hall. To what extent he lived at Hield with his family we don't know. He was included in the Tabley Poll Tax return of 1667 as a servant at a wage of '£4 plus practice'.[12] After 1670 when his wife died, he probably reverted to living at Tabley. He himself records that he went to Mobberley with Sir Peter in 1672 and returned to Tabley in 1678. He seems to have remained there until his death in March 1708, so he enjoyed many years of Leicester hospitality.

An important part of Jackson's income may have been derived from Courts. He kept the Leicesters' Manor Courts for more than 50 years. He records in his book the income he received from the Hundred Court at Halton and the Venables family's Manor Court at Kinderton from 1676 to 1685 (Appendix 3.4) which averaged over £17 a year. It is possible that the Tabley estate Courts also contributed a significant income.

About his general legal and surveying practice we know little. Clues dotted about the manuscripts in his handwriting among the Tabley archive suggest that he was engaged in much legal work, both for the Leicesters and for other people in the area. One of the few papers about his work to survive is a document of 1677 in which Christ Church, Oxford, appointed him their attorney to sell half their tithes in Rostherne, Knutsford, and Peover.[13]

An area of his affairs about which we learn a little in the Memorandum Book is his money lending. Four loans are described. On 13 August 1655, Henry and John Glover of Pickmere borrowed £5. They were to repay £1 10s 0d a year (half in February and half in July) in each year 1656–60, making five payments in all totalling £7 10s 0d. This includes an interest rate of about 16%. In a similar transaction, Robert Faulkner of Tabley borrowed £20, which he had to repay at £6 p.a. over the next five years, which was also a loan at about 16%. William, Thomas, and John Harper got slightly better terms when they borrowed £3 and were given six years rather than five in which to repay a total of £4 10s 0d. Lady Leicester was the fourth borrower. She was only charged 9%. Thomas Jackson had agreed to be bound on her behalf to pay £40 on 18 January 1664. She failed, so he had to pay:

> And thereupon she gave me assurance to receive £8 a year from John Robinson for seven years.

12 See Foster, 2003, Appendix 5.2.
13 DLT/D441.

John Robinson duly repaid him. It was evidently quite a common thing to agree to be bound for or with other people, as there are six more notes of such liabilities dated 1658–60. The following is an example:

Ralph Griffith and Thomas Jackson, both of Aston, yeomen bound to Edmund Bowden of Great Budworth, husbandman, £10 dated 11 May 1658 conditioned to pay £5 and interest 12 May 1659.

It was usual to be bound for twice the value of the debt.

5. THOMAS JACKSON'S CHILDREN: THEIR CAREERS AND PROPERTY

As they grew up the boys were probably sent in turn to Northwich school, and were then all apprenticed as framework knitters. Their mother's uncle, Edward Minshall,[14] was a framework knitter. He had originally been a member of the City of London Company of Clothworkers. When the knitting machine became sufficiently developed to be an attractive commercial proposition in the 1650s he had adopted the new trade. The London Company of Framework Knitters received its Charter from Charles II in 1663.[15] Members of other companies who had become knitters were encouraged to transfer. In August 1661 Edward Minshall had taken one of Christian's brothers as an apprentice. This boy completed his seven-year apprenticeship and became a member of the new Company and a Freeman of the City of London in August 1668.[16] It is likely that Minshall and Starkey were the masters to whom the Jackson boys were apprenticed. The boys seem to have started to learn the trade locally, so presumably one or both of their relations lived nearby. Tom was apprenticed aged 17 in 1668, Charles in July 1669 before he was even 14 years old and Peter in November 1669 just before he was 16. They did not all stay near home as the father tells us: 'Charles went to London 29 December 1671'. This was just after his 16th birthday. Peter too probably transferred to a new master as he went to Nantwich in October 1672. In December 1673 after they had been apprenticed four or five years, their father bought Tom

14 Presumably the same man as 'Uncle Minshull' in the notes 'touching my estate' on p. 92 above. Possibly a younger son of the Minshull freeholder in Appleton. See Fig. 35 below.
15 Mason, 2000, and Lewis, 1986, pp. 129–47 for the important technical improvements to these machines made in the 1650s.
16 C.L.R.O. Calendar of Register of Freedon Admissions 1668–9, 204A, p. 157b.

and Peter their knitting frames. These cost him £28 each. The next year he sent £27 to Charles to buy himself a frame in London. In August 1675 Tom became a member of the Framework Knitters Company and a Freeman of the City of London. His father noted the expenses:

	£	s	d
For his admission into the Company		14	0
To the poore man's box			6
To him that held the Bible			6
To the Clearke			6
To the Doorekeeper			6
At Guild Hall for his Freedome in the Citty		14	2
For a Coppy of the Freedome		2	6
For a box to put it in			6
To the poore man's box			6
To him that held the Bible			6
To the Clearke			6
To the Doorekeeper			6
	1	15	2
Spent on the Wardens of the Company		5	0
	£2	0	2

Tom's two brothers followed. Charles was made 'free' on 4 July 1676 and Peter on 6 March 1677. They had each served a seven-year apprenticeship. To celebrate his success Charles returned to his old home on 25 August 1676 and stayed two months. It seems likely that they each established their own business as soon as they had completed their apprenticeship. As businessmen they could contemplate marriage. Charles was the first to take the plunge, marrying Sarah Smith in London on 30 October 1677. His father sent him his portion of £100. Their first child, named Christian after Charles' mother, was born 7 November 1678. They went on to have a further seven children, the first six born at approximately two-year intervals up to May 1692, the last not until 1698. Thomas continued to send them presents: in 1679 £10; in January 1680 a 25-pound cheese; in July £5 went to Sarah and in October she received another £1 'at her lying in' for her second child.

Thomas, the eldest son, married Joane Peake in July 1678. They had nine children in the next 17 years, four sons and five daughters. Only Anne, the third daughter, died in infancy. Peter was not far behind his

98

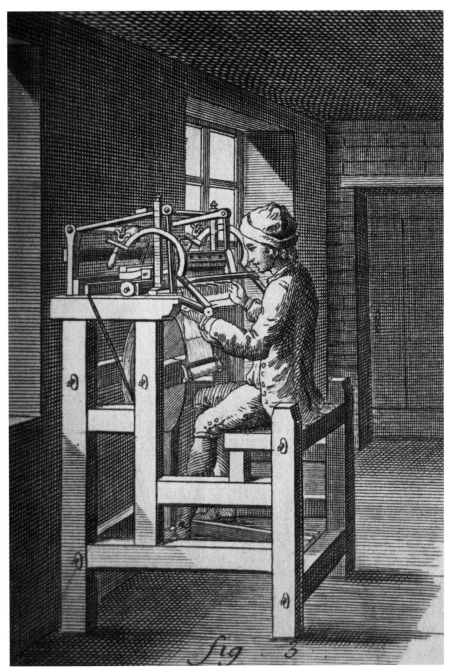

Fig. 33. The framework knitting machine had more than 2,000 parts and was the most complex machine of its time. It was capable of knitting silk stockings much more cheaply than they could be made by hand.

elder brother and married Elizabeth Bradley in February 1679. They had only four children; a son Thomas and three girls, of whom the youngest died in infancy. The difficulty of tracing individuals in historical studies of this kind without the aid of family memorandum books, like Thomas Jackson's, is illustrated by the naming of these children. In each of these three families, one son was named Thomas, so there were five Thomas Jacksons alive in the 1680s in this one family group.

To provide a portion for his second son Peter, Thomas bought the lease of another farm on the Tabley estate. This was in Wethale in Aston by Budworth. As this is a good example of a series of transactions with a three-life leasehold, I will describe them in some detail. Ralph Griffith married Thomas's sister Anne Jackson in March 1649. In February 1666, Ralph renewed his lease. He paid £50 to add two lives – his wife, Anne, and their son, Ralph.[17] Ralph Griffith, the father, died in 1678. In October 1681, Thomas Jackson bought the lease from his sister Anne and her son Ralph for £110. Their two lives remained in the lease. The farm contained about 25 acres. Thomas then paid Sir Robert Leicester £30 to change the widow's life for his son Peter's life and to add Peter's son Thomas. The three lives were then Ralph Griffith the son, Peter Jackson and his two-year-old son Thomas. The farm was valued in the Leicester survey of 1666 at £13 p.a. At 20 years' purchase – that is 20 times the annual value of £13 p.a. – its full freehold value was £260. Thomas Jackson had bought what was likely to be a 50 or 60-year lease for £140. This was about 12 times the net value of £11 11s 10d p.a. (£13 minus the £1 8s 2d annual rent).

Thomas Jackson's eldest son Thomas was destined to inherit the family farm at Hield. Between 1656 and 1679, Thomas bought Ralph and John Whalley's land field by field. He also secured possession of the land the Coppock family were renting from the Tabley estate (see Survey in Appendix 3.1, and Fig. 32). By 1680 he had increased the area of his farm to 43 acres. He does not tell us what this cost, but we know from the Leicester survey of 1716 that it was valued at £30 p.a. In October 1681 he gave it to Thomas and Joane and arranged a new lease from Sir Robert Leicester in which they and their eldest son Thomas were the three lives.

These were Thomas's arrangements for his three sons. They all seemed successful for some years. However, events did not turn out so well with his only daughter Penelope, or Penne as he called her. Since 1663 he had

---

17 For the background to these leases see Foster, 2003, Ch. 3 (ii) and Appendix 3.6.

Fig. 34. The Millington family built this house in 1630, according to a date carved on the front. Note the central chimney-stack enabling the house to have two storeys. It is now called Green Lane Farm, Appleton.

noted down the money he was setting aside for her portion. By 1674 he was able to give her a dowry of £200. He arranged a marriage with young Thomas Millington, the owner of a freehold estate of about 150 acres in Appleton. Thomas's ancestors had been freeholders of the Green Lane estate of some 70 acres since the early sixteenth century.[18] In 1668 Millington had bought an adjoining ancient freehold from the Watts family. He had paid £465 for this estate of about 78 acres, so he must have seemed a most suitable husband (see Figs 34 and 35). He was of an established family and had a good landed estate. Thomas evidently made a legal agreement that Penne's portion should be put into a marriage settlement that would provide her jointure and descend to the children of the marriage. The marriage took place on 11 June 1674 and their first child, a son called Thomas, was born on 12 March 1675. Unfortunately, Penne died a year later in March 1676, probably over the birth of her second child, Anne.

Then something disastrous happened to Thomas Millington's finances. Whether he was in business and had trading losses or whether he gambled

18 Rylands, 1882, p. 179; Foster, 2003, Appendix 3.3.

we don't know. Between July 1678 and November 1682 he had to sell more than three-quarters of his estate. It seems likely that he 'broke' in 1678, as our Thomas notes,

Thomas Millington came to my house about 15 April 1678.

The purchaser of his estate was James Moss, one of the largest woollen cloth merchants in Manchester. The marriage settlement had never been properly documented. Thomas Jackson had to take a suit in the Court of Exchequer in Chester to obtain an order that the marriage settlement be completed in accordance with the earlier agreement. By a document dated 29 September 1683 two trustees, one of whom was Penelope's brother Thomas, took over the remainder of the Millington freehold estate for the eventual benefit of the young Thomas Millington and his sister Anne.[19]

In 1669 Thomas Jackson had bought from Sir Peter Leicester for £30

19 WM Box 63.

Fig. 35. [Left] Part of the Warburton estate map of Appleton in 1765. Notice the Thorn Tree in the top right-hand corner. The Millington/Watts estates were the shaded fields *a, b, c, d, E,* etc. They were bought by the Arley estate in 1785 from the descendants of the Moss family. They were then added to the 1765 map in which the old Arley lands were either coloured or colour-edged. See map in colour p. xviii. An analysis of the deeds (WM Boxes 63–4) reveals that the land holdings in 1667 were:

Millington Freehold   Cheshire acres as in the Map

Green Lane House* E1–8	7 – 3 – 07
d3, 4, 7–9, 11, 12	14 – 3 – 33
2 Barley fields Nos 1–2	8 – 2 – 35
Cottage(s) a2	2 – 0 – 07
	33 – 2 – 02 = 70.9 statute

Watts Freehold

Cross Farm* d1, 2, 5 ,6, 10, 13, 14 in which the family lived	15 – 3 – 01
Walnut Tree Farm* c1–15 let on a three-life lease to Randle Twisse, shoemaker	12 – 3 – 08
Cann Lane Farm* b1–6 let on a three-life lease to Richard Warburton, linen webster	8 – 2 – 08
	37 – 0 – 17 = 78.5 statute

* nineteenth-century names

It is unusual to find three-life leaseholders like this on small freeholder's lands; they were normally only on the major gentry's lands.

---

the freehold of a small farm in Aston known as Berrys. This extended to nearly 16 acres and was valued by Thomas at £8 10s 0d p.a. In 1651 Edmund Berry had bought a three-life lease from the Leicesters for £90, just over ten times the annual value of £8 10s 0d. The three lives were Edmund, his wife Margery, and their son John. By the time Thomas Jackson bought the property, Edmund had died, so there were only two lives in being. The Leicesters had bought this freehold farm in 1633 because it adjoined their Wethale lands. The only rent payable by the Berrys was 8s p.a. chief rent to the Warburtons of Arley.[20] In 1679 Thomas Jackson bought two more fields from the Leicesters which had traditionally belonged to this farm, so that its total area became over 22 acres. Sometime in the 1680s the two Berrys died so that Thomas became the full

20 The small rents payable by freeholders were called 'chief' rents. The three life leaseholders paid 'old' rents.

owner of a freehold with a value of about £12 p.a. worth around £240.[21]

At the beginning of the 1680s Thomas was at the peak of his career. In his early 60s he must have been contemplating retirement with some satisfaction at what he had achieved in his working life. He had set up his three sons in business at a cost of £30–£40 each. He had given his eldest son a three-life leasehold with a rental value of £30 p.a. worth at least £300. His second son Peter had a leasehold valued at £13 p.a. worth £130. He had given his youngest son Charles a portion of £110. He had endowed his daughter Penelope with £200 and, after a struggle had secured this on freehold property for the benefit of her children. In total he had expended some £840 in setting up his children. He himself had a freehold property worth over £200 and, as we shall see, at least £200 in cash. He had therefore saved over £1,200 during his working life. In a world where the ordinary working man was earning £10 to £15 a year this was an achievement of which he could be justifiably proud.

Alas, his world was to fall apart in the next 20 years. The first signs of trouble that we find in the surviving records start in 1684.[22] Peter had his framework knitting business in Congleton. In February 1684 Thomas had to lend his son £1 13s 0d. In April Thomas had to pay £2 for Peter's wife Betty's 'cure'. In June, Peter came and borrowed a further £2 1s 0d and returned to Congleton. Unfortunately, it was not only Peter's business that was in trouble. In July 1684 Thomas had to join his eldest son Thomas in two Bonds to pay £46. In August 1685 he actually had to pay first £20 and then a further £15 8s 0d for his eldest son. Finally at Christmas 1685 or soon after, Charles came back from London and evidently told his father that he was giving up the framework knitting business.

What had gone wrong with the three sons' business we are never told. We can get some idea of the likely problems by examining the progress of the framework knitting industry.[23] A framework knitting machine was the most complex and sophisticated machine in use at the time. It had more than 2,000 parts and the fine latched needles were a triumph of the wire-drawers' and the steel forgers' crafts. Although it had been invented by William Lee of Nottinghamshire about 1590 it seems likely that it was

21 WM Box 69.
22 DLT/B100, Memorials 1684-1705.
23 Chapman, 1972, pp. 7–50; Wykes, 1992, pp. 23–54. Frames may be seen working at Ruddington Framework Knitters Museum, Chapel Street, Ruddington, Notts, NG11 6HE. Tel: 0115 984 6915.

not until the 1650s that the design was sufficiently improved to make it a commercial machine rather than an inventive curiosity. By 1664 it is thought there were only about 650 frames in England, and they were mostly in London. These were designed to produce silk stockings for the gentry[24] which they could do much more cheaply than hand knitting. In the 1650s and the 1660s profits will have been high. Minshall, Starkey and the Jackson brothers were attracted into this new business by the high rewards, but so were many others. The French are thought to have built frames and to have exported silk hose to London.[25] Most English machines seem to have been made on the Nottingham coal field and as the number in existence increased their price fell. From the £28 Thomas Jackson had paid in 1673–4 it collapsed to about £10. The cost of manufacturing the machines probably also fell as manufacturing techniques improved. The centre of stocking manufacture seems to have moved from London to Nottinghamshire. There may have been a sharp fall in the prices of silk stockings. As there were no detailed written specifications for textiles at this period, and many different qualities of every article were made, historians can rarely identify textile price movements. There is therefore no price evidence to support this thesis, but the movement of the centre of production to the Midlands is well attested.

Traditionally only Freemen could sell goods in a city or town and only members of a Company could practise a trade there.[26] These rules restricted entry to those who had served a seven-year apprenticeship and so maintained high incomes for Freemen and high prices for customers.[27] It seems likely that members of the Framework Knitters' Company (and Freemen of London) who came from the Nottingham area trained young cottagers in Nottinghamshire to operate the machines without an apprenticeship so that they did the work for much lower wages than those who had served an apprenticeship expected to earn. The Freemen then sold the products in London and elsewhere at prices that yielded them a good profit, but squeezed the incomes of Members of the Company living and working at the trade in London or elsewhere in the country, such as Cheshire. The framework knitters in London, no doubt appealed to the

---

24 C.L.R.O. RCE 152 contains rough notes of a framework knitter's silk dyeing 1670–81.
25 See Mason, 2000, pp. 86–9 for details of other European countries importing and setting up frames in the 1660s and 1670s.
26 For example see Mendenhall, 1953, pp. 79–119.
27 See Mason, 2000, p. 231.

Company to enforce the rules on apprenticeship. The Justices in London, who were mostly Liverymen and Freemen, probably supported the Company but they had no jurisdiction in Nottinghamshire. The Company's charter gave it control of the industry throughout England, but it was probably not able to persuade the magistrates of Nottinghamshire to restrict the trade to Framework Knitter Company members because they were pleased to see their local poor cottagers being employed in this new business.[28]

If this analysis is correct the Jackson brothers were faced with the choice of giving up the trade or working for the same miserable wages – probably about £10 or £12 per year – that the Nottinghamshire cottagers earned. For the three Jackson brothers who had invested in a full apprenticeship and who had therefore worked for nearly nothing for seven years and had only enjoyed the fruits of their membership of the Company for about seven years it must have been a bitter blow.

Charles was the most successful in re-establishing himself. He applied to join the Post Office, a growing business at that time. Whether his visit to his father at the beginning of 1686 had been to canvas political support among the family's Cheshire friends, we are not told. In December 1686 he was admitted a Letter Carrier and Clerk. He evidently made progress up the hierarchy because he was able to tell his father in 1690 that his salary was now £50 p.a. By October 1692 he felt sufficiently secure financially to buy a 51-year lease of his house in London for £30. The rent was £10 p.a. (notice that the relationship between rent and 'fine' was quite different in London and Cheshire). In 1693, his father recorded the tax Charles paid that year, when the rate of Land Tax was 4s in the pound, or 20%. His office was assessed at £30, so he paid £6 for that; his house was assessed at £8, which made the tax on that £1 12s 0d. His cash lent at interest was set at £100 so that the £6 interest paid £1 4s 0d tax. The total tax he paid was £8 16s 0d. In the summer of 1695 he and his wife and daughter visited Tabley. His career continued successfully at the Post Office and in August 1697 he was promoted Clerk of the By-night. In June 1698 he became Clerk of the Kent Road. He was then able to write to his father and tell him that his salary was £60 p.a. and he received another £60 a year in benefits. He transferred to being Clerk of the Bristol Road in February 1700 and Clerk of the Chester Road in April 1705.

28 See Mason, 2000, pp. 104–6 for legal activity of this kind in the 1720s and 1730s.

This progress was in marked contrast to his brothers. Peter was continually short of money. A few pounds had to be given to him and his wife Betty in 1684 and 1685 to keep them going. In February 1686 his father had to pay £12 7s 0d on Peter's account to Bradley. It was worse in July 1687 when Peter was arrested by John Perceval for a £12 debt. He was only released because Charles arranged to pay off the money at £2 a year. In fact, it seems the father paid it all. In September 1690 Peter tried a new style of life going to serve the Secretary of the Earl of Monmouth. It was not a success and 'he came away'. From 1688 to 1692 Thomas paid between £5 and £10 each year towards the upkeep of Peter's family. These gifts included a cow which cost £2 2s 6d, several items of clothing, taxes due on the farm and even 4s to the schoolmaster of Budworth to teach his grandson Tom to write. Despite this Peter ran up debts. Finally, to escape his creditors, he fled to Ireland in November 1692. There he lived at Monilea and seems not to have returned to England till 1695. He probably then lived in London for three years till he returned to his wife and family in August 1698. In October of that year his brother Charles bought him 150 needles for five shillings. He evidently made an effort to return to his old trade. Charles also paid off a 4s 6d debt and his father cleared another for 12s 6d, but the family remained in poverty. In October 1705 his father had to give Peter a coat and his wife a shirt. Sir Francis Leicester regained possession of the Wethale leasehold sometime after 1716.[29]

Thomas did not require continuous support like Peter and his family. One reason was that he was much richer since his farm was worth £30 p.a., but in the end this led to worse trouble. His father's only notes about Thomas between 1685 and 1690 record his help in collecting the rents in Whitley due on the Tabley Chapel endowment. But he was evidently running up debts in this period. In April 1690 the father had to join with his son in mortgaging the Berry freehold for £200 at 6% to Mrs Bridget Williams, a widow in Chester. Because this sum was quite close to the value of the freehold, the leashold farm was also added to Mrs Williams' security.[30] Thomas seems to have told his father that the mortgage was only for two years, but it is evident from later events that the money was probably used to repay loans taken out earlier. Thomas's family may have lived more economically after this. The older Thomas contributed £1 towards the diet of his granddaughter, Christian, in November 1691. In

29 DLT/B83.
30 WM Box 69.

1692 robbers broke into the house at Hield and stole Thomas's clothes and his sword. In May 1693 the sheets were stolen from the father's bed at Tabley. In view of what was to follow it seems that these incidents may have been the work of creditors desperate to recover some of their money. In December 1693 the father recorded:

> 3rd my son Tom took leave of me; 6th he went to Liverpool; 7th he took shipping.

By the 23rd he was in Dublin. Sadly his father recorded the money he had paid out on his son's behalf since 1685. Including the two payments in that year, it totalled £118 5s 11d.

Thomas returned from Ireland in July 1694. After six months' absence he may have known that his father had compounded with all his active creditors. Our Thomas made a few notes about his son's movements in the next three years. In July 1695 he went to work in Witton, presumably because of the flourishing salt trade there. In January 1696 he moved to Frodsham, the port from which the salt was shipped. There he seems to have taken the King's shilling and become the sergeant's mate on board the *Britannia*. From there he moved to the *Edgar* and then to the *Lennox* before returning to Chester in 1697. In September 1697 he sold the freehold of Berry's farm for £260. This involved paying off Mrs Williams' mortgage. The advantage of that may have been that he could then borrow against or sell the Hield leasehold. Whatever he did, it evidently involved the final break with his father, who never mentioned him again.[31] The family appear to have been still living in Hield in 1705, but before October 1706 they had sold the Hield property to Margaret Robinson. At that date she had a new lease from Sir Francis Leicester in her own name although the three Jacksons, Thomas, Joane, and their son Thomas, remained the three lives.

6. THOMAS JACKSON'S GRANDCHILDREN[32]

a. The Millingtons

Penelope's two children Thomas and Anne seem to have continued living with their apparently impoverished father at Green Lane House (nineteenth-century name). In May 1684 our Thomas Jackson paid £4 15s 0d for

---

31 It seems likely that he pretended to be the sole owner of Berry's farm when he sold it, but the documents show that his father had joined in the mortgage and therefore presumably also had some ownership rights.

32 See Appendix 3.5 for a list of these.

'Thomas Millington's lease', but whether this was for father or for son is not clear. On 6 November 1687 young Thomas Millington came to see or perhaps live with his uncle Thomas. This seems to have been the start of the process of getting him apprenticed in London. No doubt preliminary enquiries were made, but in April 1689 he was fitted out with new clothes and sent up to London:

	£	s	d
new clothes (suit)	2	6	0
hat		6	0
pr of stockings		2	6
new shoes		2	8
2 shirts, 4 handkerchiefs, 2 neckcloths		14	0
a trunk		9	0
his diet and carriage to London	1	0	0
given him in money		5	0
	5	5	2

He was, no doubt, originally 'on liking' with Mr Joseph Nunn, a silk dyer, at the Rainbow in Coleman Street. That proved satisfactory and he was formally bound apprentice on 14 June 1689 when he was 14 years and three months old. His grandfather sent a further £17 to finance the deal. In August 1694, aged 19, he visited Tabley again and his grandfather gave him £1. When he had done his time he seems to have set up on his own as he is referred to in a deed of July 1699 as silk dyer of St Clements, London. In this period he must have married because his grandfather notes:

25 Aug 1700 Thomas son of Thomas Millington was born and died.

Our Thomas sent the wife 10s when he heard the sad news.

Thomas Millington, the father, died 9 June 1705. His daughter Anne had presumably been living with him. When left alone by his death she went to visit her uncle at Hield. She quickly moved from there to Tabley to look after her grandfather. While she was there her two first cousins named Christian Jackson also came to visit their grandfather. He gave all three of them a guinea each. There cannot have been much money in the Millington family by this time because while Anne was with her grandfather he gave her a bible, which cost 4s 10d, and 'a sitting wheel to spin jersey on' which cost 7s.[33] These are hardly the presents that a well-off

33 DLT/4996, 2 loose sheets.

girl of 30 would need. When she left in April 1706 he gave her a shilling. At the same time Thomas sent 10s and a copy-book which cost 1s 6d to her brother in London. There was presumably a child in that family learning to write. The last we know of Thomas Millington is that in October 1707, when he was styled 'Silk Dyer', of St Martin's in the Field, London, he sold the remaining 17 acres of the Green Lane estate for £220 to John Moss, son of James who had bought the rest of the estate earlier.

b. Thomas Jackson's children

In April 1692, when his father was still looking solvent, the eldest son Thomas started at Northwich School, where his grandfather and his father had been pupils. His grandfather was an admirer of the headmaster Aaron Nichols.[34] Unfortunately the breach between our Thomas and his son seems to have included the eldest grandson who is never mentioned again, so we don't know how his education progressed. The only glimpse of him in the surviving archives is in March 1737–8. At that time John Robinson renewed the lease of the Hield property. Thomas, the only surviving Jackson life, was styled 'of Nether Knutsford, attorney at law'. He also appears in the Register of Attorneys made at that period.

There is, however, a single mention of the second son Charles. On 11 June 1700, aged 14 years and three months, he was apprenticed to Mr Ladyman, a working goldsmith at the Rose and Crown, Sherborne Lane, near the Post Office in London. The eldest daughter, Christian, may have had her first job in Chester when she went there in July 1697, aged 18. If so it didn't last long, because at Christmas that year she went to serve Mrs Venables, moving to live with her at Agden in January 1698. She left there after 20 months, in August 1699, and went to Ruthin to serve Mrs Mostin. That job only lasted till January 1700. The following summer she and her brother Charles went to London together in Mr Barnet's wagon. He was apprenticed to Mr Ladyman and she went to serve Mrs Pennuce (?). The last we hear of her is in September 1705 when she was out of service and visited her grandfather. There she met her cousins Christian Jackson and Anne Millington.

34 Cox, 1975, pp. 129–30. The grandsons Thomas and Charles are presumably the people named in the list of pupils *c.* 1696, p. 134.

c. Peter Jackson's children

On 10 April 1693 Thomas, the eldest son, went with Sir Francis Leicester to Chester and was sent up to London. He presumably stayed with his uncle Charles's family. On 12 June he went 'on a liking' to Mr Peter Martinscroft, barber and periwig maker of Aldermanbury near the Axe. He was formally bound apprentice on 4 July. His grandfather noted the money paid. The binding cost was £12 12s 0d, a new suit was £2 18s 6d. With other necessities the total came to £17 6s 6d.

On 25 January 1701 his grandfather sent Thomas £5 via his uncle Charles. This was perhaps a present for successfully completing his apprenticeship. In June that year Tom the barber, as he was known to his grandfather, went to serve Colonel Seymour (second son of Sir Edward Seymour, Bart) at a salary of £18 p.a. plus the right to the Colonel's old clothes. When not living with the Colonel he was to have 8s a week board wages. This was apparently not an occasion when master and valet formed a friendship. In January 1702 Tom was reported to have gone to serve a widow in Cannon Street at £13 p.a. plus his diet. The last we hear of him is that he got married on 8 October 1704.

Peter's eldest daughter Penelope is only mentioned twice in her grandfather's notes. On 21 September 1699, when she was 17½, she came to serve at Tabley, and on the 18 December in the same year she left.

d. Charles Jackson's children

Charles's eldest daughter Christian seems to have entered service in April 1697, when she was 18½ years old. Her first post was with Mrs Gawden (Gauden) at 'Esquire Ewen's house in Clapham'. For some reason it did not last long and she was home again in August. Perhaps she had several spells with Mrs Gawden. The only other one recorded was in May 1702, when she 'went to serve Mrs Gawden'. In September the same year she went to serve Sir Humphrey Winch's lady. Whether it was from this lady that she came 'from Stapleford in Notts' to Tabley in August 1705 we are not told. There, with her grandfather, she met her two first cousins, the other Christian Jackson and Anne Millington.

Charles's two sons, Charles and his younger brother Thomas, were taken by their father in October 1691 to a school in Chipping Campden, Gloucestershire. They were aged eleven and nine. Charles, it seems likely, stayed there until he was 14. He was then apprenticed, in March 1695, to

Mr Bradwin, an apothecary, at Redcross Street near Cripplegate Church, Aldersgate Street. In April 1696 he was turned over to Mr Richardson, another apothecary in Aldersgate Street. His father had to pay another £10 to rebind him and agree to find him with clothes. Grandfather Jackson sent £5 to his son to help with the unexpected expense.

Charles's second son Thomas was no doubt the favourite of his grandfather. From Chipping Campden, he went to St Paul's School in London in 1695 or '96. In April 1696 his grandfather noted that Dr Thomas Gale was headmaster. In April 1701 he went up to Trinity College, Cambridge, with an Exhibition (Mrs Robinson's) from St Paul's of £6 5s 0d a year. In April the next year he was elected a scholar. He got his BA in 1705 and his MA in 1708, when he was also ordained. He then spent 30 years, 1725–55, as Rector of Rushton, Northamptonshire.[35]

Two aspects of this story of Thomas Jackson's family deserve more discussion. It did not seem appropriate to interrupt the story with explanations that nevertheless are needed, so Appendix 3.6 contains notes on:

(1) the property rights of wives and children, and

(2) sending money from Cheshire to London.

35 McDonnell, 1977, p. 351.

A Survey of the Manour of Hield in Aston
juxta Great Budworth as the same was measured by Tho. Jackson
Anno Domini 1649

The value 1649				Cheshire acres		
£	s	d		a	q	p

Israel Leycester's tenement, entitled Hield House

			The house, Gardens, Outbuildings, Folds, & wasts between the house & ferny crofts	0	2	20
2	10	0	Penditons Yoard	0	0	20
			The Orchard	0	2	18
			The Fearny Crofts	0	1	18
1	10	0	The field under the house, halfe of this belongs to the Racke ground	1	1	1
3	10	0	The little meadowe	1	2	21
1	10	0	The little Moore	1	1	20
3	0	0	Holts meadowe	1	1	38
9	0	0	The nearer marled field	3	2	8
			The further marled	3	1	39
1	10	0	The Longshoote	1	2	30
22	**10**	**0**	**Summe**	**16**	**0**	**33**

Thomas Jackson's tenement

			The Hempeyoard, house, outbuildings, gardens, orchard & backeside	0	1	7
			Meadowe	0	2	36
			Barley field	0	2	36
			Little meadowe	0	2	22
			Hield Wood	1	0	0
			The Pingot	0	0	6
			The Tanny flat or further field	3	3	2
9	**10**	**0**	**Summe**	**7**	**0**	**29**

John Jackson's tenement

			The house, gardens & crofte on the backeside	0	0	28
			The Hempeyoard	0	1	11
			The further parte of the meadowend	0	0	34
			The upper side of the Geld field	1	0	14
			The lower side of the Geld Field	0	2	8
			Worralls field	0	3	5
			The greate meadowe	1	1	12
5	**10**	**0**	**Summe**	**4**	**1**	**32**

£	s	d		a	q	p
			Raphe Whalley's tenement			
			The mill, two Pooles, folds & Masts*	1	0	2
			The house, Hempeyoard, Orchard & Pingot	0	2	15
			The sandy field or loont field	0	3	11
			The higher field	1	1	16
			The Poolested at the end of the higher field	0	0	25
			The Hempe yoard in which John Whalley's house stands			
			but is parcell of Raphe's	0	0	17
8	0	0	**Summe**	4	0	7
			Racke Ground in the Manour of Hield *but now leased in 1653*			
5	0	0	The great meadow held now by Israel Leycester *in Lease*	3	3	13
2	0	0	The Wood, held by him also			
			now added to Israel Leycester's lease	1	3	8
5	0	0	The Sandy field held now by the same Israel *now in lease*	5	0	12
			The great Moore held now by the same Israel,			
			this is parte of his tenement in Lease	2	1	22
1	10	0	The Hield-croft held by John Williamson of Budworth	1	0	10
3	0	0	The Oxe-Hey held now by Peter French of Budworth	2	1	21
4	0	0	The Gorsty field held now by Richard Coppocke of			
			Budworth	3	0	20
3	0	0	The ffowle meadow held also by the same Coppocke	2	0	4
5	0	0	The Butty meadow held by Coppocke & Williamson	2	2	30
			Summe	24	1	20
			George Kirkman's Cottage *now added to Israel Leycester's tenement*			
			⌈ The House & garden	0	0	8
3	0	0	⎪ Barnecroft	0	2	8
			⎪ Mill field	1	2	30
			⌊ Hempe yoard	0	0	34
			Summe	2	2	0
[79	0	0]	**Summe, totall of all the Hield**	58	3	1

Source: DLT/B98

Notes
1. Cheshire Acre = 2.1157 Statute Acres
2. Notice the hempyard on four of the holdings

*Were these 'Masts' the poles on which woollen cloth was 'tented'?

APPENDIX 3.2

The crops grown in Hield (probably) 'at halves.'
Jackson's share in thraves

Table A

	Loont or Sandy Field	Higher	Worrals	Little meadow	Hield wood	Barley	Tanny flat	Tithe paid £ s d
1656	18 peas	32 oats						—
1657	22 barley	46 barley						10 6
1658	– peas	34 barley						
		14 oats						4 6
1659	Missing							
1660	32 oats	29 barley						11 0
1661	20 peas	30 oats						9 0
1662	18 oats	25 peas	32 barley					11 0
1663		50 barley	20 barley	14 oats	22 oats			1 0 0
1664		20 oats						
		9 peas	17 oats	24 barley	41 barley			
					– beans			—
1665				20 barley	29 barley	27 pots		—
1666				15 beans	30 beans	30 barley		9 0
1667				7 barley	38 barley	31 oats		—
1668	Missing							
1669							104 barley	
							4 oats	—

Table B

	Barley	Oats	Peas	Beans
Total crop in 12 years (thraves)	522	261	72	45
Average annual crop (thraves)	43.5	21.75	6	3.75

Improvements to house and farmyard (spelling modernized)

Feb. 1656   I made the pale about the garden

1659/60   This winter I floored the house and made the wainscot door in the parlour

May 1661   I built the Kitchen

May 1662   I did the house about with lime and hair

May 1664   I made the wainscot – in the Kitchen chamber, whited the house, did the Kitchen with lime and hair under and rebuilt the parlour chimney

Aug. 1666   I built the house of office

Sept. 1668   I then made a new window in the Chamber over the house and another in the parlour and did it with lime and hair under the floor

Sept. 1669   I then built the new Shippon, Haybay and garner and made the well in the lane

Mar. 1670   I then laid the floors of the Garners and made the stairs there

Apr. 1671   I pointed with lime and hair the garners

Mar. 1672   I pulled down and rebuilt the shoreing by the barn

Nov. 1673   I set down the pump

May 1673   I laid the pump in Colours

July 1673   I made the pale at the swinecoate

Apr. 1676   I repaired the end of the barn

I made the same summer ten thousand of brick

June 1677   I walled the side of my house with brick

Made the new windows in the house; wainscoted the house side; made the window shuts and the little chamber door; undershot the house with lime and hair

Notes

1. 'Shuts' are perhaps shutters.

2. The practice of covering the underside of the suspended timber floors of the first floor with lime and hair, which is described three times in these notes, was perhaps an innovation of the period. Whether the process was applying a thick slurry of lime and hair to the woodwork or whether it was 'plastering' on reeds we cannot be sure. The former seems more likely. Before houses had chimneys, when the fire was in the centre of the room, all the upper part of the high room would have been blackened by smoke (see Figs 17–20). The building of chimneys made possible the insertion of first-floor rooms. Whitening the underside of these floors would have improved the light in the ground-floor rooms.

Thomas Jackson's receipts from Halton and Kinderton Courts

	Halton			Kinderton		
	£	s	d	£	s	d
1676	6	0	0	6	0	0
1677	10	0	0	6	0	0
1678	8	0	0	2	10	0
1679	8	0	0	5	10	0
1680	18	0	0	4	10	0
1681	12	0	0	7	0	0
1682	17	0	0	5	10	0
1683	18	0	0	6	10	0
1684	10	0	0	7	10	0
1685	10	0	0	5	0	0
Totals	117	0	0	56	10	0

Notes
1. Halton was the Hundred Court of Bucklow Hundred.
2. Kinderton was the 'Manor' Court of the Venables family, Barons of Kinderton near Middle-wich.

APPENDIX 3.5

Children and grandchildren of Thomas Jackson
(b. = born)

Children of Thomas Jackson and Joane Peake, who married 11 July 1678
Christian, b. 14 April 1679
Thomas, b. 19 February 1680/1
Elizabeth, b. 17 May 1683
Anne, b. 13 January 1684/5, died 19 March 1684/5
Charles, b. 9 March 1685/6
Anne, b. 2 September 1688
George, b. 19 February 1690/1
Joseph and Sarah, (twins), baptized 2 July 1695

Children of Peter Jackson and Elizabeth Bradley, who married 8 February 1678/9
Thomas, b. 21 November 1679
Penelope, b. 18 March 1681/2
Elizabeth, b. October 1684
Peter, b. 20 January 1686/7, died 28 February 1686/7

Children of Charles Jackson and Sarah Smith, who married 30 October 1677
Christian, b. 7 November 1678
Charles, b. 10 October 1680
Thomas, b. 21 October 1682
Sarah, b. 26 November 1684
John, b. 15 May 1687
Samuel, b. 2 August 1689
Mary, b. 31 May 1692
Francis, b. 6 April 1698

Children of Thomas Millington and Penelope Jackson, who married 11 June 1674
Thomas, b. 12 March 1674/5
Anne, b. March 1675/6

APPENDIX 3.6

Two Notes

1. *The property rights of wives and children*

How did the wives of these three families – the Thomas Millingtons, the Thomas Jacksons, and the Peter Jacksons – continue to live in their houses and farms after the husbands had 'broken' or had fled to Ireland?

In the case of the Millingtons, we know that the last 17 acres of the estate were put in a settlement. The income of this settlement was 'for the use of Thomas Millington, the father, for his life'. The income would have been £9 or £10 a year, and that was all he had to live on except what he earned. The capital was owned by the Trustees and so could not be touched by his creditors. At his death the property descended absolutely to the son, except that he may have had to provide a portion for his sister. Settlements of this kind were common and a number of such documents are to be found among the sets of deeds of the small freehold properties that the Arley estate bought in the four townships in the eighteenth and nineteenth centuries.[1] In some cases where the family owned both freehold and leasehold property, both were settled. Full settlement with two or more independent trustees were less common where the property was only leasehold. I have not found one except in a will. Nevertheless, rights similar to those enjoyed by families with settlements of freehold property seem to have been enjoyed by families of leaseholders. It may be that simpler forms of document were adequate for leaseholds, which were

118

a 'chattel'. An agreement at the time of marriage may have been adequate to protect the wife and children.[2] It may be that traditional land law which protected the wife's dower and the heir, was important. It is also possible that custom may have protected families from eviction where their names were in the lease. Whatever the exact legal position, these examples of the Jackson family seem to show that such rights existed.

2. *Sending money from Cheshire to London*

In the course of the Jackson story many sums of money were sent from Cheshire to people in London. How was it done? It seems that there were two methods: a) Small sums could be given to people going to London – usually carriers. For example, on 8 April 1706, 'I sent by John Stretch's man to Thomas Millington 11s 6d'. (b) Larger sums made use of cheese trade 'bills'. For example, in 1689 Thomas Jackson sent by Mr Howe, cheesemonger in Thames Street, £20 for Lady Leicester and £6 to Charles for Thomas Millington. A more detailed example is: '13 April 1696 sent Mrs. Leicester a bill of exchange £40 had of Mr. Morris to be paid by Mr. John Greening in Thames Street, Cheesemonger, at 15 days sight'. Mr Morris will have been a cheese factor or farmer who had sent cheese to John Greening, who therefore owed him money. By paying £40 to Morris, Lady Leicester could draw £40 from Greening.

1 WM Boxes 48-74.
2 WM Box 69 appears to include such documents from the 1730s and '40s.

IV

The Fells of Swarthmoor Hall, 1673–8

1. INTRODUCTION

Freeholders were an important group in Cheshire and Lancashire society in the seventeenth century. These were not families based on old landed gentry estates, but who owned freehold land ranging from small farms of fewer than 20 acres, such as Thomas Jackson acquired, to hundreds of acres. A few of these families, like the Shuttleworths, came to own thousands of acres, and so became indistinguishable from old gentry families. The freeholders, as a group in north-west society, had incomes between those of the three-life leaseholders and those of the old major gentry.

I have found only one account book produced in a freeholder family in the north-west. It was written by Sarah Fell at Swarthmoor Hall between 1673 and 1678. This house is near Ulverston in Furness in the extreme north of Lancashire (now Cumbria, see Map 4), a long way from the south Lancashire–north Cheshire area, from which all the rest of the archives used in this book are drawn. Furness was an outpost, where some old ways survived longer than in the Mersey basin. Some of the farming and textile manufacturing at Swarthmoor described in this section was similar to that carried on at Smithills 80 years before.

On the other hand, the Fell family's business activities were absolutely up to date. Their coastal shipping ventures to Bristol and Cornwall were competing directly with Mersey traders. The freeholders were the richest new social group to emerge between 1550 and 1650, and this study would be missing a vital piece of the puzzle if it did not include a picture of a freeholder family. Before 1540 there were probably under 1,000 free-holder families in the two counties of Cheshire and Lancashire. Many of them lived on small farms hardly distinguishable from the farms of the tenants who became three-life leaseholders. By 1650 there are likely to have been several thousand families, who held their farms as 'copy-holders' or 'fee-farmers' or by 'tenant-right', who were economically and effectively freeholders even if their titles were legally distinct. The original

120

Map 4. North Lancashire and Furness.

Shuttleworth farm at Gawthorpe was of this type. With the owners of the farms that had been freehold in 1540 and the owners of the small farms that people like Thomas Jackson had bought from the major gentry the total number of freeholders was even larger. All these 'freehold' properties had increased in value around 20 times between 1540 and 1650, so all these families owned an income-producing capital asset. Whereas the 'freeholders' usually owned at least 90% of their properties, the three-life leaseholders usually had only about 50%, so the freeholders were the richest group.[1]

My analysis of the occupations of country families living near Smithills in the 1580s and '90s has suggested that many of them were in business. Unlike the landed gentry who rarely involved themselves in trading, these other families were interested in increasing their wealth through their businesses. With their greater capital resources, the freeholders were able to extend their activities more widely.

2. THE FELL FAMILY AND THEIR ESTATE

The Fell family's estate around Swarthmoor[2] appears to have been built up by purchase from the middle of the sixteenth century. Before 1536 four landlords owned most of this part of Furness. These estates were Conishead Priory, Furness Abbey, Nevill Hall and the lordship of Muchland, and the Fells were probably tenants of one of these. All these estates passed to the Crown between 1536 and 1570. When the Duchy of Lancaster confirmed their 'tenant right' in 1564–73 the tenants became virtually freeholders of that land in a similar way to that in which the Shuttleworths' copyhold land at Gawthorpe became effectively freehold.[3] Like the Shuttleworths, they then bought more land from other 'freeholders'.[4] Thomas Fell was admitted to Gray's Inn in 1623.[5] He became a judge and Vice-Chancellor of the Duchy of Lancaster under the Commonwealth, and no doubt increased the size of the estate. In 1632 he married Margaret Askew. She and her sister were heiresses of the Marsh Grange estate about four miles west on the other side of the Furness peninsula. Her share of this estate was worth about £3,000 at the time of her marriage.[6] It probably contained, therefore, some 300 acres. Thomas and Margaret Fell had nine children between 1633 and 1653 and eight of them, one son and seven daughters, survived into adult life. Judge Fell died in 1658. His son George married Hannah Cook in 1660. The Judge

1 See Foster, 2003, Ch. 3, for a more detailed account of these new property owners and the rising value of their land.
2 Two excellent biographies of Margaret Fell provide much of the background – Crosfield, 1913 and Ross, 1949.
3 Hoyle, 1992, pp. 197–8 for Furness, pp. 241–7 for Clitheroe.
4 See VCH Vol. 8, p. 354, note 89 for an early purchase.
5 See D.N.B.
6 Crosfield, 1913, p. 4.

Fig. 36. Swarthmoor Hall in the eighteenth century.

left his wife a life interest in Swarthmoor Hall so that she could bring up her seven daughters there. George and his wife Hannah were allotted Marsh Grange House with some land around it.[7] George was a lawyer like his father and the young couple actually lived mostly in London. He died in 1670, leaving a seven-month-old son and a two-year-old daughter.

In the summer of 1652 George Fox, a preacher, visited Swarthmoor. He made a great impression on the Fell family, especially Margaret. Swarthmoor Hall became a centre of the religious movement that came to be known as the Society of Friends or Quakers. George Fox and Margaret Fell were among its most important leaders as it spread rapidly in Britain, America, and continental Europe. After the Restoration of Charles II in 1660 the so-called Cavalier Parliament passed a number of Acts against Quakers and other religious groups who did not conform with the Established Church and whose attitudes to the traditional social order were thought to be subversive. Between 1660 and 1689 their preachers and their meetings were severely restricted and many Quakers spent months in jail. In 1669, after she had been more than ten years a widow, Margaret Fell and George Fox were married.[8]

7 See Appendix 4.1 for a discussion of the arrangements on this estate.
8 Ross, 1949.

Fig. 37. George Fox 1624–91, as he may have looked when he arrived at Swarthmoor in 1652.

At the time the account book begins in 1673, the Swarthmoor Estate was owned by the trustees for the three-year-old Charles Fell, the only son of George.[9] The estate consisted of some 420 acres of land together with manorial rights in Ulverston and Blawith. There were also common lands, urban property in Ulverston, and corn mills.[10]

Margaret Fox, aged 59, had a life interest in the Hall and at least 81 acres around it.[11] Four of her daughters had married by this time. The three unmarried daughters, Sarah, Susannah and Rachel, were living at Swarthmoor as were their married sister Mary and her husband Thomas Lower. All these girls had had their portions which had probably come from rights to the Marsh Grange lands under Margaret Fell's marriage settlement. Sarah and her sisters appear to have been the owners of Marsh Grange House with about 100 acres in 1673. In 1676 they sold it to Mary and Thomas Lower, who appear to have moved there in 1675. Sarah and her sisters also owned the important Force Forge which is

9 Charles Fell also owned, via trustees, the Manor of Osmotherley, which had earlier belonged to his grandfather. Ross, 1949, p. 227.
10 See Appendix 4.1.
11 See Appendix 4.1.

described below. How much else they owned is not known, but they were definitely persons with property.[12]

In June 1673 Margaret Fox with her daughters, Sarah and Rachel, and her son-in-law, Thomas Lower, went to Bristol to meet George Fox on his return from a tour in America. Sarah soon returned to Swarthmoor as she seems to have been the main manager of the house and farm there. In December George Fox was arrested and imprisoned at Worcester. Thomas Lower stayed in Worcester, but Margaret and Rachel returned to Swarthmoor. The next year Margaret went again to Worcester; some member of the family seems to have cared for George Fox in prison until he was released in February 1675. By June that year Fox and his wife had arrived back at Swarthmoor and they stayed there for nearly two years.

In 1673, when the account book begins, Sarah was aged about 31 and evidently a person of considerable character, confidence and intelligence. Her two unmarried sisters, Susannah and Rachel, were about 23 and 20. In the four to five years covered by the account book there were almost always some family members living at Swarthmoor. Sometimes there were only two or three; sometimes there were as many as seven or eight.

3. THE ACCOUNT BOOK[13]

This account book was originally one of several kept by Sarah Fell, but is the only one to survive. She appears to have been the business manager of the family who kept the family cash box. The account book is a record of this cash, itemizing every payment in or out. She received money on behalf of other family members and she paid money out to them. What makes the record of particular interest is the detailed reason she wrote for each item. Thus she did not write just 'paid out to Thomas Lower', but instead she wrote:

19 Feb 1677   By money lent to Brother Lower to pay off little Margery Lower's nurse, when the child was wained (weaned) 12s 6d.

12 There are hints in the account book that Sarah and her sisters and her mother had an income from rents as well as from the two farms. Some of these rents may have come from corn mills.
13 Penney, 1920. This is a well edited book with a large amount of additional information in the Notes.

Sarah evidently also kept account books for each member of the family. The 12s 6d in the item given above was transferred to the account of Thomas Lower. There the money she received for him and the money she paid for him were brought together so that a balance could be struck from time to time, and a payment made to settle what she owed him or vice versa. In the surviving account book only the money paid in or out was recorded. Payments made in other ways, for example by transfer between accounts, are not, so no overall figures appear. We never discover what Margaret Fox or Sarah's total income was, nor what in total they spent in a year. Nevertheless, the account book tells us a great deal about how families like the Fells conducted their affairs and much also about the people who worked for them and with them.

4. THE STAFF AND THE FARMING

One aspect of the old-fashioned way of life in Furness was that the arrangements with the staff and other workers were very similar to those we encountered at Smithills Hall in the 1580s and '90s. Whereas at Tabley in the 1670s the people who came to do farming or building work for a day or two were paid a full cash wage of 8d to 1s a day, the visiting adult workers at Swarthmoor were paid 4d a day for most agricultural work and 5d or 6d a day if they were building craftsmen. They were evidently having their meals in the Hall in just the same way as we saw that people working at Smithills were treated in the 1580s and '90s. This analysis is confirmed by entries on 17 and 19 May 1674. Edward Brittan was paid 6d a day for mowing at Gleaston and because this was not near Swarthmoor, Sarah Fell paid James Kendall's wife 8d a day for tabling him. We have seen at Smithills that mowing was usually highly paid work.

The main farming work was not done by casual workers but by full-time employees who lived in Swarthmoor Hall or Marsh Grange. Before 1676, when the Lowers bought Marsh Grange, Sarah Fell seems to have managed both these farms. The male farming staff seem to have worked the two farms together. This staff normally consisted of two or three young men and two or three boys. Edward Braithwaite, who earned £2 15s 0d a year, was the most highly paid. Others earned £2 10s 0d to £2. As these rates were only about 2d a day, it seems likely that they were provided with all their clothes as well as their meals, although the accounts

126

only hint at this.[14] The boys earned between 5 and 17 shillings a year depending no doubt on their age. Their wages often included clothing as part of the contract. On 12 May 1675 Sarah hired John Hird for a year and arranged 'to give him 12s and a shirt'. These young people did not stay long with the Fells. In these four or five years a total of 17 young males worked for Sarah Fell. When she ran both farms there were usually about six of them; when she only had Swarthmoor, three was enough. This suggests that the two farms were of similar size.

As well as young men, girls were employed.[15] The most trusted and highly paid was Ellin Pollard who evidently ran the dairy at Marsh Grange. She received £2 p.a. As well as providing for the house she sold her butter and cheese in the market at Ulverston. There seems to have usually been another older girl at Marsh Grange like Ann Bayley, who was paid £1 10s od a year, and a younger girl earning 12s a year. At Swarthmoor there must also have been a dairymaid. Ann Standish earned £1 17s 6d a year and may have done that job. As at Marsh Grange, the usual staff at Swarthmoor seem to have been one or two senior girls and a junior one. Like the boys they did not stay very long, so it is hard to discern a pattern. The principal work done by the casual staff was shearing the corn. In 1673 this work on the two farms cost £3 10s 6d and in 1674 it cost £2 14s 2d. There is no figure for 1675 because the appropriate pages are missing from the book. In 1676 £3 6s od was paid to the shearers and in 1677 they cost £5 19s 4d.

The land of these two farms was near sea level. They enjoyed a climate similar to the Much Hoole lands of the Smithills estate so they could grow anything: wheat, barley, oats, peas, beans, hemp and flax. The extent of the farming can only be gauged approximately from the account book. Each farm seems to have had one or two pairs (yokes) of oxen, which did the ploughing and carting. Each farm had a herd of milking cows[16] and there was at least one bull. There were calves, heifers and steers. Some cattle were fattened and slaughtered each year for meat and their hides sold to the tanners to make leather. There may usually have been 15 or 20

---

14 E.g., 17 October 1674, 'Paid for Scotch cloth I give to the servants'. See textile section below. Compare these rates with those at Tabley, 1648–51, in Appendix 2.2, p. 85

15 The editor N. Penney has established the date of birth of some of these girls. This reveals that they were all over 18 years old.

16 Most of the cheeses sold were around 8 lbs in weight. We can calculate this because 2d per lb was the usual price of cheese. They would therefore have been made from the milk of four or five cows. As the milk of one or two cows was probably required in the house each day, the milking cows are likely to have numbered at least six or seven at each farm.

cattle on each farm. Both farms also had a small flock of sheep. There were a couple of cart-horses and most members of the family seem to have had a riding horse on which they travelled about the country.

From the clues provided in the accounts one may estimate that each farm had 20–30 acres under crops each year. A number of their neighbours had more cows than arable land so the Fells were able to purchase manure to put on their wheat and barley fields. The Fell family's farming was different to the farming we have seen at Smithills and Tabley. These gentry farms were simply intended to provide for their own households. For the Fells farming was a business. Their land generated an important part of their income. As well as providing for the needs of the family, their living-in staff, and their casual visiting workers, the farm had to provide cash income from the sale of produce. Due to the limitations in the information available in the account book, which have been mentioned already, no total figures for sales each year are available, but adding up the value of the sales recorded gives some idea of the scale of the business.

In the year beginning 1 May 1674 each farm seems to have sold more than £50 worth of grain. Some was sold in Ulverston market, but most seems to have gone to people who called at the house. This indicates that it was an established practice to sell grain at Swarthmoor. This was an exceptional year because prices were high and there were not many family members at home. In other 12-month periods each farm seems to have sold only £10 to £20 worth. As well as corn the Swarthmoor farm made net sales in the year beginning 1 May 1674 of about £40 worth of live-stock – cattle and sheep. The Marsh Grange net sales were nearly as much. Again the figures were exceptional because in other years sales seem to have been only about half these sums. Both farms sold butter, cheese and wool. In the exceptional year of 1674–5 Marsh Grange sold nearly £10 worth of dairy products. In that year Swarthmoor even sold vegetables – cabbages and onions – out of the garden. In May 1678 26 stones of Swarthmoor wool was sold in Leeds for £6 10s 0d and 21 stones from Marsh Grange for £4 16s 0d. Over how long a period this wool had been accumulated we are not told.

Perhaps the most interesting information about farming in these accounts are the details of the co-operation between the Fells and their neighbours in farming matters. One constant activity was the use of the Fells' bull to service other people's cows. In the year beginning 1 May 1675 nearly 100 cows were brought in for bulling at 6d a time. So the bull

128

earned nearly £2 10s 0d in fees. This is evidence also of the large number of neighbours who kept a few cows. Many seem to have had only one or two. The Fells also hired out their plough oxen on a number of occasions. On 2 February 1675, for example, Isabel Jackson, widow, paid 19s 'for ploughing 3 acres of ley with Mother's draught, they were 5 days at it'.[17] In the spring of 1674 George Fell, weaver, paid 5s to have an acre or two of his land ploughed. Other arrangements were more complicated. An entry on 4 May 1674 shows that Henry Townson had made a deal with the Fells to 'hold the plough' on some of their land in return for being able to use their oxen to plough his own land. How many more of such barter arrangements were made we don't know. This one only enters the account book because something went wrong and Sarah had to pay Henry Townson 6s 3d so he could hire another plough team. It is interesting to note that there was no mention of these co-operative farming practices in the detailed accounts at Smithills. Whether this was because the Lord of the Manor lent the services of his bulls and oxen freely to his tenants or whether it was because he never did we don't know, but the latter seems more likely.

5. TEXTILES

There is a mass of information in the account book about textiles. It can be divided into two parts. We begin with the textiles they made, and go on to those they bought. The Fell family organized the production of all the textiles listed in Appendix 4.2. The hemp and flax were grown on the farm. Much of the processing was done by the permanent staff. Some help was provided by casual workers, so we find items for a day or two of work weeding the hemp or line, pulling, rippling, braking and swingling it, in short, performing all the tasks described at Smithills (pp. 28–35). Spinning took the most time, being carried out both by the female servants who lived in and by the family. Rachel Fell, the youngest daughter, bought a Dutch spinning wheel in March 1678.[18] Some 15 women and one man appear in the account book because they were paid for spinning in their own homes. One woman was paid 4d a week for the seven weeks she spent spinning at Swarthmoor.

---

17 3 Lancashire acres = 4.9 statute acres.
18 William Stout, another Lancashire freeholder, records his mother spinning. Marshall, 1967, p. 175.

The hanks of yarn were then sent out to the weavers. George Fell of Trinkelt was their favoured weaver. He did all types of cloth – hemp, linen, and woollens – except huckaback and ruggs.[19] As it was probably the custom to reserve a loom for each sort of cloth (because this reduced the time required to 'set up' the loom to produce a piece of material), he was likely to have had a business with several assistants or apprentices. In contrast two of the other weavers employed by the Fells specialized in only one cloth type each. William Hobson of Cartmel only did huckaback and John Fell of Tarne Close only did coarse hemp and tow for sacks. In a change from Smithills practice the better grades of hemp and linen were normally taken after weaving to be whitened by Richard Stable. It may be that part of this process was carried out at Swarthmoor because on 17 June 1676 Sarah paid 'the servants for watching the whitening clothes several nights 1s 2d'. Or perhaps this was only bleaching dirty clothes after washing them. Like the whitener the Fells bought 'bucking ashes' (at between 2s and 2s 8d a bushel) which they evidently used for washing and bleaching linens.

After the woollens were woven they moved on to James Walker, the 'Walkster' or fuller, who 'milled and dressed' them, or in other words fulled them and sheared them. This woollen cloth was not usually dyed in the piece but the clothes made from it were dyed individually by Thomas Benson the local dyer. For example, on 31 May 1678, he was paid 1s for dyeing three items: a) $2\frac{1}{4}$ yards of cloth, black; b) 2 waistcoats for Ann Calow and Elizabeth Briggs; and c) a pair of stockings, green.

The commonly used varieties of hemp and flax were made in pieces of 20 to 40 yards long at intervals over the four years of the account book. As we saw at Smithills households tried to keep a stock of common cloth. At Swarthmoor they often ran out, so they had to buy from their neighbours who were also making these cloths. The account book there-fore gives us the prices. Coarse hemp or harden for sacks and bags usually cost between 7d and 9d a yard. The weaving cost about $1\frac{1}{2}$d a yard out of this price. Spinning the hemp cost 4d a hank. When the Fells bought yarn it cost between $10\frac{1}{2}$d and 1s a hank, so the hemp when prepared for spinning was worth between $6\frac{1}{2}$d and 8d a hank. Unfortunately we are never told the weight of a hank, but this cloth evidently contained about half a hank per yard. This coarse tow cloth was also used for sheets and

19 Coarse woollen cloth.

shirts for the boys. It also made frocks (i.e., smocks or aprons) for them to work in. Teare of hemp cost 9d to 1s a yard and made stronger shirts and sheets. Weaving it cost 2d to 2½d a yard. Huckaback for towels cost 2.6d a yard to weave. Finer linen cost between 3d and 5d a yard to weave, and whereas the spinning of coarse grades of hemp and flax always cost 4d a hank, spinning a hank of fine linen cost 8d.

The most common woollen cloths are described as blankets and kersey which were probably similar. The wool came from the family's flocks of sheep. It seems that it was usually sorted and spun at Swarthmoor because only two of the outside spinners ever handled wool. On those occasions in September and October 1673 the wool for kersey cost 2½d per lb to spin and the wool for blankets only 1½d per lb. George Fell usually charged 1½d per ell for weaving both blanket and kersey, and James Walker charged just over 1d a yard for milling and dressing. When the Fells bought kersey or sold some from their stock the price was usually 1s 8d to 1s 10d a yard.

The Fells sometimes, as we have seen, had to buy small pieces of the cloths they normally produced themselves, but the majority of their textile purchases were of materials they did not make. A range of finer linens was made in Scotland. They made a number of purchases of 'Scotch cloth' at prices ranging from 8d to 1s 5½d a yard. Still finer 'Holland' linen was bought for George Fox at nearly 2s a yard. Superior grades of woollen cloth were also bought. Cumberland cloth and Lancashire plush both cost 2s a yard. Serge cost 2s 2½d.

Materials made of imported fibres were attractive. Cotton and silk were much easier to dye than hemp and flax. Ribbons and tapes of all kinds could be made more economically on special looms, so manufacturers produced a great range of prettily coloured items of which the Swarthmoor household were frequent purchasers. For example, on 16 October 1673, Susannah Fell bought 18 yards of black and sky coloured ribbon for 4s 9d. Fustian was a cloth with a linen warp and a cotton weft. Rachel Fell bought two yards of coloured fustian at 9d a yard.[20] Three and a quarter yards of white fustian at 1s a yard were bought for sleeves and drawers for Sarah's little nephew. Handkerchiefs were attractive to the young women. These seem to have been coloured cotton squares originally imported from India, sometimes with printed designs on them. They were probably worn around the neck. One cost Ann Bayley, a servant at Marsh

20 20 August 1674.

Grange, 2s 2d in April 1677. The quality or colour range of the dyeing available locally from Thomas Benson was less good than that available in textile manufacturing centres like Kendal. The Fell family frequently sent their own clothing to be dyed in Kendal. The Fell sisters bought small pieces of materials probably made of silk. 'A la mode' cost 3s 6d a yard and sarsenet cost 7s 4d a yard.

Clothing

Both Thomas Lower and Sarah Fell employed boys as personal servants. It seems to have been the fashion to provide smart clothing for them. This was presumably in imitation of the gentry's habit of putting their servants in livery. George Jackson, Lower's boy, was given three shirts made of teare of hemp at 11½d and 1s a yard. His doublet and breeches were made from three yards of Kersey which together with the buttons, silk, and thread cost 6s 9d. A pair of stockings for him cost 1s 8d and his hat cost 1s 10d. Tom Harrison, Sarah's boy, had a coat and a pair of stockings made from three yards of woollen cloth at 1s 8d a yard. The total cost of these, including the making up, was 5s 6d. He also had sheepskin pockets and a leather apron. This was evidently not smart enough, because a few months later in April 1677 he had a new coat made of 1⅞ yards of broadcloth at a cost of 7s 2d. James Longe, a servant at Swarthmoor, had a new suit in October 1677 made of 3⅞ yards of Kersey at 1s 10d a yard, part of which was charged against his wages.

Both sexes seem to have worn knitted woollen stockings. These normally cost 1s to 2s 6d a pair. When William Taylor came from Aberdeen to visit the family at Swarthmoor he sold Thomas Lower a pair for 10s. Were they embroidered or tartan? Or is the text of the manuscript corrupt?

6. THE BUSINESSES OF THE FELL FAMILY

The distinctive character of the Fell household, in comparison with those we have examined so far, was its involvement in business. The Shuttleworths and the Leicesters were certainly not businessmen. The Leicesters' corn milling business was part of the traditional style of the old gentry, most manorial lords having corn mills. Thomas Jackson's children were all in business, but no details of their activities have survived. Sarah Fell's account book provides plenty of little details even if, unfortunately, there is no full picture of any of the family businesses.

132

We have already examined the extent to which the farming around their two houses was conducted as a business. The other major continuous business in which they were involved, the Force Forge, has also been mentioned. It was 12 miles north of Swarthmoor in the hills at Grizedale (see Map 4) and had been acquired in 1658 by Judge Fell. His son George sold it to his four unmarried sisters in 1666. It was an important and unusual industrial operation in the 1660s. Three wheels turned by water from a dam drove 2 pairs of bellows and the hammer. Charcoal was provided from the coppice woods surrounding the site.[21] Iron ore was brought by strings of packhorses from the Dalton area four or five miles south of Swarthmoor. Iron was made by heating the ore in a hearth fired with charcoal and blown to a good heat with the bellows. The emerging iron was repeatedly hammered to remove the impurities. The iron that was produced was sold to local smiths and in nearby towns like Lancaster. From 1673 until the middle of 1676 Reginald Walker was the commercial manager of the forge, followed by William Wilson. Technical management seems to have been in the hands of Robert Russell, 'our hammerman'.

Sarah Fell's uncle Richardson, who was married to Margaret Fox's sister (the other heiress of Marsh Grange), had property near Dalton. Sarah bought some ore from him in May 1674 but we are given no details. She bought 30 quarters from Thomas Preston of Holker for £6 in February 1676 and another 40 quarters from two other men for £9 in March 1678. John Tubman, presumably a local smith, bought two stone and $2\frac{1}{2}$ lbs of finished iron in November 1675 for 7s 2d. At the same time William Yeates bought one stone and 5 lb for 3s 3d. The price of iron in both of these transactions works out at just over 2d per lb. Much larger quantities seem to have been bought by merchants from further away. William Bickerstaffe of Poulton le Fylde[22] bought £26 10s 0d worth in 1674, and Henry Coward of Lancaster paid £30 on account of iron sales in 1675. The latter was one of the most active merchants in Lancaster.[23] The business of the forge brought the Fell family into contact with some of the major traders in the north-west.

With this background, it is easier to understand the next large business adventure of which we get knowledge from the account book. On 17 November 1673, Sarah made an agreement with Joseph Sharpe that she

21 Awty, 1977, pp. 98–101.
22 Penney, 1920, p. 555, note 154/1.
23 Marshall, 1967, pp. 74–5.

and her sister Susannah would be partners with him in buying and selling grain. Joseph Sharpe had, as a young man, been a servant of Judge Fell, who left him £2 10s 0d in his will. He and Sarah had been partners together in a business venture before (see below). In November 1673 they must have agreed that there was going to be a shortage of grain in the next year which would cause a sharp rise in price. They therefore agreed to act together to buy stocks. Sarah's part was to provide the money while Sharpe did much of the buying. When they decided that the best sale prices would be obtained in Liverpool and Bristol we don't know. No doubt her sister Isabel, who was married to the Bristol merchant William Yeamans, played a part. Fell family friends among merchants and Quakers probably provided the rest of the necessary information. The venture seems to have gathered more partners as it grew. Margaret Fox, the Lowers, and Rachel all joined in. So did James Lancaster of North Scale on the Isle of Walney, a great friend and Quaker. Sarah raised at least £75 in loans from six local people including £7 from her tailor, Matthew Fell.

It seems they sent one shipload of barley to Liverpool and another of wheat, oats and groats to Bristol. They were evidently not practised in the administration of such ventures. The ship for Bristol was held up in April 1674 by the Customs officers and Sarah had to go to Dalton to sort it all out. Also, they bought more grain than the ship could carry, so some was left behind in a warehouse on the quay. This did not matter because they sold it from there in the following months. It must have made a profit because the price had risen. The partners' original estimate of the market position was fully confirmed by events. From the prices for which oats were sold at Swarthmoor we learn that oats were 1s 1d a bushel in December 1673.[24] This was a common price in ordinary years. By April 1674, the price had risen to 2s and it reached a peak of 3s 4d in June. From there it declined to 1s 6d by January 1675. It rose again to 2s 5d in March and remained at that level until May 1675 when the last of the Fells' spare oats was sold. They did not sell any more until June 1676 by which time the price had returned to 1s 1d a bushel. The prices of the wheat and barley sold at Swarthmoor between January 1674 and May 1675 followed a similar pattern to that of oats.

Some part of the return cargo on these voyages seems to have been bought by the Fell partners in Bristol. Wine bottles were certainly bought

---

24 These prices are all for Winchester or statute bushels. Swarthmoor used Carlisle bushels, containing three Winchester bushels.

there. They were sold in June to two local gentry families – Miles Dodding of Conishead and William Kirby of Ashlack. Thomas Lower was selling pepper and cumin in the area in July 1674 so perhaps he invested in a parcel of spices in Bristol. He may have overestimated the size of the market in Furness for such goods because Sarah paid 10d in April 1675 to transport some of his pepper to Lancaster for sale.

Thomas Lower, like his elder brother Richard, had trained as a doctor. Richard was at one period 'the most noted physician in Westminster and London'.[25] Thomas was an active Quaker and was living at Swarthmoor to be a support for his wife and her parents, George and Margaret Fox. When not engaged in Quaker activities he earned part of his living by seeing patients. As well as the spices he probably bought a range of items from the apothecaries in Bristol so that he could provide drugs for his patients. His family had property in Cornwall where he was brought up. It was probably in order to take possession of a property there that he had inherited from his aunt, Loveday Hambly, that he went to Cornwall in March 1677. This visit led to the second coastal trading venture of which the account book tells us. At the end of May 1677 a vessel, captained by a local friend Gawen Kirkham, was loaded with grain and iron from the forge and despatched to Cornwall. The freight for the round trip cost £53. On the return voyage, it carried blocks of tin, slate, wine and brandy. The last two had been exchanged for some of the grain sent to Cornwall. These proved to be more than the market in Furness could absorb and much of the wine had to be taken to Lancaster for sale.

The first of these two voyages certainly made a profit, because some of it passed through the account book. There is less information about the second. The return cargoes illustrate the immature nature of coastal trading on the west coast at that time. All the items we know about were either imported from abroad – spices, wine, brandy – or were not made in north Lancashire – glass bottles, tin, and slate. With such simple knowledge of their local market the Fells and their partners were able to trade successfully.

These two trading ventures and the forge were the major business activities of the Fell family, but the account book provides evidence of several minor ones. In November 1673, before they decided to buy grain together, Joseph Sharpe and Sarah had bought some £15 worth of coal on the quay at Rampside. They sold this off, retail, over the next few

25 D.N.B.

months. Another little business the family owned was a malt kiln. They roasted their own barley there to make malt to brew their own beer, and they also sold barley in the form of malt to many local people. Sometimes they hired the malt kiln out to people who had their own barley. On 2 March 1676 Thomas Greaves paid 3s 6d for making 42 bushels. The kiln required maintenance. A new set of timber laths was made by a carpenter and haircloth to hold the barley during the process was purchased.

Perhaps the activity that tells us most about the commercial life of the area was the primitive banking service the Fells provided. A number of people deposited money at interest with Sarah Fell. This was a secure loan because she owned freehold property. For example Susannah Fletcher lent £100 in 1673 at 5¾% for a year. She was then unmarried and this was probably part of her portion. On 1 February 1675 it was repaid with interest to her husband Edward Harrison. Sarah used the money to help pay for their purchase of the Marsh Grange property. In the accounts she kept, which have not survived, the interest on these loans was evidently charged against the income from the farm as she always referenced the interest paid in the account book to 'Marsh Grange account'.

Sarah not only took money in on loan, she also lent money out. One of her most frequent customers was William Benson, whose business was probably to buy harden (coarse hemp or flax cloth) from families who were making it. Almost every family in the plain of Furness was probably a potential supplier, and he would have sold their cloth on to the travelling salesmen (chapmen). They carried it to those parts of the country that could not grow their own hemp and flax and sold it there. This William Benson was often in need of small short-term loans. On 14 June 1677, for example, Sarah lent him 10s for a week. On 28 June she received the 10s back again. He does not seem to have paid money interest, but he no doubt recompensed Sarah in some way. Sarah did little services for other local traders. On two occasions she bought needles for her tailor Matthew Fell. In one instance she bought 150 for him in Bristol at a cost of 1s 8d.

Sarah's banking activities did not extend to a full participation in the system of trade bills. However, she often received money that had been moved in that way. On 13 December 1677 Henry Coward of Lancaster paid her £30 that he had received by a bill from one of the purchasers of the corn and iron sent to Cornwall. At the same time she received £7 that her sister Yeamans had sent from Bristol for the credit of her account with Sarah. On other occasions Sarah paid out money on behalf of a distant merchant in the confident belief that it would be repaid to her via a trade bill. On 30 July 1677 she paid 10s to a ship's captain for William Meade of Essex. She probably did not know him at that time, but four years later she was to marry him.

This brief description of the Fell family has emphasized their close involvement with business. One indication of the extent to which a belief in the importance of business was at the heart of Quaker culture is shown by the following list. This gives details of the occupations of the husbands that the seven Fell daughters chose. All were members of the Society of Friends when they married. The only non-businessman soon left the Society.

The seven daughters of Margaret Fell and their husbands

Margaret (1663–1706) m. 1662	John Rous, sugar merchant, London area, son of Col. Rous of Barbados, sugar plantation owner
Bridget (1635–63) m. 1662	John Draper, freeholder in Durham who left the Friends before 1671[26]
Isabel (1637–89) m. 1664	William Yeamans of Bristol, merchant (see D.N.B.), d. 1674
m. 1689	Abraham Morrice of Lincoln, silk merchant
Sarah (1642–1714) m. 1681	William Meade, linen merchant, London and Essex
Mary (1647–1720) m. 1668	Thomas Lower, MD from Truro area, Cornwall, medicine and business
Susannah (1650–1710) m. 1690	William Ingram, tallow chandler, London
Rachel (1653–1732) m. 1683	Daniel Abraham, merchant, Manchester

This list is in striking contrast with earlier social habits. The parents of these girls had been brought up in two houses only four miles apart and most country girls married men who lived locally. Even landed gentry married locally. Peter Warburton's six daughters, who shared the Arley estate from 1626 to 1643, had married gentry from Cheshire and the neighbouring counties of Lancashire and Staffordshire. By contrast the Fell daughters' husbands came from all over England. Their shared interest was the Society of Friends, most of whose members seem to have been engaged in national and international business. They were a new

26 Ross, 1949, pp. 149–50.

social group that had come into existence in the seventeeenth century. In a period when discussion of morality, the nature of society and the good life was cast in a religious mould and relied greatly on quotations from the Bible, members of the Society were seen to be joined together by their religious beliefs. At the present time when discussion of social phenomena is often about interest groups, cultures and shared norms it may be sensible to see the Society as a vehicle created to reflect the interests, the culture and the morality of this new social group. In Chapter 8 of my forthcoming *Capital and Innovation*[27] the connection between Quakers and business is examined in greater depth.

27 Foster, 2003.

The ownership of the Swarthmoor and Marsh Grange estates and the
Fell family property arrangements 1632–91

Many of the legal documents have not survived. In this note I attempt to describe the likely situation based on the existing documents and knowledge of the typical legal procedures of the period. When Thomas Fell married Margaret Askew in 1632 one or more Marriage Settlements would have been made. The normal pattern would have been for the Fell property to be settled on the eldest surviving son of the marriage. The husband, Thomas, would have the income of his estate for his life. Some lands would have been earmarked as a jointure for Margaret to provide her with an income for life if she were left a widow. Margaret's share of the Marsh Grange estate would have been settled on the children of the marriage, with Margaret getting the income for her life. There would have been powers to provide portions for younger sons and daughters in both settlements.

When Thomas Fell died, the freehold of Swarthmoor Hall would have passed to his son George under these settlements. As the Judge's wife and seven daughters were living in the house, that would have been uncomfortable for them. Therefore, Thomas in his will gave his wife a lease for her life of the Hall and the 82 acres[1] around it that were its 'home' farm. Margaret probably also came into possession of her jointure lands on the estate. George, the son, probably inherited the rest of the Fell estate. When George became engaged to Hannah Cook in 1660 a legal agreement would have been made about her portion, her jointure and the land to be settled on the children of the marriage. George Fell entered into a Bond of £6,000 to implement this agreement. On the basis of this agreement the marriage took place, but the appropriate Marriage Settlement was not provided by the Fell lawyers. So Hannah's father, Edward Cook, draper of London, took legal action under the Bond. The judgment he obtained in his favour in Hilary 15/16 Chas 2, is referred to in Swarthmoor Deed No. 1.[2] The reason why the Fell family had not produced the Marriage Settlement was probably because Margaret Fell was occupying Swarthmoor Hall. It wasn't easy to find suitable jointure

---

1 50 Lancashire acres in the will which is reprinted in Ross, 1949, pp. 398–400. The words used in the will would not, I think, have conveyed a freehold interest.
2 Friends House Library, London.

and settlement lands. The compromise that seems to have been arrived at was for the Marsh Grange trustees to exchange the Marsh Grange house and approximately 100 acres around it for the manor of Osmotherley, which was part of the Fell estate. This allowed George Fell to settle the Marsh Grange land on his wife in his Marriage Settlement and placate his father-in-law.

When George died in 1670, leaving a son and a daughter, the trustees of this marriage settlement were left holding the Fell estate on behalf of the infant Charles, subject to his mother Hannah's jointure and his grandmother Margaret's interests in Swarthmoor. In 1671–2, they appear to have transferred the Marsh Grange property to Sarah Fell and her sisters, and in 1678 they seemed to have re-acquired the manor of Osmotherley. These transactions were probably provided for in the arrangements made in 1661–2 over George and Hannah's marriage settlement.

The Marsh Grange estate had to be used to provide portions for the seven daughters. The four daughters who married in the 1660s probably each got a part of the old Marsh Grange estate that had not been exchanged with George. After his death the exchange was unwound so as to provide portions for the three unmarried daughters. Sarah and her sisters acquired the Marsh Grange property in 1671 for £1,250.[3] In 1666 they had acquired Force Forge from their brother George. They may have acquired other property. When Charles Fell came of age in 1691 and gained control of the Fell estate he sold the main Swarthmoor land to Rachel (Fell) and her husband Daniel Abraham. This document, Swarthmoor Deeds No. 2, describes these lands in detail (summarized here on p. 124). Two documents dated 5 and 6 March 1666 giving Margaret Fox rights over part of the land are noted. These rights were undisturbed by the sale. Of the total sale price of £4,500, Charles Fell and his wife got £3,900, and the six surviving Fell daughters got £100 each. This was probably in settlement of their right to inherit the whole property (under the 1632 Marriage Settlement) in the event of their brother George Fell's children not having any heirs.

3 Ross, 1949, p. 224.

APPENDIX 4.2.

Cloth manufactured locally for the Fell family appearing in Sarah Fell's account book 1673–1678

Cloth	*Uses*
Hemp	
152 ells teare	shirts, shifts, saddle panels
139 ells tow	sheets, pillowcases
44 ells coarse	grain bags, ore bags
9 sacks	grain bags, ore bags
Linen	
95 yards huckaback	towels
60 ells teare	better quality shirts, shifts, sheets, etc.
44 ells feather-bed ticking	dense to prevent feathers poking out
13 ells fine	even better quality shirts, etc.
3 whites	tablecloths?
Woollen	
94 ells blanket	blankets
35 ells kersey	outer clothes – coats, doublets, etc.
16½ ells plain	outer clothes – coats, doublets, etc.
10 ells coarse	outer clothes – coats, doublets, etc.
7 ells mixed	linsey-woolsey? It was 'milled and dressed' like a woollen cloth
8 ells stuff	linsey-woolsey? Linen warp but 'milled and dressed' for a screen
3 happins	covers – for beds? A specially spun yarn. 'Dressed and washed'
2 ruggs	better quality woollen cloth woven and dressed by Francis Crofts of Lancaster

Note
1 ell = 1¼ yards.

V

Richard Latham in Scarisbrick,
1716–67

1. INTRODUCTION

Richard Latham owned a three-life leasehold of 20 acres on the Scarisbrick estate from 1716 to 1767. He is interesting because he was the least rich man we know about who left an account book.[1] He married Ann (Nany) Barton in August 1723 and the account book appears to show every penny they spent from the beginning of 1724 until his death in 1767. Between 1726 and 1741 Nany gave birth to eight children all but one of whom survived to adulthood. Sadly for the parents their only son died aged 20. This chapter, therefore, presents a picture of Richard and Nany bringing up a large family on a small farm in south Lancashire.

The question that immediately arises is how representative or typical was the Latham family. In my *Four Cheshire Townships*, I listed the owners and some of the occupiers of every property in over 8,000 acres in the 1740s. About two-thirds of the owners were three-life leaseholders. In the more rural townships of Aston and Budworth perhaps about half of these leaseholders were resident. These townships, running south from Warrington, were close to the Mersey valley – the commercial heartland of Cheshire and Lancashire. Scarisbrick, about 15 miles north of Liverpool, was more remote. Probably more of the leaseholders were resident in Scarisbrick so Latham is likely to have had a number of neighbours living on similar small leaseholds. The majority of the land in Scarisbrick was probably in use for commercial dairy production.[2] Some, perhaps many, of the small

---

1 Weatherill, 1990. As the reviewers in H.S.L.&C., Vol. 140 (1991) make clear, this is not an entirely accurate transcription of the manuscript. These reviewers also found the editor's introduction disappointing. I agree with them. The picture presented here differs from that editor's in many ways. Nevertheless, as the manuscript is fragile, this account is based almost entirely on the printed text. This text is particularly defective in its transcription of the notes and jottings on the endpapers at the front and back of the account book. These provide important information. I carefully examined these pages of the original manuscript. The manuscript and the Scarisbrick estate papers are in the Lancashire Record Office, Preston.

2 Foster, 1998, p. 8.

resident leaseholders like Latham had decided not to rent their land to commercial farmers. They continued to use their land to produce food to support their own households as their predecessors on these farms had been doing for centuries. It has been the traditional view of historians that these families were farmers with bye-occupations. This account book suggests that description may have misplaced the emphasis. They may have been people with other occupations who did a little farming in their spare time like the two leaseholders whose land appears in Fig. 35 above on p. 102–3. Another point worth mentioning is that Latham seems to have shaped his household's lifestyle in traditional ways, so his account book may present a picture of how life was lived on these small farms in the seventeenth or even in the sixteenth century.

Richard Latham was about 26 years old when his father died in 1716 (see family tree in Appendix 5.1). From then on he was the owner of capital which was mostly invested in the three-life leasehold. The privileged nature of these leases, in which the payments to the landlord were much less than the full market value of the land, allowed the family to live comfortably. Except in one year the farm produced all their basic food. Although Richard and Ann brought up eight children (including their orphaned niece) they were never short of food. They were always able to afford a few luxuries, like sugar, and they bought new fashionable clothes for the girls as they grew up. Yet in almost all the first 32 years of his marriage, until he was about 58 years old, Richard Latham was in debt. The account book provides an unusual insight into the financial practices of the rural community. Richard borrowed £34 from relations and neighbours to pay for renewing his lease. He slowly repaid his debts at about £2 a year. If one lender wanted repayment he was always able to find a replacement. All this lending seems to have been without formal security. The interest rate was always 5%. The succession of these long-term unsecured loans, on which interest was regularly paid, tells us much about the honesty, integrity and trust that existed in rural society.

In the final section we see the major place the production of textiles occupied in women's lives. It filled a much greater part of their days than farming did for men. Ann Latham may have spent the whole of her first year of marriage spinning flax and cutting out and sewing up her sheets and pillowcases and all the other textiles needed to furnish her house. Her daughters were spinning for their livings by the age of 12 or 13. Apart from a little farm and garden work this seems to have been their occupation. The women controlled the family's textiles but producing them dominated their lives. Richard Latham, unlike most of my account book authors, was not a successful man. He did not improve his family's wealth. He did, however, maintain his family's position in society and he left his widow and daughters in a similar position to that in which his father had left him 50 years before. His may have been the average, the typical experience of three-life leaseholders.

2. THE ACCOUNT BOOK AND THE PROPERTY

The account book describes in detail the cash paid out each year. For example, the first entry for 1727 reads:

	£	s	d
for sugar 4d; salt 2d; Betty new shoos 8d		1	2

There is no mention of money received by Richard Latham nor are any of the other arrangements of his business affairs set out. It is therefore necessary to do a good deal of detective work to reconstruct the Latham family's way of life.

The property was on 'Barrassell' Green. This was enclosed before 1820 so it is not shown on modern maps, and I have not found the early estate maps. The estate rentals show that it was in the Asmall and Harleton area south of Scarisbrick Hall. The lease of 1767[3] lists the field names, and these same names occur in the account book. The lease gives the total area as nine Cheshire acres which is about 19 statute acres. The rent was 9s 9d a year and the tenant had to do boon works:

provide 2 hens or 12d
1 day heaving dung or 6d
2 days shearing or reaping corn or 20d
make ½ acre grass into hay or 3s 4d.

On the Arley and Tabley estates by the eighteenth century these boon works were always taken in cash. But Latham's account book provides examples of these works actually being performed in Scarisbrick. For example, in 1725 'boon hens' cost 1s, and in 1726 two hens were bought for 1s 4d.[4] In 1727

3 DDSc 27/288.

'boon hay working by Thos. Oliverson 3rd of July'

cost 3s 8d.[5] In addition to this 19-acre holding, the rentals show Richard Latham paying 16s (presumably a rack rent) for land in Bescar Meadow. Work on this also appears in the accounts. In 1730

'mowing half an acre in Bircher meadow by John Prescot; he went 3 times 1s 6d.'[6]

In the 1767 lease the buildings on the farm are described as a dwelling house consisting of three bays and outhousing of five bays.[7]

3. THE FAMILY AND THEIR JOBS

Richard's father Thomas (see p. 166) bought the lease with only one life remaining from the Maudsley family in 1699 or before. In 1699 he paid Robert Scarisbrick £30 for a new lease in which the three lives were his sons Richard, Edward and Thomas.[8] The property would have been worth around £10 p.a., so the lease would have had a capital value of about £140.[9] Thomas is therefore likely to have paid the Maudsley family about £100. Thus he was a man with money. Almost the only other information we have about him comes from a lease that was cut up and used as the endpapers of the account book.[10] This lease, of which a large part can be read, was made in 1711 between Henry Valentine of Ormskirk and two partners, Thomas Latham of Scarisbrick and George Holding of Ormskirk, miller. Henry Valentine evidently had a long lease of the water corn mill, windmill, and malt kiln at Eggargate in Lydiate, five miles south-west of Ormskirk (see Map 1). In this document, he let it to the two partners for seven years at £7 p.a. The two partners had to maintain the machinery at their expense, but Valentine would pay half the cost of repairs to major items.

4 1725 line 25; 1726 line 41.
5 1727 line 52.
6 1730 lines 38–40. Latham's acre was a Cheshire acre, so the meadow was approximately 1.1 statute acres. In 1723 Richard rented it to his brother John for 16s (p. 127 line 194. 'Acer' in original mistranscribed as 'doer').
7 These were timber-framed buildings. A 'bay' was usually between 12 and 18 feet square and could be one or two storeys high.
8 DDSc 27/97.
9 See Foster, 2003, Ch. 3 (ii), and Appendix 3.6. for more information on these leases.
10 The endpapers also have a bond dated 1685 in which Thomas was to be paid 50 shillings in 10 quarterly instalments.

These mills were major capital works at this period. Sir Peter Warburton spent between £200 and £300 each on renovating his mills at Arley and Warburton in the 1750s. Even after this, repairs costing between £5 and £20 a year were not infrequently required. So it can probably be safely inferred that Thomas Latham knew something about milling and that, as the first-named partner, he had the financial strength to be able to keep the machinery in repair during the seven years. Unfortunately he died after five years. His will, if he made one, has not survived. We know that the practice was to provide portions for all the children, and the evidence we have suggests that it was followed in this case. The endpapers show that Ellen had at least £22.[11] Thomas's main asset was probably the leasehold property. If all Thomas's five children got an equal share they could perhaps have had as much as £30 each. There was often not much cash in deceased persons' estates at this period. It was common to make the eldest son, who inherited the property, pay part of the portions from the 'unearned' income (i.e., the annual rack rental value) of the property. It is likely that Thomas's will obliged Richard to make payments to his brothers and sisters. It is probable, therefore, that the property income of £10 p.a. was used by Richard during his first seven years of ownership, 1717 to 1723, to pay the balance of their portions to his siblings. The three younger brothers certainly had spare cash in the early 1720s. Richard borrowed £4 from Edward and Thomas, probably in 1722.[12] At a similar time, he borrowed at least £2 5s 0d from John.[13]

Thomas got married in June 1717, and it was unusual for girls in this society to marry men who had no money. His bride, Elizabeth, was nearly six months pregnant, so the relationship had evidently become serious quite soon after his father's death. I have found no evidence for Thomas's occupation. When Edward died in 1724 his probate papers described him as 'miller'. He had evidently learned this business from his father and presumably he found another job in milling after the Eggargate contract ended. The surprising fact is that both these young men, Thomas and Edward, died in their early 30s, in 1724. Thomas's wife Elizabeth had died only two years after she married. Her son Thomas died aged five, just a

11 P. 127, line 201. Line 200 should read 'owing to my sister the 1st of May more £4 0s 0d – in part for cows'. A note (omitted in the printed text) beside the start of the 1711 lease reads, 'I paid to Elin my sister ye 25 of August 2 pound now owing her 20 pound and no more from this time 1723'. It is possible, therefore, that she had more than £22.

12 P. 126, line 158.

13 P. 126, line 149 should read, 'I borrowed of John'. Also line 157.

146

year before his father. Richard's only sister Ellen died in 1725. Thomas's surviving daughter Elizabeth seems to have gone to live with Richard and Nany. She must have been the 'Bety' who had stockings for 5d, and shoes for 8d and 7½d in 1726, when Richard's own Betty was only a baby.[14] It is tempting to attribute the early deaths of Richard's younger brothers, his sister, and his nephew to their going to work in Ormskirk. The well-known contrast between the high mortality in towns and the health enjoyed by country dwellers would have been neatly illustrated. However, although they were all buried in Ormskirk, we do not know where they lived.

We know more about Richard's youngest brother John and his wife Kety. Their names appear in the account book frequently. John did work around the farm in 1722 and 1723[15] and he rented two fields in 1723.[16] He evidently did more work in 1724 and 1725 because in 1726 Richard

'reconed the 29th January with John my brother, paid with butter, milk and cheese [and] corn £2 1s 0d,'

and,

'paid to John my brother the 18th February 1726 £1 19s 0d.'[17]

John and Kety evidently lived very close to Richard and Nany because later that year

'to Katy John's wife the 30th of September for 1 day work in hay [and] washing, milking when Nany was sick 25th of July 1s 11d.'[18]

At the end of the account book there are rough notes on the costs of making 15,000 bricks in 1723.[19] Both John and Richard joined in this work. This was the year Richard married and it may well be that the property was improved at that time to provide a dwelling for John and Kety and another for Richard and Nany. The three bays of dwelling house in the 1767 lease may have been in fact two dwellings. This supposition that there may have been more than one dwelling on the property is strengthened by later evidence. Before 1809 the Scarisbrick estate had

---

14 Lines 26, 98, and 100.
15 P. 124, lines 90–95; p. 126, lines 150–2, 154, 160–6.
16 P. 127, lines 193–4.
17 Lines 14–5, 22.
18 1726, lines 87–8.
19 Pp. 124–7, lines 88–110, 169–91.

acquired the Latham family's interest in the property. Rentals show two cottages that had been 'part of Lathams' being let. The land, and perhaps other buildings, was let to a third tenant.[20]

If we accept the hypothesis that John and his family had a dwelling on the site, it helps to solve two more puzzles. The first is that nowhere in the account book is there any record of rent paid. Yet we have seen that the lease specified rent and the estate records show that it was regularly paid. How could this have been? A note in the endpapers[21] gives a clue.

> 'I set or sold hay to Hugh Boondel for or in the year 1725 to pay ye 1 day of November ye rent is £1 1s 6d. Hugh paid ye 13 of November.'

Perhaps the rent was paid by special barter arrangements of this kind, but to make such arrangements steadily over 40 years seems arduous. If John were renting his dwelling from Richard it would have been much easier to ask him to pay the Scarisbrick estate rent as part of his rent to Richard.

A similar puzzle exists with the tithes. The payment of tithes is only mentioned in the account book on three or four occasions. This is strange because we know tithes were regularly paid by all farmers. Someone must have paid tithes so this could have been another of John's duties. As the corn tithes seem to have been owned by the Scarisbrick estate the arrangements to pay them may have also been part of the Manor Court day. In the rough notes at the end of the account book there is a list of what John owed Richard in 1723. One of the items is 'for small tithes which I paid', which seems to confirm that there was an arrangement that John should pay the tithes. The only time that Richard paid was in 1738 when he recorded

> 'for the tythes to John Longworth and his companions £3 18s 6d.'[22]

This wording suggests a deputation to gather in arrears. As the tithes on a 20-acre farm would probably have been between 10 shillings and one pound per year,[23] this £3 18s 6d probably represented arrears built up over four or five years. Apparently John had failed to pay, so the collectors had recourse to Richard, who cleared off the debt. Richard must have made a better arrangement with John after this because he never paid

20 DDSc/25/84.
21 Omitted in the printed text.
22 Line 55.

148

tithes again. A similar puzzle exists over who paid the land tax and other local taxes. I have found no information on this.

If John and Kety were living in a dwelling on the site and were paying the leasehold rent of 9s 9d a year, the Bescar meadow rent of 16s 0d and the tithes averaging about 15s a year, their total payments would have been about £2 per annum. That was about the market rent for a cottage and garden. We have no clear indication of John's occupation. He did one or two days work around the farm in some years until 1761. He dug turf, filled dung, threshed and mowed, so he evidently remained physically fit. He cast bricks and 'skilled' them in 1723.[24] This may mean that he set them in the kiln (often spelt 'kill') so he may have been a brickmaker. He did thatching and possibly sawing[25] in 1749, so it seems likely he was mostly a building worker.

The next major puzzle is the occupation of Richard Latham. Was he a full-time farmer? From the account book we get a good idea of the farming operations. They normally kept two cows and some young stock. Calves were bought and sometimes kept for a period. Heifers were occasionally bought. Sometimes there were three or four cows. Richard seems to have traded in cattle as the names of the cows often change. There was always a mare and sometimes there were one or two colts. Some land grew grain each year: wheat, barley and oats are all mentioned. Wheat seems to have been grown in most years so they presumably ate wheat bread. Oats were probably grown every year. Some may have been eaten as oatmeal and some was dried for the horse. Barley occurs less often. From the clues provided it would seem that three to five acres was the usual extent of the arable. This suggests that 15 to 25% of the land was usually in crops and the rest was grass or hay to feed animals. This pattern of farming is similar to that practised in north Cheshire and described in my *Cheshire Cheese* on pages 63–76.

From the figures given there which set out the time required for the various farming activities and their cost one can see that Latham's farm of 20 acres would have required between £5 and £7 worth of work a year. There was not therefore enough farm work to keep a man fully employed

23 Foster, 1998, pp. 63–70 and 102–5.
24 Pp. 124–5, lines 96 and 97. These seem the same two operations that are described in lines 104 and 105 as 'casting' and 'making them bricks'.
25 1749, lines 21–5.

since a farm worker earned about £12 in a year.[26] In fact, the account book shows that Richard usually spent £1 to £2 a year having farm work done for him. So he and his wife apparently only did £3 or £4 worth of farm work a year. This analysis is confirmed by what is recorded in the accounts after 1755. In 1756 Richard fell ill and although he evidently recovered partially, he was never as fit as before. The costs of assistance with the farm work rose to three and four pounds a year. Perhaps as much as £5 was paid in 1763 but it is difficult to be sure when the work was carried out that was paid for. One reason for the increase was that before 1756 Richard and his family seem to have done all the threshing. After 1756 they often paid others for threshing.

So if Richard did not occupy himself fully with farming, what did he do? The clues are few. An important one is what we learn about the mare and the cart. There was always a mare on the property yet almost every year other people were paid to do ploughing and carting. On many occasions when the horse was required for farm work, it seems that it was not available. The most likely reason for this would be that Richard was using the horse on other business. The cart was also important to Richard. In 1736 expensive repairs were made to it costing a total of £2 6s 2d.[27] This was the only piece of his equipment on which a significant sum was spent on repairs. The mare was regularly shod – between two and six times a year. One of the indications that Richard's active life was finished was that the mare was shod for the last time in June 1760.

Another clue that suggests a business other than farming occupied the horse and cart is provided by a series of entries such as 'to James Forshaw looking after goods in moss ground 6d'.[28] These entries suggest that 'goods' had been temporarily warehoused on the moss ground before being transported elsewhere. They might have been goods in which Richard was trading or they may have been in transit and waiting to be joined with other goods to make a full load to some destination. We never discover what the 'goods' were so we do not know whether Richard was a trader or a carrier.[29] Or he may have been a bit of both like the Widder

---

26 Foster, 1992, p. 10.
27 1736, lines 42–8, 56, 58.
28 1736, line 120. Other examples are at 1731, line 97; 1732, line 76; 1736, line 11; 1738, line 3, etc.
29 1731, line 97 has 'looking (after) hor or cheeses in moss ground 1s.' Does this tell us anything?

brothers of Great Budworth.[30] Richard's attitude to Manor Courts also suggested he had, or might have had, important business that he needed to be available to do. He went to considerable trouble and expense not to attend them. The rent was always paid on Manor Court days and so probably, on the Scarisbrick estate, were the tithes. We have seen how Richard avoided direct payment of both. The account book has a number of entries like

'to Wm. Wilkin to free me from Darby Court for 3 years, new baly: 7d.'[31]

All these clues do not make it certain that carriage or trading were Richard's business. However, these occupations were common among the leaseholders of small farms. They had control of the land that would provide grass and oats for their horses. This kind of work provided an opportunity to employ their small capital and a chance of making profits.

4. RICHARD LATHAM'S INCOME AND EXPENDITURE

At the end of each year between 1724 and 1735 Richard Latham added up the money he had spent. In the following years he left a blank for the annual total. L. Weatherill has added up each of these years for us in the printed text.[32] At first glance one is tempted to think that these totals represent Latham's annual expenditure. Closer analysis reveals that this is not so. They include capital payments of two kinds. First there are capital payments to renew the lease and to repay loans. In order to find the £41 10s 0d that it cost him to renew the lease in 1728 Richard had to borrow £28. He received loans from four individuals. When any of the lenders required their money back Richard borrowed from someone else to repay them. The payment to each old lender was included in the account book but not the new loan (see pp. 155–9 below for a full account of these loans). The second kind of capital payment was connected with the farming. It was said earlier when enquiring into Richard's occupations that one of them was cattle dealing. In the account book the cost of each cow purchased was recorded but not the value of the corresponding sale. Another type of capital expenditure on the farm was marling.[33] Richard

30 Foster, 1998, pp. 79–80.
31 1730, line 27.
32 Listed on p. xxii. The 1741 total there and on p. 49 is misprinted as £51 19s 0d, and should be £30 19s 0d.
33 Foster, 1998, p. 59.

did this on only three fields in 43 years. In 1740 it cost £5 9s 10d, in 1746 it cost £4 4s 10d, and in 1753 it cost £2 5s 0d.

In addition to these capital payments we should also exclude a few other exceptional payments. Richard spent some £30 on setting up the house and farm in 1724–5 when he was newly married. He spent £12 9s 6d on three cows and a heifer, and £10 4s 6d on a mare. The remainder went on carts, plough, harrow, saddle, churn, cheese vat, etc., and a feather bed, which cost £2 3s 0d. It is also sensible to exclude a few other exceptional payments. The £3 18s 6d paid in 1738 for arrears of tithe which was mentioned earlier; the £2 6s 2d for repairs to the cart in 1736; and £1 10s 10d for the funeral of Alice in 1736 have therefore been left out.

After all these exclusions the size of the family's normal cash expenditure on running the household as recorded in the account book each year is revealed (see Appendix 5.2). From 1724 to 1739 it varied between £6 and £12. From 1740 to 1758 it varied between £14 and £27 and from 1759 to 1766 it was between £11 and £18. However this cash expenditure is not a good indication of Richard's total income. The best way to understand this is to examine Richard's position. The property was worth about £10 a year. He could have let it to someone and received £10 a year rent. However, he and Nany chose to do around £4 worth of work on it each year. They also paid others to work on it. The farm will have yielded them value of about £16 a year.[34] This consisted of the value of the grain and vegetables grown, the value of the milk, butter and cheese produced by the cows, the value of the horse's work and the value of the animals when sold or eaten (less the cost of their replacement). In addition to this there were Richard's earnings in his business. For it to be sensible for him to be in business rather than doing agricultural work we must assume that he earned at the rate of about £16 a year instead of the £12 p.a. a farm worker received. So for the 75% of his time spent in this business he may have received around £12 a year. We shall see on pp. 159–65 below that Nany did textile work worth about £2 a year, so their total income was possibly of the order of £30 a year. The account book is therefore only listing a part of their total annual consumption. Nevertheless, the three periods identifiable there accurately correspond to phases in the Latham family's life cycle.

34 See Foster, 1998, pp. 63–76 for a detailed discussion of the costs and values of this type of farming.

In the first 16 years to 1739, while all the children were small, the farm provided all their basic food – grain, meat and dairy products. The minor purchases of these which are recorded were probably for convenience. Many of the food entries in the accounts record the acquisition of little extras to their main diet – sugar and treacle, salt, dried fruits and spices. Another category of purchases was the household needs: soap and candles, repairs to furniture, the house and the farm equipment. Seed corn and help on the farm were often significant expenses. So were textiles and the interest paid on loans which we will examine more closely in the next sections. In the early years of this period Richard may have sold farm produce and rented out fields. The endpapers show that his brother John and his sister Ellen both rented fields in 1723. George Harrison bought grain and paid 'land money' (presumably rent) in 1726.[35] As the children grew up and ate more, this phase probably passed. Richard's income from his business, if the previous analysis is correct, was often more than the cash he recorded that he paid out. What happened to the excess? As we have seen, he was slowly paying off his debts at the rate of about £2 a year. He was also perhaps accumulating a little capital to operate his business. There is an entry on the endpapers saying

'Henery Bell had of me the 13 day of February 1731 the some of 6 pounds,'[36]

so there was some loose money about by that time.

In the second phase, 1740–58, the house was full of teenage children. This had advantages and disadvantages for the finances of the household. The disadvantage was that they ate more. In 1740 on the only occasion recorded they had to buy significant quantities of 'corn'. They bought about 20 measures at the mill. Each measure made 60–75 lbs of bread. It is likely that one reason for these purchases was that their own crops had yielded badly. There was a poor harvest in the area that year. The price of this 'breadcorn' from the mill approximately doubled in the first six months of 1740. Richard paid 3s in December 1739, the usual price of barley.[37] The price slowly rose until in June and July 1740 he paid 5s 5d. Perhaps it was the poor yield in his own fields that encouraged him to start marling. In July 1740 he did his first field at a cost of £5 9s 10d.

The advantage of a large family of teenagers was the work they could

35 P. 127, lines 192–7 and p. 125, lines 140–7.
36 Omitted in printed text. Should be before p. 122, line 25.

do and the money they could earn. In 1739 the girls had started spinning cotton (see 'Textiles' below). The children will also have done more around the farm and the garden. They dug turf (peat) for fuel. Usually the only farm work paid for in the 1740s was a little ploughing. It would seem that it must have been the money the children earned and gave to their father that allowed the cash expenditure to rise to more than £20 a year. Much of this extra money was used to buy clothes for the children (see 'Textiles' below). We are not able to work out details of their diet despite the apparent wealth of accounting evidence. Richard's liking for barter arrangements makes any estimates meaningless. We have already seen how the payment of rent and tithes was made without using cash. Another example appears in the jottings in the endpapers. In 1747 Richard sold a cow to Jonathan Rogers for £3 10s 0d. He was paid £2 in cash and then received meat worth 18s 9d between 30 January and 1 June. We don't know whether the balance was paid in meat or cash. Other account entries show pigs and calves being slaughtered. We don't know how much meat there was, nor whether it was eaten, bartered or sold. Other clues suggest more bartering. The mare that was bought in 1724 for £10 4s 6d cannot have remained at work for 40 years. Yet a mare was shod each year until 1760. There must have been at least one replacement, perhaps two or three. The replacements may have been foals grown up, they may have been bartered for cows, or they may even have been bought with cash and not recorded in the account book. We will see more bartering in 'Textiles' below. The loan of £6 in 1731 to Henry Bell, mentioned above, is not in the regular annual accounts. In short, the more one examines the Latham family's accounts, the clearer it becomes that the account book is just recording the movement of money out of a purse called 'housekeeping expenses'. Business or trading activities were perhaps dealt with in another book that has not survived.

Despite these problems it is possible to see that the standard of living in the Latham house while the children were growing up was well above subsistence. Every year there were numerous purchases of sugar and treacle. More than 60 were recorded in 1746, costing £1 9s 2d. Even the low quality sugar, which Latham bought at 3d to 5d a lb, was a luxury product.[38] Quite a lot of meat was eaten; a range of vegetables was grown

37 Compare with Tabley, pp. 84–6 above, and with the crops Richard usually grew, p. 149 above.
38 1724, lines 84, 90, 93.

154

in the garden and so were fruit trees.[39] Ducks and chickens were kept, and geese were bought.[40] Turf was dug and 40–50 baskets of coal were bought every year to keep them warm in winter. The children were all sent to school. This never cost more than 5s a year as village schools were not expensive. In Appleton, John Caldwell charged 1d a week for teaching reading and 2½d a week for writing. Presumably this was part-time.[41]

In 1747 Betty, the eldest daughter, went to work for a Mr Richard Parks in Ormskirk. (Dicy), the only son, died in 1748. Between 1748 and 1756 Sarah, Rachel and Ann followed Betty into service. Thus the size of the household diminished. From 1756 Richard, by this time probably in his middle 60s, was not able to do as much. The mare may have been let out to Peter Maudsley that autumn[42] and much more was paid for work on the farm that year. Richard may have done a little work in the next three years but the mare was never shod again after 1760. Around £4 a year was spent on the wages of farm workers in the 1760s.

So a third phase can be distinguished. After 1758 cash expenses were being reduced to match the reduction in the family income caused by Richard's retirement from full-time work. In this period it seems that one or two of the youngest daughters may have stayed at home and their cash earnings perhaps replaced most of what Richard had made. The family may well have started selling a little farm produce or renting a field to increase their cash income. The account book records one major difference between this period and the '40s and early '50s. Then Richard bought the daughters' clothes probably with money they had earned and given to him. After 1758 the daughters, if they were still at home, bought their own clothes.

5. THE MANAGEMENT OF THE FAMILY'S CAPITAL

When he inherited the farm in November 1716, it is likely that Richard Latham was obliged to pay portions to his brothers and sister. He may well have had to pay out £10 p.a. or more – the full value of the farm – for the first seven years of his ownership. By 1723 he seems to have cleared

---

39 Seed beds in the vegetable garden are described in a part of the endpapers omitted in the printed text. 60 gooseberry bushes were bought in 1726, line 9. 1735, line 109 mentions a pear tree.

40 E.g., 1733, line 7.

41 At Arley Hall, Captain Hore's invoice, 1 July 1760.

42 P. 122, lines 1–24.

off the debts so that he was in a position to take a wife. It is probable that his marriage with Ann (Nany) Barton was a social arrangement rather than a love match. She probably came with a portion of £20 or so which would have been appropriate for a marriage with a 20-acre leaseholder. It seems likely that her portion was the source of most of the £30 that they spent on setting up the farm and the house.[43] Richard repaid £8 of loans in 1725–26. These loans may have been taken out to supply the rest of the money they needed to start their household. The accounts suggest that there was a honeymoon period in 1724. They drank more ale in that year than they ever did in later years and a lot of sugar and candy was bought. In almost the only intimate note in the whole book Richard says, 'Nany my wife going to the Filde the 3rd June [1725], I did lye with her the same morning'. This was almost exactly nine months before their first child Betty was born on 19 February 1726. They had been married for about 21 months by June 1725. Was this the first time? There seems a striking contrast with the behaviour of Richard's brother Thomas and his wife.

When Richard and Nany got married in 1723 he was the owner of a lease in which three young men were the 'lives'. It must have seemed that they would not have to renew the lease for many years. Fate decided differently as his brothers Edward and Thomas were both dead by April 1724. Richard's was the only life remaining. The family was in a dangerous position. If he were to die they would lose the farm. Nevertheless, Richard waited until his son was born and had survived his first winter and was seven months old before he renewed the lease. The two new lives seem to have been Nany and their son Richard (Dicy). The cost was £40 plus £1 10s 0d for the lawyers. To find so much money Richard had to borrow £28 from four people (see Appendix 5.3). As his sister Ellen's executor since her death in 1725, he had about £6 that she had left in trust for her two nieces.[44] The remaining £7 10s 0d had presumably been saved by Richard from his income in the previous two years.

43 There may seem rather much inference and deduction in this account. It is difficult, however, to see what other explanation for the facts there could be. Richard owned the farm for seven years before 1724. At the beginning of that year, he had no farm animals or equipment and no store of grain. They bought bread, butter, and milk in the early entries in the account book. He can only have been letting the farm either as a whole or field by field. The endpapers, lines 193–7, show that he rented fields to his brother John and sister Ellen in 1723. He had no capital in 1724. What could he have done with seven years rent but pay portions? He was not profligate; he must have had a reputation for steadiness or he could not have borrowed £28 at 5% in 1728.
44 See Latham family genealogy, p. 166.

Appendix 5.3 sets out the names of the lenders and the amount of their loans each year. It shows the total of these outstanding loans slowly reducing from £34 in 1729 to £19 in 1739. As we have seen their harvest in that year was bad and they had to begin buying grain to eat by December. Richard also decided he must marl a field to improve fertility. So he borrowed a further £5 to bring the total of the outstanding loans up to £24 again. From there these loans were steadily reduced and the last ones paid off in 1748. Richard paid interest on all these loans over the 20 years at 5% p.a. (one shilling in the pound). The annual interest payments therefore were 28 shillings in 1729–31 and slowly declined thereafter. They were a significant part of his annual expenditure (Appendix 5.2, column E). He did not pay annual interest on the money he held as trustee for his nieces. He probably paid them the accumulated interest when he gave them the capital.

It is interesting to see who the lenders were. So far as we know anything about them, they would seem to have been of two main types – old and retired, or young and unmarried people. William Aspinwell, James Asmos and James Sunner were definitely of the first kind. Aspinwell's loan was repaid to his executors in 1735 and Sunner died in January 1748.[45] Alice Parker, Jane Hesketh and Alice Clarkson were of the second type. All had their loans repaid at the time of their marriage. Two other lenders were trustees investing children's or dependant's money. Family connections played a part in some of these loans. Alice Parker was the widowed sister of Nany Barton. Her £5 loan was repaid in January 1733 when she married John Forshaw. She lent money to Richard Latham again in 1743 after Forshaw died and she had become a widow again. William Parker, who lent money in the 1740s, may have been a relation of her first husband. John Barton, who introduced Alice Clarkson as a lender, was also probably related to Nany. Perhaps the most surprising fact revealed by Appendix 5.3 is that 13 different people made long-term loans to Richard Latham in these 20 years. This reveals how very widely a small capital was distributed in this society. That the rate of interest was only 5% throughout is also surprising. The standard rate of interest on mortgages secured on landed property was approximately 4½% before 1730 and 4% thereafter. The relations and neighbours of Richard Latham who lent this unsecured money to him must have been very confident of

45 1735, line 125 and 1748, line 22.

his integrity to be content with such a small premium over the rate of interest on secured money.

From 1748 to 1760 Richard had no long-term debts. In 1753 his eldest daughter Betty married Charles Heys, a saddle-tree maker in Ormskirk. Charles may have been a cousin.[46] Richard provided his daughter with a portion of £10.[47] He had to borrow £6 to do this but repaid it by the end of 1754.[48] In 1760, no doubt conscious of his failing health, he decided to renew the lease again. Dicy's death in 1748 had meant that he and Nany were the two lives left in the old lease. In May 1760 he added Alice as the third life. He paid £40 for the new lease, £1 12s 0d legal fees, and a guinea to Mrs Scarisbrick, which, as he commented, was a new custom.[49] On this occasion Richard seems to have had nearly all the money to pay for the lease in cash. In 1761 he had loans outstanding of £10 from Thomas Tomson and £5 from Elin Wright, but he repaid them both by the end of 1762. Whether this £42 12s 0d was the capital he had been using in his business or whether it represented his savings during the 1750s we do not know. It was evidently nearly all the cash he had because in his will, written in 1764,[50] he requested his wife to raise £20 to add Martha's name as the third life in a new lease. She duly followed his wish.

His will makes it clear that the lease was his only significant asset. He left it to his wife for her life. After her death the five unmarried daughters were to have £10 each to make them equal to Betty Heys and then the six girls were to share the balance equally among them. In this way all six girls became joint owners of shares in the lease after Nany died in about 1783. They did not sell the lease. The Scarisbrick estate rentals list the tenant as 'Ann Latham's successors' until 1797 when there's a gap in the records. By 1809 the estate owned the property. We do not know whether one or two of the daughters lived in the house and paid rent to the others or whether there was a tenant who paid rent to them all.

The way in which these three-life leases provided a favourable economic background to the lives of the tenants is well illustrated by this story of the Latham family. In the century from 1699 to around 1800 their payments to the Scarisbrick estate, apart from the 9s 9d rent and the 6s

46 1724, line 3, refers to 'Thomas Hey my brother'.
47 His will, WCW 1767.
48 Lines 128–9.
49 This comparatively high price for adding one life may have reflected the growing realization that the age of lives was important.
50 WCW 1767.

6d boons, were £30 in 1699, £40 in 1728, £40 in 1760 and £20 in 1767 – a total of £130. If the property had been rack rented at £10 p.a. the total rent in this century would have been £1,000. As rents rose after 1750[51] real rack rents would probably have exceeded £1,300. The Scarisbrick estate actually received 100 x 16s 3d annual rent = £81, plus £130, plus interest on £130, which would be about £100. This makes the total only £311 for the whole century.

6. CLOTHING AND TEXTILES

This was the part of the household activities dominated by the women. In the Latham family, with seven or eight women to one or two men, this was particularly true. There is a mass of information about the production of textiles in the account book. This account will only sketch the principal features.

As with other areas we have examined we start with a puzzle. Throughout the book there are innumerable purchases of flax in many forms – tear, tow, mumpins, strikt and so on. No loom is ever mentioned, nor any part of one. Weaving is paid for only rarely. What was going on? On closer examination, one finds that sheets, towels, pillowcases and material for shirts and shifts were never bought. Suddenly light dawns. This was another of Richard Latham's bartering arrangements. One of their neighbours, perhaps even a member of the family, was a linen weaver. He did all their weaving in exchange for farm produce or other services. It cannot have been Richard's brother John because he was charged 1s 8d in 1723 for 'weaving of linen cloak 20 yards'.[52] We never discover who the weaver was, because he was never paid in cash.

Nany evidently made the production of the household textiles her first job in the matrimonial home. In the third and fourth entry in the account book she bought six lbs of tear of flax at 8d per lb and 24 lbs of tow at 2d per lb. She must have started spinning with an old wheel, because later in the year the purchases of new equipment for the household included a new wheel and three bobbins bought in Kirkham and new cards for tow from London.[53] Towards the end of the year she bought another 19½ lbs of flax priced between 3d and 4¾d per lb. We never get any clues as to

51 See Foster, 2003, Chs 2 and 3.
52 P. 125, line 130. Note 1d a yard.
53 1724, lines 91 and 131.

the weight or value of the cloth that was made from her spun yarn, but it is likely to have made a reasonable stock of sheets, towels and shirts. If she spun two to four hanks to the pound it might have taken her 150 working days. At 4d a day, that was worth £2 10s 0d.[54] In subsequent years she did less, particularly when she was surrounded with small children. In due course she taught her daughters to spin. The account book shows that between 30 and 60 lbs of flax was bought in most years. Some yarn and cloth will no doubt have been sold to oblige neighbours, but the majority was probably used as cloth in the household. From the 1730s onwards she often bought large amounts of flax at Kirkham. For example, in 1730 she bought two stones (28 lbs) at Kirkham for 10s (4¼d per lb). The reason that Nany bought her flax in Kirkham was that Baltic flax, which was cheaper than flax grown in England, was imported there in large quantities.[55]

The household also needed other textiles. Woollen cloth seems always to have been bought whether it was blankets or clothing. Serge, kersey and frieze were bought for outer garments, usually priced between 1s and 2s a yard. Cheaper and perhaps better-wearing than woollen cloth was 'linsey-woolsey' – a linen warp and a woollen weft. Nany couldn't spin wool, so after they had bought 11 lbs of wool for 5s 3d, Elizabeth Herst came and stayed in the house for ten days and spun it for them for 1s. The usual linen weaver couldn't handle it so they paid

'for making 16 and dyeing 14 yards of linen and wool 2s 4d.'[56]

Nany bought worsted (combed) wool and knitting needles and had someone spin it for her. What she knitted is not clear as she often bought the children's stockings.[57] She didn't attempt to make clothes – other than

54 Young, 1776, pp. 117–61, has various descriptions of the types of linen made there. Stephenson, 1757, has much discussion on the types of linen that were and could be made and how these depended on the type of yarn that was spun. See particularly pp. 64, 110–11, 119–20, 187–8. Crawford, 1972, gives numerical shape to these general principles. No one seems to have recorded the actual weights of the hanks typical in various English districts. In the trade, the specification of linen cloth was described by its price. See Beckman, 1956, for orders, invoices, and letters of complaint on quality and price. Durie, 1996, has information on the Scottish linen industry. The Nicholson papers 920 NIC in Liverpool R.O. are those of a firm which imported Irish linen yarn to Liverpool *c.* 1740–70.
55 See Singleton, 1977, pp. 73–108 for the importers of this Baltic flax. See Foster, 2003, Ch. 9, for the sailcloth manufacturing industry that used this Baltic flax.
56 1726, line 63; 1727, lines 3, 4, 22.
57 1728, lines 31, 34, 35, 51; 1735, lines 35, 72, 105.

shirts, shifts, pillowcases, etc. A tailor was always paid to make outer clothes, breeches, vests or gowns. All the family's shoes were made for them by shoemakers but they sometimes bought 'steel hemp for thread' to repair them.[58]

From 1724 to 1735 providing textiles for the family never involved a cash expense of more than £2 p.a. In two or three years it was under £1. By 1736 Betty, the eldest daughter, was ten and her uncle Thomas's daughter Betty was 16. (It is seldom possible to distinguish between these two in the account book.) For the next 20 years there was a house full of young people who were interested in their clothes. The annual spending on textiles grew steadily and reached a peak of £9 10s 1d in 1747. One aspect seems to have been a demand for clothes that looked more interesting. Perhaps there were new fashions in Ormskirk. In 1735, and almost every year thereafter, the children had to have handkerchiefs. These seem to have been coloured, printed, or check cotton squares, which were worn at the neck or on the head. Cotton and wool could be dyed in a much wider and brighter range of colours than was possible with linen, and this seems to have been the charm of handkerchiefs. It also led in 1736 to the family buying some cotton. They probably wanted to make their own coloured cotton checks. They bought 3 lbs at 1s a lb and tried to spin it. This was evidently not totally successful as they bought more and employed other people to spin their cotton for them at 8d a lb. They bought black flax and Dutch flax and paid for quite a lot of dyeing. Finally in 1739, by which time Betty was 13, they made a really determined assault on the problem of spinning cotton. A new cotton wheel was bought for 2s along with new cotton cards and a spindle. A cotton wheel was mended and more steel spindles and whorls were bought. Twice more new spindles and whorls were bought as well as another new cotton wheel. It must have all been successful in the end, because they never paid to have cotton spun again and they bought yet another new cotton wheel, spindles and cotton cards in 1740.

From 1740, then, there were four wheels for spinning cotton in the house. Yet the total amount of cotton purchased in the next five years was only about 14 lbs. Despite this they bought new cotton cards in 1746, 1750 and 1754. Sarah had a new cotton wheel in 1753 and Martha had one in 1754. It seems a fair inference that these cotton wheels were used to spin cotton on 'outwork'. We know that the spinning of imported

58 1731, line 29.

fibres was organized by the 'putting out' system . Fibre was 'put out' to families who carded it into a sliver, spun it in their homes and returned it. This is evidently what the Latham daughters did and the money they earned paid for their new clothes. The 1740s and '50s were a period of rapid expansion for printed and check cotton manufacture in Lancashire, and the Latham family played a small part in it.

1741 saw another improvement in the equipment available for textiles. An iron pot (cast?) weighing 34 lbs, capable of holding 6¾ gallons, was acquired and bricked into a corner with a hearth area beneath. It cost 7s 9d.[59] This allowed a large amount of water to be heated for washing. It also permitted experiments with dyeing for which logwood was bought four times in 1742. There was a purchase of 'holick roots', evidently another dye, but logwood appears only once more, so these trials were presumably not successful.[60] A pair of scales was also bought for 1s 6d but this was probably for checking the weight of the hanks of spun cotton they were producing.[61]

Richard and Nany's daughter Betty was 16 in 1742 and the family's new source of income was reflected in her clothes that year. She had new stays for 4s 3d. Stays were usually made by the tailor from whalebone, buckram, stuff and blue serge and often cost twice as much as this. She had a new shag hat, which cost 5s 1d; a

'new blue gown – 11½ yards of floweren demask at 1s 8½d a yard £1 os 4d';

and 'new caps and handcharfs 1s 2d.'[62] Nany had to be suitably dressed to accompany her to show it all off. She had a

'new gown – camblet 9½ yards, 1s 2½d yard, 11s 4d.'[63]

The next year Betty had a cambrick apron and sleeves for 7s od, and a white hat for 1s 2d. Nany had a new petticoat of four yards of tammy for 4s 6d.[64] Dicy was not far behind and had a new coat made from 3½ yards of bearskin cloth at 2s 2d per yard, for a total of 7s 7d.

59 1741, lines 95, 105–6.
60 1742, lines 61, 62, 64, 77, 83.
61 1742, line 24.
62 Lines 55, 60, 69–70, 120.
63 Line 113. Camblet was a plain woven cloth of wool and other fibres often made with a number of different coloured pre–dyed yarns. Montgomery, 1984.
64 1743, lines 56, 73, 84.

As the girls' gowns became more showy the minor items in their costumes had to keep step. A better quality of linen was needed for the small parts that were exposed. Two yards of linen cloth for caps was bought for 2s. Two silk handkerchiefs cost 4s in 1743 and Sara had one in 1744 which cost 3s 1d. Lace for a cape cost 1s 1½d and Sara had 1¾ yards of fine cloth for an apron which cost 6s 4d.[65] All these prices were only the cost of the fabrics and tailor's work was required to make them into clothes. The Master Tailor seems to have been paid about 8d a day, while his assistants, presumably boys, got much less. 7s 8d was paid to the tailors in 1743.

As the years went by and the other girls grew up they too had similar clothes made for them. However they were all working women. A frequent item in the accounts was for brats.[66] In 1745 the family decided to grow their own flax. They bought three quarters of a bushel of seed for 4s 3d. They probably sowed it on about a quarter of an acre. They must have pulled it, laid it in bundles in the water and taken it out and spread it to dry themselves, as there is no mention of payment for these processes. As we have seen at Smithills it was traditional to have a communal party at the next stage of processing, so the account book records

'at braking the 11th October 6 brakers, 13 swinglers, 1 dryer 11s 1d.'[67]

There were evidently a number of families in the area still growing their own flax, and they each sent members to these parties. The girls seem to have heckled their flax themselves that winter as there were no payments for dressing flax in 1745/6. In 1746 they must have sown less as the cost of braking and swinging on 20 October was only 3s 10d. There is a payment of one penny in January 1747 for dressing flax and Elin Taylor dressed 20 lbs in February for 10d.[68] They grew more in 1747. Their total harvest for 1745 and 1746 was probably between 100 and 150 lbs.[69] They only grew flax again in two years, 1748 and 1761. They probably decided that there was only an advantage in growing their own flax when the price of Baltic flax was unusually high.

65 1742, line 105; 1743, line 132; 1744, lines 52, 64.
66 A coarse apron for working in, often made of blue linen.
67 Lines 120–1.
68 1746, line 133; 1747, lines 2, 25.
69 Calculated from seed sown and other clues.

In January 1746 the girls widened their technical expertise in textiles still further. They bought a new spinning wheel for 7s and new wool cards in Preston for 1s 3d.[70] Some of the younger daughters must have learnt wool spinning. They bought 12 lbs of wool in early 1747 and in April paid 2s 11½d for 'working and dyeing' 20 yards of 'linen and wool'. Whose clothes were made of this linsey-woolsey we do not learn but Ann had 7½ yards of 'linen and wool' later in the year, which cost 1s 1d a yard. At least four yards of this were used for a coat. Sara also had four yards that year.[71]

We get a clearer idea of the importance of pre-dyeing in different colours when they next made linsey-woolsey in 1752/3. After they had bought and spun the wool, they had it dyed on five different occasions. One was blue and another green but other colours are not described. Cotton and linen was also pre-dyed. Finally they paid for 'making and dyeing 15 yards'.[72] One can envisage that the resulting cloth might have resembled some of the simpler stripes and checks on sale in England in this period.[73] This type of material was certainly popular with the younger girls. They made it again in 1754, 1755 and 1760.[74]

Richard's illness in 1756 seems to have brought an end to the years of heavy spending on clothes, or at least a change of organization. In 1756 the household expenditure on textiles dropped to £1 5s 10½d. No new clothes were bought for the girls, but perhaps promises had been made to the younger girls. In 1757 Richard recorded,

'I laid down Rachel's 2 stampt gown 16s 10½.'

In 1758 12 yards of worsted was bought for Martha's gown at 11s 3d. Black and white printed and quilted cloth costing £1 6s 2d, purchased at the same time, may have been for Ann or Alice.[75] Printed fabrics seem to have had great attractions. After this, almost no new clothes for the girls were bought.

It appears that Alice and Martha stayed in the house to look after their old parents. Richard was about 70 in 1760 and Nany was probably over 60. The daughters would have been able to keep the farm going, to do the

---

70 1746, lines 4, 7.
71 1747, lines 3, 20, 22, 41, 56, 99, 104, 118–9.
72 1752, lines 18, 118; 1753, lines 6, 12, 14, 24, 43.
73 Montgomery, 1984, has 64 pages of coloured illustrations D1–D104.
74 1754, line 57; 1755, line 15; 1760, line 65.
75 1757, line 94; 1758, lines 30, 32–4.

milking and help with the harvest. They could have kept up the supplies of fruit and vegetables from the garden. The old couple's income would presumably have been from rent or the sale of farm produce helped out by whatever work they could do. For Richard to have been able to spend the £15–£16 shown in the account book it is likely that his daughters were paying him something from their earnings as spinners. Whatever they had left they were able to spend for themselves on their clothes now that they were adults.

7. CONCLUSION

This study of the Latham family shows how an ordinary rural family on a typical small three-life leasehold could live a comfortable life. The wealth that this privileged tenure provided allowed the family to educate their children and to give each one a small capital with which to start their own adult lives. It shows how such a family was able to save enough money to renew their lease. Both Richard Latham and Thomas Jackson, described in Chapter 3 above, were brought up on these small farms. Both went to 'primary' school where Richard learnt enough to run his business and keep his account book. Thomas Jackson was evidently a more able pupil who was sufficiently promising at Latin to go on to Northwich School aged 12. So one can understand how an 'average' person like Richard Latham was able to maintain his position and how those with greater abilities were able to rise in the world either as professionals, like Thomas Jackson, or, more commonly in the North-West, as businessmen like Thomas Hough.[76] These two detailed stories enable us to see how the many three-life leaseholders who have only left us a will and an inventory were able to make the money they often possessed, and they help to fill out the picture of the three-life leaseholders of Lancashire and Cheshire as a large group of families who each possessed a small capital. It is well known that a large number of families from these two counties emigrated to the colonies on the Delaware river, particularly Pennsylvania, between 1675 and 1725.[77] The costs of this migration were all borne by the families and friends of those who made the journey. It was the possession of capital by large numbers of three-life leaseholders and small copy-holders/freeholders that made it possible.

76 Foster, 2003, Ch. 8 (ii).
77 Fischer, 1989, pp. 419–603.

APPENDIX 5.1.
Latham family in Scarisbrick

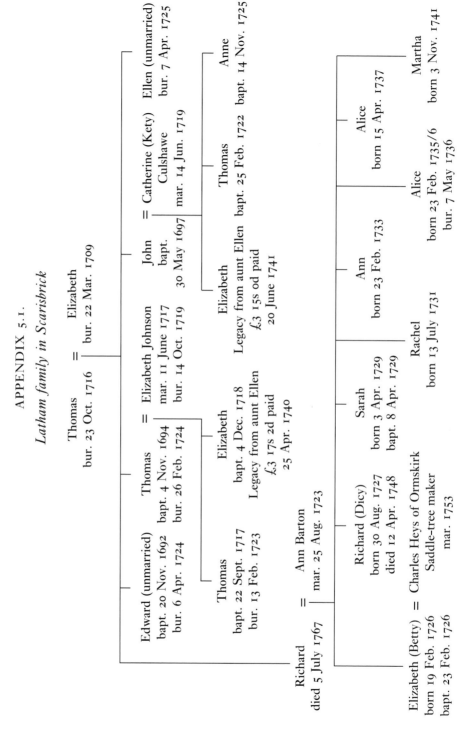

Notes

1. There are many differences between this chart and that printed in Weatherill, p. xiii.

2. Ormskirk Parish Register transcripts in Manchester Central Library (LPRS) provide all baptism, marriage and burial dates. Births and deaths are from the account book.

3. Richard's baptism does not appear in Ormskirk P.R. That he was the eldest son is inferred from three facts: (a) in the 1699 lease the three lives are Richard, Edward, and Thomas, sons of Thomas – in that order; (b) Richard inherited this lease and it was usual for eldest sons to inherit these leaseholds. In the Scarisbrick estate rentals, Thomas Latham's name appears up to 1717. From 1720 the rentals list Richard Latham; (c) his birth in 1699, as suggested by Weatherill, is unlikely. Babies were very rarely put as lives in these leases because of the high risk of death in the first year or two.

4. Weatherill's suggestion that Richard's mother died in the 1740s is based on 1743, line 39, 'me going to the buring of our mother...'. This is almost certainly Nany's mother. This usage of 'our' occurs several times, e.g., 1725, line 88, 'Doly our sister', meaning Nany's sister.

5. We do not know the amount of legacies left by Ellen to her nieces. Some part of the payments in 1740 and 1741 are probably interest. There may have been 'advances' earlier – for example, for clothes.

The Latham family's cash expenditure on housekeeping from the account book

	A. Total expenditure			B. Capital payments on lease and loans			C. Capital payments on the farm			D. Other unusual payments			E. Remainder of household expenditures		
	£	s	d	£	s	d	£	s	d	£	s	d	£	s	d
1724	37	14	11				21	17	9	3 cows 1 mare cart, etc.	2	3	0 bed	13	14	2
1725	16	19	2	1	0	0	5	18	5	cows mare, cart etc.	1	1	10 prove will	8	18	11
1726	16	19	8	7	0	0	3	4	0 cow				6	15	8
1727	14	6	4				3	0	6 heifer				11	5	10
1728	55	2	6	41	10	0 lease	6	8	0 cattle				7	4	6
1729	12	1	9				3	4	6 heifer				8	17	3
1730	12	8	7	2	0	0	3	1	0 cow				7	7	7
1731	9	12	9				1	7	4 calf				8	5	5
1732	24	2	11	16	0	0							8	2	11
1733	19	11	9	10	0	0	1	14	0 calves				7	17	9
1734	19	15	0	6	6	0	3	8	10 cattle				10	0	2
1735	24	7	8	9	10	0	4	10	3 cattle				10	7	5
1736	15	2	9							1 10 10 funeral 2 6 2 carts				11	5	9
1737	9	18	3	2	8	0							7	10	3
1738	16	18	0	1	0	0	1	9	3 calves	3	18	6 tithes	10	10	3
1739	23	19	5	10	0	0	3	10	0 heifer				10	9	5
1740	31	3	6	8	17	2	5	9	10 marling				16	16	6
1741	30	19	0	13	15	0							17	4	0
1742	30	15	10	14	0	0							16	15	10
1743	33	12	6	15	0	0	4	9	6 cow				14	3	0
1744	17	10	9				1	6	6 calf				16	4	3
1745	21	12	6	1	0	0	3	3	0 heifer				17	19	6
1746	31	6	2	6	0	0	7	2	4 cow and marling				18	3	10
1747	24	18	9	2	0	0							22	18	9
1748	31	4	5	11	3	1	3	4	6 cow				16	16	10
1749	28	0	4					19	6 calf				27	0	10
1750	19	18	6				1	9	0 cow				18	9	6
1751	21	3	4				6	4	0 cows				14	19	4
1752	24	6	10				4	2	2 cows				20	4	8
1753	25	3	1	3	6	0	3	15	0 calf and marling				18	2	1
1754	29	16	9	8	0	0							21	16	9
1755	19	1	7				4	2	6 cow				14	19	1
1756	20	5	6										20	5	6

	A. Total expenditure			B. Capital payments on lease and loans			C. Capital payments on the farm				D. Other unusual payments			E. Remainder of household expenditures		
	£	s	d	£	s	d	£	s	d		£	s	d	£	s	d
1757	17	17	8											17	17	8
1758	26	15	1				4	10	0	cattle				22	5	1
1759	15	2	10											15	2	10
1760	54	14	4	42	13	0 lease	1	0	0	calf				11	1	4
1761	30	2	9	15	0	0								15	2	9
1762	17	14	9	5	0	0								12	14	9
1763	16	3	1											16	3	1
1764	21	1	1				2	15	0	cow				18	6	1
1765	18	3	5											18	3	5
1766	24	5	3	3	0	0	5	2	9	cows				16	2	6

Notes
1 To nearest penny.
2 1741 total expenditure amended as text.

Long-term loans taken by Richard Latham to finance the purchase
for £40 of two additional lives on his lease in April 1728

Total loans outstanding for most of the year (£ s d)	Principal lenders and the amounts of their loans
1729 34 0 0	Mr. Gill for Ned Fryer – 10 William Aspinwell – 8 Alice Parker – 5 James Hesketh – 5 Himself as trustee for Latham nieces – 6
1730 34 0 0	same
1731 34 0 0	same
1732 29 0 0	Alice Clarkson – 10 W. Aspinwell – 8 J. Hesketh – 5 Latham nieces – 6
1733 29 0 0	Clarkson – 10 Aspinwell – 8 Joseph Coppoe for W. Baume – 5 Latham nieces – 6
1734 20 0 0	Clarkson – 5 Aspinwell – 8 Elin Bond – 1 Latham nieces – 6
1735 20 0 0	Same Aspinwell dies. Executors, line 125
1736 20 0 0	Clarkson – 5 Bond – 1 James Sunner – 8 Latham nieces – 6
1737 20 0 0	same
1738 19 0 0	Clarkson – 5 Sunner – 8 Latham nieces – 6
1739 24 0 0	Clarkson – 5 Sunner – 8 Latham nieces – 6 James Asmos – 5
1740 21 0 0	Sunner – 8 William Parker – 10 One Latham niece – 3

Total loans outstanding for most of the year (£ s d)				Principal lenders and the amounts of their loans
1741	18	0	0	Sunner – 8
				Thomas Bond – 10
1742	18	0	0	Sunner – 8
				William Parker – 10
1743	18	0	0	Sunner – 8
				Alice Forshaw – 10
1744	13	0	0	Sunner – 8
				Forshaw – 5
1745	13	0	0	same
1746	11	0	0	Sunner – 6
				Forshaw – 5
1747	7	0	0	Sunner – 2
				Forshaw – 5
1748	Nil			Sunner died Jan. 1748.
				Forshaw repaid May 1748.

Notes

1 The rate of interest was always one shilling on the pound per annum, or 5%.

2 There were a number of more short-term loans taken and repaid.

3 Loans were taken and repaid on various dates in all years. The above figures are simplified. The original gives a more complicated picture, but is not significantly different.

VI

George Dockwra in Aston by Budworth

1. INTRODUCTION

The survival of a little group of papers at Arley Hall allows me to provide a vignette of an impecunious gentleman. Such scions of propertied families, given a good education and with the manners and habits of gentry society, were not uncommon. As well as the younger sons of the major gentry who were often in this position, there were others whose careers in the church, the Law, the army, the navy or the civil service had not progressed as well as was hoped. Such people often found themselves living on a small fixed income provided by a settlement or an annuity. George Dockwra was just such a person.

One of the purposes of this book is to describe the different cultures that developed in various groups in north-western society between the sixteenth and the eighteenth centuries. People who thought of themselves as gentry and lived on modest incomes of around £50 a year or less were a significant group. There were other groups who had similar sized incomes but behaved in very different ways.

2. GEORGE DOCKWRA'S GRANDFATHER AND FATHER

George was the grandson of the London merchant William Dockwra (see p. 225) who is famous among philatelists for starting the London Penny Post in 1680.[1] This organization used local shops as post boxes and claimed to deliver letters all over central London in a few hours for one penny. It was so successful that James, Duke of York, later James II, claimed that it infringed his Patent as Postmaster General and he seized it in 1682. After William and Mary had ascended the throne Parliament awarded William Dockwra a pension of £500 p.a. in 1690 for seven years, in recompense for the loss of his business.[2] Between 1692 and 1697

---

1 Todd, 1952.
2 Ibid., p. 58.

172

William Dockwra ran a large copper-manufacturing business with works near Esher, Surrey.[3] From 1690 to 1702 he was also Registrar and Secretary of the East New Jersey Company.[4] At the time of his death in 1716 his principal assets were parts of two 'proprieties' in the East New Jersey Co. A 'propriety' was a twenty-fourth part of the whole province of East New Jersey.[5]

His six surviving children, two sons and four daughters, each inherited an equal share of this property. Richard, the elder of the two sons, may also have been a businessman. His marriage, before 1704, was unusual. His father William tells us:

> My son Richard married to Mrs. Ann Warburton, one of the sisters of Sir George Warburton, Barronett, unknown to their Parents on either side being both blameworthy for it. She had a daughter born and died an infant before I know of their marriage. Afterward it came to be known to me and my wife about ... they came to my house and she with child again. A son was born in Cloak Lane on Thursday 14 Sept 1704 – a quarter past eleven at night. And christened Thomas by Dr. Offspring of Blackhall. The Godfathers Thos. Dockwra of Putteridge Esq. ye great Grandfather, and myself Wm. Dockwra, Grandfather. The God-mother was the Lady Martha Warburton Dowager, the Grandmother.[6]

This son Thomas must have died, because when Richard Dockwra died in 1741, his only living son by his wife seems to have been George. He also had a natural son, James Dockwra Felton, apparently by his housekeeper, Mrs Ellen Felton. In his will he divided his capital of some £1,200 between George and the Feltons, mother and son. His capital consisted almost entirely of loans at interest to seven gentlemen. The largest, of £315, was to Sir William Stanhope. As well as these sound loans his Executors made a list of another £1,200 of dubious debts that seem not to have been paid. Some £800 of these dated back to the 1720s and included £167 owed by Lord Gage. The list provides no clue as to the nature of his business. Perhaps he just lent money at interest to gentlemen. George's £600 was given to Peter Warburton (later 4th Bt)

---

3 Hamilton, 1926, p. 103, 119.
4 Pomfret, 1962, p. 187.
5 Canterbury will. Prob 11/554, folder 250. East and West New Jersey made up what is now the state of New Jersey. These proprieties were valuable assets. However, the independent spirit of American colonists made them controversial.
6 Paper in Large Box 10, Arley Hall. Note early eighteenth century 'Mrs.' where we would write 'Miss'. See Appendix 7.1, p. 225 for genealogy.

Fig. 38. This painting has always been known as a portrait of Anne Dockwra, but it is not clear whether the sitter was the sister of Sir George Warburton, 3rd Bt, and mother of George described here, or the mother of Sir Peter, 4th Bt. See genealogy in Appendix 7.1, p. 225.

and Thomas Slaughter as trustees to purchase an annuity for him. This account of George's way of life from 1741 to his death in 1757 is based on the trustees' papers.[7]

3. GEORGE'S WAY OF LIFE IN ASTON BY BUDWORTH

I have found nothing about George's early life. His handwriting on several of the surviving invoices shows him to have been a well-educated man. He cannot have been older than about 35 when he arrived at Arley in October 1741. At first he lived in Arley Hall with his aunt Anne Warburton and her son Peter, who was heir to the Arley estate (see Appendix 7.1). His annuity was £40 a year and he was charged £12 p.a. for his board. When Peter Warburton inherited the estate and the baronetcy from his uncle Sir George in June 1743 his way of life changed dramatically. From being a bachelor gentleman living quietly on a small allowance he became the owner and manager of a great estate. George Dockwra seems to have felt that his presence in Arley Hall was no longer suitable, so he moved into Lower Feldy Green Farmhouse with Jonathan and Ann Beswick.[8] He paid them £12 a year for his board and a further £3 p.a. for the 'ley' (grazing) of his mare. Presumably he had a bedroom of his own but ate with them. He was evidently happy with this abode because he stayed there for the next nine years.

George's largest expense was his clothes since he had to be dressed as a gentleman. He bought the material for his shirts and handkerchiefs from Peter Hill, linen draper, in Warrington:

		£	s	d
Jan 1742	24 yards Irish linen at 2s yd	2	8	0
	1¼ yards cambrick at 4s yd		5	0
June 1745	6 linen hanks @ 1s 6d and making 6d		9	6

The linen seems to have been made into seven shirts by Mary Leigh for 10d each, the cambrick decorating the neck and wrists. There may have been enough linen left over to make some stocks.

7 At Arley Hall. The Arley Estate provided the annuity.
8 See Map 2 in Foster, 1992, pp. 30–1 and 56.

George chose the material for his suits from Thomas Deacon, the mercer, in Great Budworth.[9] Sometimes they were of quite inexpensive cloth such as:

	s	d
June 1743 5 yards Ratteen (a thick woollen) @ 3s 8d	18	4
2¼ yards black plush (wool velvet) @ 5s 6d	12	4½
5¼ yards shalloon (lining) @ 1s 4d	7	0

At other times – perhaps for Sir George Warburton's funeral – they were much more expensive:

	£	s	d
June 1743 4¾ yards superfine black broadcloth @ 17s 0d	4	0	9

These were made up into clothes by John Leigh, a tailor in Budworth. He bought all the rest of the materials he needed, such as trimmings of velvet and silk, the stiffening of canvas and buckram, and the buttons and thread, from Thomas Deacon on Dockwra's account. He charged his time as in the following example:

	s	d
June 1743 Myself 4 days making cote and breeches	2	8
July 1743 Making black sut of clos	5	0

John Leigh also often repaired Dockwra's clothes with materials bought at Deacons. As well as his suits Dockwra also needed a few accessories: shamy (chamois) gloves at 2s 6d; white gloves at 1s 3d; 2⅜ yards of broadest hatband crepe at 1s 6d a yard. Over the five years 1742 to 1746 George had two expensive suits and four cheaper ones and ran up a bill of £29 11s 6d with Mr Deacon. Deacon was, no doubt, glad to be paid in 1746 by the Arley estate accountant. It is difficult to judge from the incomplete figures that survive whether this expense was wholly paid out of George's annuity.

On his legs, George wore 'black woollen hose' at 1s 6d a pair. His shoes were made by John Kerfoot, a Budworth shoemaker and came in an amazing variety:

9 Foster, 1992, pp. 46, 61.

			s	d
Feb 1742	Strong shoes		4	6
Apr 1742	Thin shoes		4	0
Jan 1743	Slip shoes		4	0
Mar 1743	Spatter-dashes		6	0

To complete his appearance, on his head he wore:

Supplier	£	s	d
Mr. Siddall Apr 1742 A new wigg	1	12	6
John Wrench Sept 1743 A new Hatt		9	0
Charles Buckley Oct 1743 A full grisel Bobwigg	1	5	0

From these descriptions, we get a picture of George walking up the High Street in Great Budworth very much the gentleman. What did he do all day? Perhaps many days began with a visit to John Snelson, who kept a barber's shop and ale house at what is now 53 High Street. George had an arrangement with John to shave his head and beard and powder his wig for 10s 6d a year. George evidently often lingered after his shave and had a glass of ale or cider. When John was paid in May 1747 by Sir Peter Warburton, he was owed a guinea for two years shaving in 1745 and '46, and 17s 10d for ale and cider in those two years. John Snelson was apparently a good friend of George's, because Sir Peter also reimbursed him for 10s he had lent George for a journey to Chorley in Lancashire,

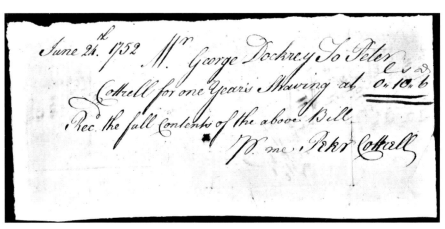

Fig. 39. An invoice from Peter Cottrell, the barber.

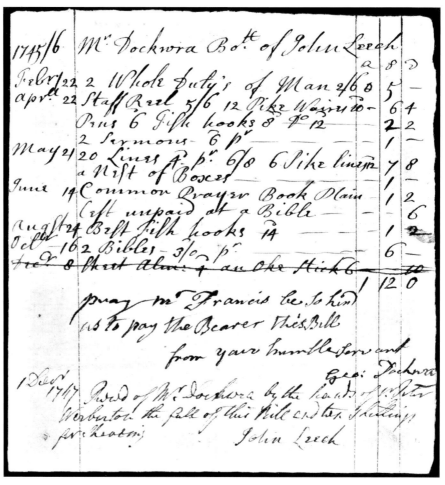

Fig. 40. John Leech's invoice for bibles, prayer books and fishing tackle. Apparently Mr Francis Bartholomew, the accountant, didn't pay the bill at the end of 1746 so it was paid by Sir Peter Warburton in 1747.

and 5s for another to Tarvin. In addition, he had lent George 1s to buy pictures and 6d for a basket to carry his fish home one day. Snelson's was not the only hostelry in Budworth that George frequented. On his visit to Budworth in May 1747 to tidy up George's unpaid bills, Sir Peter Warburton also paid John Heath, probably at what is now 42 Church Street, 14 shillings for wine, rum, cakes, and 'veittless'. When Sir Peter paid bills, he often noted on the back of the receipt the coins he had given. His payment to the Beswicks on 15 May 1751 was:

	£	s	d
4 moidores	5	8	0
9 guineas	9	9	0
Silver		3	0
	15	0	0

Perhaps George found drinking in Budworth inns a bit expensive because in the summer of 1744 he experimented with home brewing. In the next 12 months he bought £8 15s 6d worth of malt from Ralph Kinsey, a farmer in Aston by Budworth. He bought 5¼ lbs of hops from Ann Beswick for 6s 5d, and she probably brewed the ale for him at Lower Feldy Green. He bought glass bottles, a cork and a parcel of glasses from Thomas Poole, the glazier in Knutsford at a cost of 13s 11d. Whether this was a success and his Budworth friends, who presumably included many of the people mentioned in my *Four Cheshire Townships*, were willing to go out to Feldy Green for a game of cards, we don't know. There are no more bills for malt or hops.

As well as drinking and chatting, George played games and sports. In November 1743 he bought

'a pair of Battelers and 2 pairs Shuttlecocks'

from Peter Hill in Warrington for 6s. John Barrow supplied him with

'a hunting thong with a silk cord to it'

presumably for use when following the hounds chasing hares. He bought a pound of gunpowder in 1747 so he may have done some shooting. His real enthusiasm appears to have been fishing. He bought a rod from Joseph Fothergill in Warrington in May 1742 and had it repaired more than once. Fishing was also an interest of John Leech, the bookseller in Knutsford. From him George was able to buy two copies of *The Whole Duty of Man*, two bibles, two sermons and a Book of Common Prayer, as well as a staff reel for 5s 6d, 12 pike 'Waires' for 10d, 20 lines at 4d each for 6s 8d, six pike lines for 1s and 2s 8d worth of fishhooks. The other activity that must have brought variety to his days was riding around the country. His mare needed new shoes every month and frequent repairs to the girths, stirrups and bridle, so he must have covered many miles.

As Sir Peter and Lady Elizabeth Warburton's family grew up, George no doubt found that playing with the children made life at Arley more attractive. Perhaps also his health was failing. The bills from Henry Penney, the apothecary in Knutsford, become more frequent in the late 1740s. After 1752, there are no more bills for boarding with the Beswicks, and he seems to have moved back to Arley Hall. He died in 1757 at Aston Park, where the Warburton family was living while Arley was being rebuilt.

VII

Sir Peter Warburton, 4th Baronet,
1708–74

1. INTRODUCTION

The estate management papers left by Sir Peter are the largest of the seven archives used to create these portraits of family life. This chapter therefore provides information on a wide range of subjects. The first section continues the examination of the culture of the gentry, a world in which a number of positions of wealth and influence were well established. The eldest sons of gentry were the only people who knew for certain that they would inherit such a position, though daughters and younger sons all hoped to get themselves into one of the choice places. As well as the great estates that could be inherited or acquired through marriage, there were many lesser positions in the Church, the Law and the government service that could be secured by influence or by friendship or perhaps even by a little merit. All that a young man or woman, without the right to a place by birth, could do was to manœuvre themselves into a position so that chance might carry them to the prize. We see Thomas Slaughter, an illegitimate son, profiting from his father's affection to secure a good estate. We also see several men waiting their turn. A few, like Sir Peter Warburton 4th Bt, and Sir Robert Grosvenor 6th Bt, were lucky while others waited in vain. Unable to marry where they loved, they died without wives. Some were provided with sufficient money to allow them to marry. Sometimes they did not have enough to do the same for their children who had to be apprenticed into business. This was a different culture from that in which their parents had raised them. We see that the family of Warburton of the Gore was unable to make the transition and instead sank irrevocably into poverty.

In the next section, the style of life of Sir Peter and his family at Arley are briefly described. There were many similarities with earlier centuries. Tradition and custom were powerful forces in gentry life. On the farm, by contrast, there were great changes. Under Sir Peter the last vestiges of the system of self-sufficiency were abandoned. First meat and then grain were bought. Farm workers no longer lived in the big house. Similarly, textiles were no longer made at home, but were all bought from the great variety of shops in the area. Some unusual archives provide a description of the standard of living of the servants and allow an approximate comparison with that of farm labourers and of the tenants who farmed the land on full market (or rack) rents.

Finally some examples are given of the greater complexity of the economic life that had developed in the area. The first group are all from the building industry. They illustrate how much technology had improved and how this led to a wide variety of products being available from many different sources. These changes in turn required a greater movement of goods. It is suggested that the Arley estate may have transported as much as 1,000 tons of materials a year on the country roads. Some of the reactions to this increased traffic are examined.

2. THE POSITION OF YOUNGER SONS OF THE GENTRY

The difference between an eldest son inheriting a large estate from his father and its inheritance by any other member of the family is vividly shown in the first 35 years of the life of Sir Peter Warburton, 4th Bt. The Arley estate had been settled by Sir Peter, 2nd Bt, on his three sons and their descendants in succession (see Appendix 7.1). Sir George Warburton, 3rd Bt, uncle to Peter, later 4th Bt., had the misfortune to lose his wife when he was only about 30 years old. Their only son died the following year in June 1706. Diana, the only daughter, was sent off to live with the estate manager, Hamlet Yate, at Arley. Everyone must have thought that Sir George, an MP living in London, would be sure to find another wife. So young Peter, though he was heir to the Arley estate from his birth, can have had little confidence he would ever inherit it. He seems to have been brought up in Hertfordshire near his uncle's Putteridge estate. However Sir George remained unmarried. His daughter Diana married Sir Richard Grosvenor, 4th Bt of Eaton, in 1724. Many people at the wedding must have thought that if the 16-year-old nephew Peter were to die, the Eaton and Arley estates would be combined in the hands of Sir Richard and Diana's eldest son. Events were again to follow a different pattern. Diana died childless in February 1730 and Sir Richard followed her to the grave in 1732, making way for his younger brothers Thomas and Robert to become the 5th and 6th Baronets.

Fig. 41. Anne Slaughter, 1706–75, sister of Sir Peter Warburton 4th Bt.

After his daughter's death, Sir George reorganized his affairs. In the early 1730s he sent young Peter to live at Arley Hall. About the same time, he also despatched his natural son Thomas Slaughter to live at Arley. I have not found anything about Slaughter's mother; perhaps she was Sir George's housekeeper in London. Sir George seems to have introduced both young men into Cheshire society without any embarrassment.

Thomas Slaughter, who must have had some legal training in London, took over as Steward of the families' Manor Courts after Sir George sacked Hamlet Yate in 1732/3.[1] He also played some part in the management of the estate. An accountant called Francis Bartholomew seems to have had charge of all the routine business of the estate.

Around 1734 Peter fell in love with a Miss Lewis. He tried hard to marry her, but Sir George would not give her a jointure (secured on the estate) of more than £300 p.a. Her father would not agree to such a small sum. Even Sir Francis Leicester, who seems to have been Sir George's best friend, could not make Sir George change his mind.[2] It seems that Sir George did not want to alienate a significant slice of the estate's income to a young woman who might be left a childless widow to enjoy the income for 50 years. Anyway he evidently had other hopes about who would eventually inherit the estate. In the late 1720s Sir George sold the Dockwra family estate around Putteridge and also the neighbouring Alington lands which he had inherited from his wife.[3] From these sales Sir George accumulated a substantial cash sum, and it appears to have slowly become apparent that he was likely to leave it to his natural son Thomas Slaughter. Although he never married again Sir George continued to have affairs with various women including a Mrs Fanny Richmond, an affair which nearly resulted in a lawsuit in 1726.[4]

By September 1738 Peter Warburton had abandoned hope of marrying Miss Lewis. Perhaps he recognized that he would not be able to marry until he inherited the estate – if he ever did. He became increasingly concerned about the future of his sister Anne (Fig. 41). If he were to die before he inherited, she and their mother would be in an unhappy position. So he wrote to his friend Sir Francis Leicester at Tabley, asking his advice about a scheme he thought of proposing to Sir George. The plan was that his sister Anne should marry Thomas Slaughter. The existing settlement should be altered to put the Slaughters next in line after himself and his children to inherit the estate. He had spoken to his sister, who was 'very willing to leave herself to the Discretion of her Friends', but he had not even hinted at the project to Slaughter or Sir George. We only have Peter's letters to Sir Francis, but they show us that the scheme

1 Foster, 1992, pp. 17–19.
2 WM Box 24, items 5–12.
3 Clutterbuck, 1827, pp. 87 and 121.
4 DLT/C35, item 22.

Fig. 42. Sir Peter Warburton, 4th Bt, 1708–74.

advanced slowly and steadily by carefully thought-out steps to a successful conclusion.[5] The marriage followed soon after.

Sir George Warburton died in June 1743. As Sir Peter wrote to Peter
Legh of Lyme after the funeral and after the will had been read: 'He has
left all he could from me but 20 guineas for mourning – even to husbandry

5 WM Box 39.

utensils as well as livestock.[6] The opinion of the Arley family 50 years later was that Thomas Slaughter had received at least £50,000 from Sir George. This may be an exaggeration but the Slaughters were certainly well off. They bought a large house in Chester and he became High Sheriff of the county in 1755. He competed with his horses at many of the race meetings in the area in the next 20 years.[7]

For Sir Peter the great thing was that the long uncertainty was over and he was at last in possession of the estate. Now there was no shortage of proposals for his hand in marriage. Lord Barrymore wrote suggesting Lord Granard's daughter. We do not know if they ever met.[8] The girl he fell in love with was Elizabeth, eldest daughter of Edward Stanley, 11th Earl of Derby and they were married in February 1746. Her portion was £6,000 and her jointure £600 p.a.[9]

Sir Peter was one of a small number of lucky sons of younger sons of gentry estate owners. Most were not so fortunate. In 1673, the first baronet, Sir George Warburton, had settled the bulk of the Arley estate on Peter, his eldest son by his first wife, and his male heirs, just before Peter's marriage. In a second settlement the same year, he gave the manor of Winnington to Thomas, his eldest son by his second wife, with succession to his younger sons by his second wife.[10] The three younger sons by the second wife never married and lived all their lives like George Dockwra, on modest allowances. Their eldest brother, Thomas of Winnington, had four sons, so they had no chance of the inheritance. They were too poor to attract a wife. Yet they were required to live as 'gentlemen' so that they were ready to inherit if called upon. The second son of Sir George by his first wife was luckier. His mother was Elizabeth, daughter of Sir Thomas Myddleton of Chirk Castle. He was more generously provided for by his father and became a student at Gray's Inn in 1666. He matriculated at Trinity College, Oxford, in May 1667, was called to the Bar in 1673 and married a widow. His father gave them a three-life lease of the Gore Farm, Aston by Budworth (approximately 192 acres).[11] They probably brought up their family there – two sons and a daughter, who survived to adult life (see Appendix 7.2).

6 WM Box 24, item 19.
7 Foster, 1992, p. 15; Harrap's *Manchester Mercury* 7 May 1754, and many more.
8 WM Box 24, item 18.
9 Certificate of Marriage, Arley Large Box 10, item 21. Settlement WM Box 40.
10 WM Boxes 38, 39.
11 See Map 2 in Foster, 1992.

Sir Peter Warburton 4th Bt enquired about their descendants between 1743 and 1751 because a male descendant from either of the sons was probably heir to the Arley estate if he were to die without a son. His lawyers discovered that, though both sons were dead, they had both married and had had children. The only surviving child of Thomas, the elder son of George of the Gore, was Anna Maria. She was married to a shoemaker called William Hudson. George, the younger son, had lived at the Gore with his wife in the first decade of the eighteenth century. They had two sons and three daughters there.[12] Their eldest son George was apprenticed to a vintner, but 'afterwards worked at the lead Mills in Goodman's Fields', and died a bachelor in about 1747. Their only other surviving son was Robert who had been apprenticed to a printer in Manchester. In 1751 he was a waterman in Milford Lane, London. He was married and his only child was Susan who, in 1751, had 'lately been apprenticed by St. Clements Parish to a Turner in Bond St.'. Elizabeth, the only daughter of George of the Gore, received a legacy of £100 from her godfather Sir Thomas Myddleton. She married 'Mr. Gee, a stationer, who was afterwards Collector of Excise'. Their four children in 1751 were:

a) William, 'an Exciseman at Colchester'.
b) Dorothy, 'housekeeper to a Clergyman somewhere in or near Hertfordshire', unmarried.
c) Elizabeth, 'who married one Parker, an attorney in Hertfordshire. He left her and went into the West Indies'. She is now dead, but her only daughter Elizabeth is 'servant to a Hair merchant near Tower Hill'.
d) Hester, who 'is not in her senses and is in the Workhouse in Tring in Hertfordshire'.[13]

The survival of these unusual records illustrates how quickly the families of younger sons and daughters of the major gentry could descend into poverty when the support of inherited wealth was withdrawn.

3. FAMILY LIFE AT ARLEY

As soon as they were married, Sir Peter and Lady Elizabeth Warburton moved into Arley Hall. Elizabeth, who was known to everyone as Lady Betty, had six children. The eldest daughter, Elizabeth, born a year after

12 Great Budworth P.R.
13 WM Box 24, Folder 9, subfile 4.

Fig. 43. A coach and horses with outrider.

the wedding, died aged 12. The next daughter, Ann, was a much admired 21-year-old when she and her sisters caught smallpox. Despite intensive nursing, she died although the other girls all survived. The only son Peter, born in 1754, and his three remaining sisters lived long lives, the three women all reaching the age of 70 or 80. This was a much better record of child-rearing than that of Sir Peter's sister Anne Slaughter. She had the misfortune to lose at least four of her children in their early years during the 1740s. The reasons for the difficulties that the upper classes had at this period in bringing up their children do not seem to have been discovered. Less well-off people living around Arley brought up large families with few losses in childhood.

The Warburtons lived all their married life in Aston by Budworth. They moved out of Arley Hall for about eight years, between 1755 and 1763, while it was being rebuilt. They went to Aston Park, a much smaller house one-and-a-half miles to the south which had been built for Hamlet Yate, the estate manager between 1705 and 1715, when he was looking after Sir George's daughter Diana.[14]

As Sir Peter had been left with an empty purse when he succeeded to the estate their style of living at first was as simple as convention allowed. 'It is a much pleasanter thing to increase than retrench; this was the rule I laid down to myself when I first married,' Elizabeth wrote to her sister Charlotte in 1751.[15] The Warburtons' position at Arley Hall demanded that they had a coach for Lady Betty to go about in. She drove it to Knutsford or Warrington to do her shopping and was always accompanied by her footman when she descended from the coach to go round the

14 Foster, 1992, p. 19, for illustration.
15 Arley Large Box 7, item 47/1.

188

Fig. 44. Thomas Whittingham's elegant invoice for the dinner he served at Kinver to the party from Bath. The coachman and postillion from Arley, with their eight horses, had eaten earlier at a cost of 15s 10d. The two men on their horses had brought the six coach-horses from Arley.

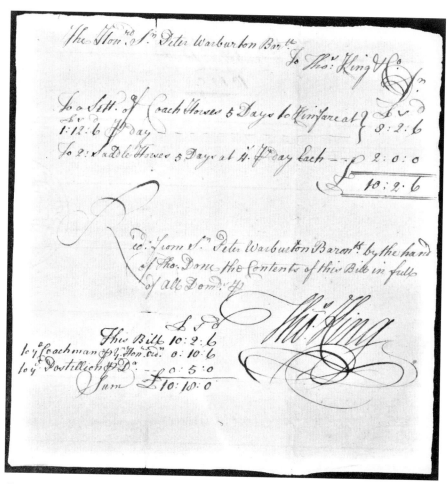

Fig. 45. Thomas King's bill for the hire of the six coach-horses who had drawn the coach from Bath to Kinver. Notice that he also charged for the two-and-a-half days it would take them to return to Bath. The two saddle horses were for the coachman and postillion to ride back to Bath. These two-and-a-half days of horse-power for the coach cost Sir Peter nearly the same as an agricultural worker received in a whole year.

shops. In a similar style, Sir Peter was normally accompanied as he rode about the estate by 'his man' Thomas Byfield. These formalities employed four men. In addition Lady Betty needed a maid to help her dress in the elaborate fashions of the day. Apart from these five, the staff at Arley in 1750 was the minimum that could operate a house with 18 people living in it.[16]

16 See Foster, 1992, p. 35 for a list of servants in 1750. See below p. 201 for a list in 1766.

190

In the summer months, when the unpaved country roads were hard, the coach also took Lady Betty to dinner with neighbouring gentry. In the winter the family may have ridden, accompanied by the groom, to the closest of these houses. As well as these local journeys, the coach took them to Bath in October 1751, where they spent the winter with their two young daughters and then returned to Arley in May 1752.

Unusually, all the bills for this return journey to Bath have survived because Thomas Done, the estate manager, was with them, thus providing a vivid snapshot of travel in this period. The coach set out early each morning and paused after two or three hours for a 'morning bait'. In the middle of the day they stopped again for dinner. The afternoon drive took them to the inn where they were to spend the night (see Map 5 on p. 192) The following bills describe their expenditure on the journey home.[17]

	The journey and its costs	£	s	d
May 4	Left Bath; 2 turnpikes		2	10
	Bait at Cross Hands		1	6
	Dinner at Petty France		15	9
	Turnpike on Frocester Hill		1	11
28 miles	Night at Frocester	2	8	3
May 5	Turnpike from Frocester		1	11
	Turnpike from Gloucester		1	11
	Bait at Corslawn		4	0
	Dinner at Upton on Severn		17	2
	'to go through some grounds' near Upton		2	0
	Turnpike into Worcester		1	5
37 miles	Night at the Bell Inn, Worcester	1	19	11
May 6	Turnpike from Worcester		1	5
	Dinner at Kinver		13	0
	At the New Inn at Rudge Heath 'sider & ale'		1	0
	Turnpike from New Inn			11
46½ miles	Night at the Red Lyon, Newport	2	13	1
May 7	Dinner at the Red Lyon, Whitchurch	1	2	11
	At Beeston Brook for ale and hay		1	0
36½ miles	The servants at Oulton per Your Honour's orders	2	3	0

Lady Betty, her maid and the two children travelled in the coach. Sir Peter, his groom and Thomas Done rode beside the coach. Their luggage

17 A.R.I.. Bath journey, 1752 folder.

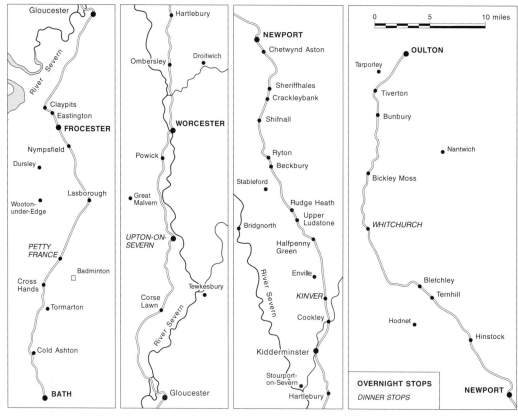

Map 5 The journey from Bath to Oulton in May 1752.

was carried in William Widders' wagon, which had come down to Bath specially to bring them back. In his wagon he also carried five newly hired maids who were probably destined to work at Knowsley or other friends' houses. They were each paid one guinea on setting out from Bath.[18] Widders charged £28 for the round trip. Sir Peter's own coach-horses had spent the winter at Arley. They came south to Kinver to collect the coach on its way home so the hired horses, which had drawn the coach from Bath, were paid off there. The Warburton party was no doubt happy to be with their friends the Egertons at Oulton on the last night of the journey – but the cost was no less (see Figs 44–7).

18 This suggests that labour was already scarcer and more expensive in Cheshire than in Somerset. See below Section vii, and Gilboy, 1934, p. 220.

192

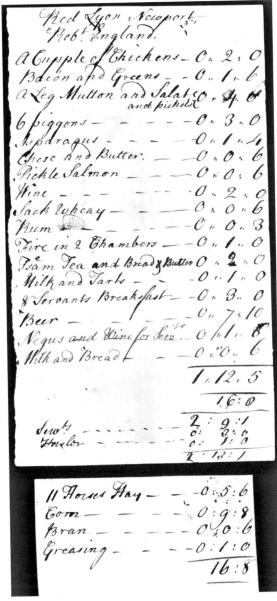

Fig. 46. This bill gives a good idea of the variety of food and drink consumed at the evening meal. The eight servants who had breakfasted separately from the family were presumably the coachman and postillion, the groom and the five new maids. The eleven horses were – six for the coach, three for Sir Peter, his groom and T. Done and two on which the coachman and postillion had ridden from Arley. Notice that no charge was made for the bedrooms. This was typical of an innkeeper's practice at this period.

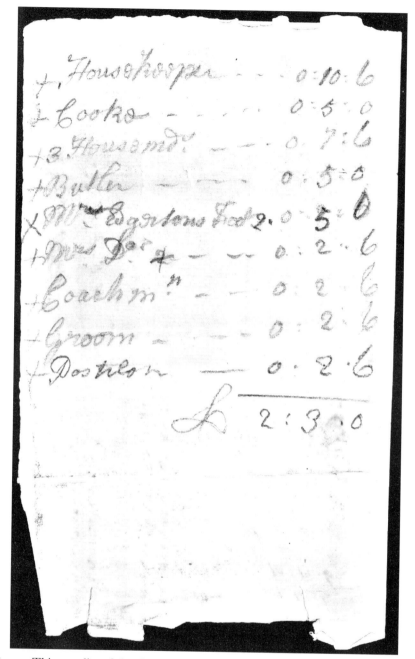

Fig. 47. This rare list of the tips paid by T. Done on Sir Peter's instructions to the servants at Oulton illustrates their hierarchy. The housekeeper there was well ahead of the butler and the cook. Tips like these made a significant difference to the incomes of the servants of major gentry families (see below Sec. 7, p. 201).

The Warburtons went again to Bath in the spring of 1755. Lady Betty returned in the autumn of that year via Lord Stamford's and Sir Richard Acton's in Shropshire.[19] They also made visits to Scarborough, Buxton, Chester and London. They went to stay with her parents and her un-married sisters at Knowsley at least once every year. Of Lady Betty's five sisters the only one who married was Charlotte. She eloped with John Burgoyne, a charming young soldier whose fortune, in the opinion of Lord Derby, was inadequate for marriage with his daughter. The elopement in the summer of 1751 caused a major upset in the family. Lord Derby forbade all his other children to communicate with his disobedient daughter. Betty, from the security of her marriage, strongly opposed this view and openly flouted her parents' wishes. She even arranged for her sisters to meet Charlotte in Oxford. Burgoyne later became famous as the English general who surrendered his army to the Americans at Saratoga in 1777.

The unmarried Stanley sisters were not very happy at home, perhaps due to the excessive discipline and strict routine of the household. Lady Betty, on a Christmas visit in 1758, wrote to Charlotte: 'Supper bell rings and we are the same regular piece of clockwork that you formerly knew us, so I have only time to say ...'[20] Margaret suffered with asthma there and eventually in 1755 got permission to go and live permanently at Arley, where she could breathe easily and liked looking after the children. The other three sisters made frequent visits to Arley. When their father died in 1776, it appeared that he was not one of those notorious spendthrift noblemen. He had saved £117,000 from the estate's income during his tenure. Did he ever worry in his declining years that he had been too severe with Charlotte about John Burgoyne's small fortune?[21] He left most of the money to his four unmarried daughters. Margaret died soon after her father, so the other three daughters received over £33,000 each.[22]

No visitors' book for Arley survives from this period but Granary Books, which note the issue of grain to visiting horses, provide similar information. In the seven years between 1763 and 1773 for which these books exist, 119 visits are recorded: 48 were by the family such as Lord Derby, his son Lord Strange and Lady Betty's sisters, the Slaughters and General Warburton of Winnington. Almost all the rest were neighbouring

19 Arley Large Box 7, item 47/3.
20 Arley Large Box 7, item 47/4.
21 He evidently did because he left her £25,000 in his will, but she too died in 1776.
22 WM Boxes 29, 30.

gentry, Barrys, Egertons, Grosvenors, Leghs, and so on. The only person clearly not in either of these categories was Mrs Raffald. She had been Lady Betty's housekeeper from 1760 to 1763 and seems to have driven out from Manchester in a post-chaise to ask permission to dedicate her book, *The Experienced English Housekeeper*, to Lady Betty.[23] There is no evidence of house parties composed of several families of guests, nor of balls or other large gatherings. Perhaps large parties only assembled for dinner in the middle of the day and the horses brought their own food with them.

4. THE ARCHIVES

Sir Peter left a large archive at Arley which has provided much of the material for my two earlier books in this series. Detailed estate accounts exist for most years from 1750 to 1774. There are many thousands of receipted invoices[24] which amplify the entries in the accounts. Although all this provides a huge amount of information it does not permit an exact description of how the annual income was spent. One reason for this is that invoices frequently cover a period of a year or more. There was not the modern interest in prompt payment, so it was often several months before they were paid. Sometimes invoices covered several years – occasionally up to five or even nine years. Thomas Topping, a seedsman of Warrington, was paid in November 1762 against an invoice for the supply of goods between December 1753 and April 1761. The total was only £7 9s 4d. There is no evidence that he had sought payment earlier. Servants also used the Warburtons as a bank. John Burgess, the coachman, drew £80 on 21 November 1768, which was his pay for the five years 1761 to 1765 inclusive. He drew £64 in May 1770 for the four years 1766 to 1769 inclusive.[25] Such habits make it impossible to state accurately the amount spent annually on different categories of expense such as transport or textiles.

Another practice that prevents us obtaining a total view was that Sir Peter handled all capital transactions personally. Such activities as the purchase of a farm, the taking of a mortgage, and the receipt of the capital sums paid for the renewal of life leases were always done solely by him.

23 See below, p. 206.
24 Footnoted as A.R.I. (Arley Receipted Invoices) with date. Where a date is given in the text there is no further footnote.
25 See also p. 204 below.

In addition he always took several hundred pounds a year of the estate income in cash, but no account of this cash survives. Presumably he and Lady Betty used the money for their personal expenditure – clothes, horses, coach, furniture, books, pictures and so on. They also paid for the expeditions they made to Bath, London and other places.

Only traces of such items appear in the estate manager's accounts. In the first ten years of her marriage Lady Betty was her own housekeeper. In 1755 she began delegating this work to her maid Ann Worsley. House-keeping bills then started to be paid by the estate and soon a specialist housekeeper was appointed. So this type of expenditure appears in the estate account from the mid-1750s onwards. The surviving accounts therefore only cover the expenses of the way of life at Arley Hall. They describe the farm, the horses, the wages of the staff and everything else that the family and the 20 other people who lived in the Hall consumed. They also describe the money spent on repairing old buildings and constructing new ones. This building work seems to have cost between £500 and £1,000 p.a. throughout the period. The largest single item was the rebuilding of Arley Hall between 1756 and 1763. The gross estate income was about £2,500 in 1750[26] and by the early 1770s, because rental values had increased sharply, it had risen to between £3,500 and £4,000.[27] The next sections show how the way of life at Arley Hall in the 1750s and '60s was different from that seen earlier at Smithills between 1582 and 1600 or at Tabley in the middle of the seventeenth century.

5. THE FARM[28]

We saw earlier[29] that as late as 1626 there were over 200 cattle at Arley. In the 1750s there were just a dozen milking cows. All the meat eaten in the Hall was bought from the butcher. After 1757 this butcher was always Thomas Gatley of Knutsford. He usually delivered to the Hall three times a week and in a typical year he brought a total of between £200 and £250 worth of meat. The price was always 3d per lb. The land upon which the cattle had grazed in 1626 had been let to dairy farmers since the Restoration.

26 Foster, 1992, pp. 8–10.
27 Rents and casual profits were about £3,000 p.a. and fines for renewing leases around £600 p.a. WM Box 20, Estate Accounts. See Foster, 2003, Ch. 2.
28 The detailed operation of the Arley Hall farm, 1750–53 is described in Part 3 of Foster, 1998.
29 Chapter 1, p. 59.

So where did the butcher get his supplies? The answer appears to be that there had developed a major drift of cattle every year from the north and west of Britain to the south and east. Cheshire fed this stream with its surplus calves and worn out cows. It drew its meat in exchange.

Another change was that the farm workers no longer lived in the Hall as they had still done at Swarthmoor in the 1680s. Many in the 1750s were married men with families living in rented accommodation.[30] They were able to live without land on which to grow their own food because grain was now sold retail. Arley Mill, for example, had become a grain shop. Smithills had a mill in the sixteenth century, but except in famine years, it did not sell much grain. Arley Mill in 1762 sold its entire toll grain by the peck (four pecks in a bushel) to some 80 different customers, many of whom only bought occasionally. If supplies ran low the estate sent more from the granary. Amongst the most frequent purchasers were seven Arley labourers. Isaac Barker bought most – 59 pecks or nearly 15 bushels. This was probably not enough grain to feed his family for the whole year because, according to the List of Poor for 1762, he had a family of six. There were clearly other suppliers in the area. The Arley labourers bought mostly barley and only a little wheat, which suggests that barley bread was still the common food. The labourers may also have eaten oatmeal. Arley Mill did not grind oats at this period but Warburton Mill ground large amounts, which were carried into Manchester for sale. There would also have been supplies on sale in Great Budworth.

We have seen that gentry houses traditionally grew all their own food. A significant change was under way at Arley in the 1750s and '60s. The granary books that survive from between 1758 and 1773 show that less and less grain was being grown.[31] The supplies of wheat and oats required for the Hall were partly being provided from the tithes the estate bought. The rest was purchased either from local farmers or from dealers selling grain brought into the Mersey estuary by ship. In some years no grain at all was grown at Arley. Most of the malt required to brew beer in the Hall was acquired from dealers who brought it from the Derby-Loughborough area. William Widders brought some as part of his carrier business but the principal suppliers in the '60s were John Bancroft of Weaverham and Charles Ollyer of Great Budworth. The barley that came to Arley was made into malt at Harper's or Ellam's kilns in Appleton. It seems that by

30 Foster, 1992, pp. 28–9, List of Poor.
31 WM Box 22.

198

1770 confidence that the 'market' and its transport arrangements would always provide supplies allowed the estate to abandon self-sufficiency.

6. TEXTILES

We have seen that Sir Peter Leicester was still able to call on the services of a network of textile workers in the middle of the seventeenth century. By the 1740s almost all these people had disappeared from the Arley area. Basic linen yarn seems never to have been spun at Arley Hall in Lady Betty's time. This must have reflected her 'modern' views when she married because employing maids to spin seems still to have been the practice in her parents' household at Knowsley. They had 'yarn bleached and woven into 144 yards of flaxen cloth' in July 1750 and again in November 1751. On both occasions it cost £3 4s 0d.[32]

Lady Betty bought her flax and hemp cloth in shops. The cheapest grades came from the Baltic and the more expensive from Ireland. Some of the medium grades may have been made in England (see Table A below).[33] The maids still evidently cut up the cloth and made it into sheets, pillowcases, towels, shirts, and so on, as there are no invoices for sewing.

Table A. Examples of linen bought for Arley Hall 1757–76

Date	Type of linen	Supplier
27 Feb 1751	21 yards Russia at 5d yd	
	32 yards Russia at 6d yd	Hannah Neild, Knutsford
12 May 1755	144 yards hemp at 12d yd	
	72 yards huckaback at 12d yd	
	168 yards fine flax at 1s 10d yd	Mr. Jordan
30 May 1757	25 yards Irish linen at 2s 11d yd	Bridget Tootall
22 Feb 1758	12 yards English linen at 1s yd	Peter Hill, Warrington
27 Mar 1776	47 yards English sheeting at 15d	Mary Clare
	48 yards English sheeting at 13d	

The only craftsmen (or women) manufacturing complete textiles in the north Cheshire countryside seem to have been the makers of rope, twine and nets. Like their ancestors two centuries earlier, they grew

---

32 Lancs R.O. DDK 2012/1 John Bibye's cashbook.

33 Robert Stephenson says huckaback made in Yorkshire and sheeting made in Lancashire was better than Irish. Stephenson, 1757, pp. 119–20.

hemp and flax in small plots beside their houses. By the 1750s they may have augmented these supplies with the cheaper fibre imported from the Baltic. Ropes were made whatever length and type was required – wagon rope, black double corded rope, etc., costing 5d to 6d per pound. Net yarn, being finer, cost 1s to 1s 2d a lb, and knitting cost a few more pence per lb. Richard Hind in Aston by Budworth[34] was one maker, but the Warburtons bought from at least four others in the 1750s. There were nets for game – partridge nets and glade nets. There were fruit nets and nets to cover the poultry house, and nets for fishing – draught nets, brook nets, and drum mill nets. The Hind family also did fishing with their nets. Many of the old uses of hemp had disappeared. For example, leather had replaced hemp in the harness of horses so that saddlers provided all the requirements of the stables.

All other textiles were bought in shops. Outer garments were made by tailors. Thomas Riley and John Leigh made and repaired clothes for the servants, the children and even Sir Peter in the 1760s. Mary Caldwell who made dresses for the teenage girls called herself a Mantuamaker. The procedure seems to have been that the family went to the mercer's shop and chose the main cloth. William Jackson and John Kinsey in Great Budworth, John Peacock in Warrington or John Skellorn in Knutsford provided 'ordinary' items. Manchester and London were probably the source of some of the cloth for the family's own use. The tailor came to measure and then went to the shop and bought everything required – the cloth, linings, stiffenings, trimmings, buttons and thread. Some of the larger shops like Skellorn's must have had a huge range: cloths from all over England and perhaps Europe and India; wool, linen, cotton, silk, and many mixtures and colours. Skellorn's invoices list 300 or 400 items in a year. These were general shops. There were also specialist shops and specialist tailors. Ann Fowden in Warrington seems to have stocked materials that appealed to young girls. Ann Burgess in Great Budworth made them into dresses. Jonathon Goldsmith specialized in leather breeches, which could be calf, buck, lamb or ram skin. These were worn by the servants for riding and cost from 6s to £1 1s od a pair. Shoemakers were also specialized. One made the children's shoes while another was an expert in boots. There were also several suppliers of hats and caps. There were milliners in Knutsford and Warrington. One shop sold men's caps, another the livery hats with

34 Foster, 1992, pp. 26–7.

gold loops that servants wore. Shopping for clothes was an important and time-consuming operation for those who could afford them.

7. SERVANTS AND STANDARDS OF LIVING IN THE RURAL COMMUNITY

In the early years of their married life Sir Peter and Lady Betty kept their staff to a minimum. By the 1760s there had been some expansion. The list in Table B of the 25 servants in 1766 can by compared with the 15 of 1750.[35]

Table B. *The staff at Arley and their pay in 1766*

Position	Salary		
	£	s	d
Thomas Byfield, Sir Peter's man	20?	(unknown because paid by Sir Peter personally)	
Butler	20		
Housekeeper	16		
Cook	10		
Lady Elizabeth's maid	8		
Lady Elizabeth's footman	8	8	0
Brewer	6	10	0
Miss Ann Warburton's maid	6	10	0
Miss Harriot and Emma's maid	5		
Two laundry maids	5	each	
Two house maids	5	each	
Kitchen maid	5		
Odd job man	5		
Coachman	16		
Groom	8		
Post chariot postillion	7		
Coach postillion	4		
Undergroom	5		
Carter/foreman of the farm	8		
Dairymaid	5		
Gardener	21		
Game keeper	16		
Accountant/Estate manager	40		
	260	8	0

35 Foster, 1992, p. 35.

The cost in 1766 totalled £260 8s 0d compared with only £107 in 1750. Some part of this resulted from the additions. A housekeeper became necessary when Lady Betty gave up doing the job herself. The butler appeared when the family moved back into the new splendour of Arley Hall in 1763. The maids for the daughters were required when fashion decreed that the young ladies were old enough to wear elaborate hair-styles and clothes.

The rest of the increase arose partly from recruiting better qualified people to do the work, and partly from a general increase in pay. As new trades and industries multiplied in the north-west in this period the wages of all skilled people increased sharply. As can be seen when comparing the lists, almost everyone was paid 50% more in 1766 than their predecessors had got in 1750.[36] Maids got £5 instead of £3 and the coachmen got £16 instead of £10. Peter Harper, the estate manager, was paid £40 instead of the £20 that young Thomas Done had received in 1750. Peter Harper, probably in his late forties, was a fully experienced manager. He was the brother of Thomas, who not only leased the Warburtons' largest farm (172 acres) in Appleton, but also had freehold property in Grappenhall and interests in mills, malt kilns and other businesses. John Phipps, the head gardener was an accomplished nursery-man who had worked at Croome Court in Worcestershire under 'Capability' Brown. He had come to Arley on the recommendation of William Emes who began creating the Park in 1763. The high-class gardeners who had been employed in the 1750s had all left to get married. In order that John Phipps could stay at Arley after his marriage Sir Peter built him a house beside the garden where he could bring up his family.[37]

The excellence of Peter Harper's accounting has led to the survival of some unusual papers about the diet of these servants. While Arley Hall was being rebuilt, 1755–63, a skeleton staff remained in one corner. This normally consisted of Peter Harper, the surveyor of the building works, Matthew Glanham, the head gardener, the farm foreman, a cook/housekeeper and a maid. Others like the rat catcher, the basket maker and Kitty Humphrey, who dressed feathers, came for a few days. Harper meticulously recorded everything that was bought for them in the four years 1758 to 1761. He also recorded the exact number of days for which

36 Compare Gilboy, 1934, p. 220.
37 See my article on the development of the Arley gardens in *Garden History*, Vol. 24, No. 2.

each person was fed. An alternative arrangement to provide for this group during the building works would have been to give them 'board wages' of 6d a day each so that they could stay in nearby farmhouses. Six pence a day is £9 2s 6d a year. It seems that Harper originally intended his accounting to show that the group in Arley Hall cost no more than this. Actually it showed the costs were just over £10 a year. The figures in Table C have been adjusted so that each person's food cost exactly £10 per year. This means that when the sums of money are shown in decimal pounds they can easily be converted into percentages. Thus £5.69 spent on meat can be seen to be 56.9% of total expenditure.

Table C. *Average housekeeping expenses per person per year at Arley Hall 1758–61 (A.R.I.)*

	£	%
455 lbs meat at 3d lb in large joints	5.69	56.9
165½ lbs Cheese at 2d lb	1.38	13.8
6⅘ bushels (about 470 lbs) wheat at 4s bushel	1.36	13.6
17¹⁄₁₀ lbs sugar at 8d lb (approximate average)	.57	5.7
21⅗ lbs butter at 5d lb	.45	4.5
1 lb tea at 6s 5d lb (approximate average)	.32	3.2
Salt and spices	.18	1.8
Other, mostly fish and fowls	.05	0.5
	10.00	100

In addition to the above, they will have had vegetables from the garden and probably some milk from the 12 cows the dairy maid was looking after at Aston Park.

More difficult to assess is the amount of beer or ale they drank. Throughout the 1760s around £10 worth of malt seems to have been brewed into ale each month. When Sir Peter gave a bonfire party on Budworth Heath in 1759 to celebrate Wolfe's victory at the Battle of Quebec, he bought 40 gallons of ale from local innkeepers at 1¾d a pint.[38] This was probably strong ale. If similar ale were brewed at Arley and equally distributed among the family and servants, each person might have got 1½ pints a day. However it is likely that the brewing at Arley was done in the same way that it was done in the Shuttleworth

38 A.R.I., 29 November 1759.

household (described on p. 52 above). Only a small amount of strong ale was brewed. Most of the beer brewed was small beer. However it was shared out it seems that the average cost of the beer per head must have been about £4 p.a.

Although at first glance a twenty-first century person is amazed at the amount of meat our ancestors consumed, it may have been less than it seemed. The tidy meat that we are accustomed to see might weigh only half as much as the carcass it was cut from which would have included a lot of bone and gristle. If the bills surviving from the Bath journey (above p. 193) are a good guide, they had two cooked meals a day, probably consisting of roast meat and greens or stew with onions and root vegetables. Sometimes there were potatoes, and there was always bread and cheese. It was all washed down with beer. Very occasionally there was a sweetmeat of some kind or a cup of tea. Once or twice a year there was fish or chicken. The housekeeper's monthly bills show that the family enjoyed fish, game and fowls much more frequently than the servants did. They also had more sweets, tea, coffee and chocolate.

That 6d a day was thought an appropriate level for 'board wages' seems to demonstrate that this was the usual standard of life in farm-houses. These were normally the households of rack-rented tenant farmers in this period. It was in one of these households that George Dockwra went to live. He would have enjoyed a similar diet to that eaten by the servants at Arley, perhaps without the beer.

The servants also seem to have received all their clothes from the estate. It was because he was provided with everything he needed that John Burgess, the coachman, was able to refrain from drawing his salary for nine years (p. 196 above). When the value of their food, beer and clothing was added together, each servant may have been receiving some £12 to £15 per year in benefits. Even with a wage of only £5 p.a. plus tips (see p. 194 above) a servant was much better off than a labourer who was lucky if he could earn £12 a year.[39] But a labourer had freedoms, in particular the freedom to marry, which was denied to servants. Some married labourers must nevertheless have wondered, after they were married and had two or three children to bring up, whether they hadn't paid too highly for their freedom. Out of his £12 the labourer would have had to pay rent for a cottage or a room in a farmhouse. The Overseers of

39 Foster 1992, p. 10.

the Poor rented several cottages from the estate at £1 10s 0d p.a. After firewood or coal, boots and clothes, and food for the children, it is difficult to see how the married couple, even if the wife earned a little, would have had more than £7 or £8 for their food. Oatmeal porridge, bread, cheese, and vegetables are likely to have been all they could afford. This analysis shows why the Warburtons regarded their agricultural workers as 'Poor' and why they gave them a Christmas present of meat and money every year.[40] It should also be noted that the appearance of a group of landless labourers in the area with a lower standard of living seems to have occurred between 1642 and 1750.[41] At Smithills, Tabley and Swarthmoor farm workers all lived in. They probably therefore had a diet similar to that enjoyed by the Arley servants. It was the cessation of this practice that turned the estate's farm workers into 'Poor'.

It would seem that in rural Cheshire before the Civil War ancient Manor Court rules prevented the estate's tenants, who were all three-life leaseholders from letting their lands to 'strangers' who did not own a three-life leasehold. This custom limited the supply of casual agricultural labour to the families of three-life leaseholders and reinforced the gentry's habit of employing living-in servants to farm their large demesnes. After about 1642 these old rules were slowly relaxed and 'strangers' came to live in rural townships as rack-rent paying tenants of three-life lease-holders.[42] By 1750 the 'strangers' had divided into three groups. The first group were the rack-rent paying tenants of farms who were mostly engaged in producing cheese as described in my *Cheshire Cheese*.[43] The size of a viable dairy farm was between 65 and 100 acres whereas the pre-1650 farms averaged only 25–30 acres, so the redundant buildings and cottages, if not demolished, were available to house the other two groups. The second group were skilled workers or people with capital ranging from a doctor of medicine to a clockmaker and a tailor. The third group were poor people with low skills like labourers and thatchers together with the retired, the sick and the widowed. As this new group slowly emerged the gentry and others with farms largely abandoned the practice of employing living-in agricultural workers and took to supplying many of their needs on a daily, weekly or monthly basis from among these poor people. The

40 Foster, 1992, pp. 28–9.
41 See Foster, 2003, Ch. 5 (iv), b, for the evidence for these statements.
42 Those in Aston by Budworth are listed in Tables 6–9 in Foster, 1992, pp. 27–33.
43 Foster, 1998.

only living-in farm worker at Arley in 1750 was the farm foreman. Many of the Arley servants seem to have belonged to families who possessed a little capital. A number of them are known to have left to get married and start their own businesses. Peter Swinton, the Arley farm foreman in 1750, became a tenant farmer on the estate.[44] John and Elizabeth Raffald went to Manchester in 1763 where he ran a plant nursery and she a 'take-away' food shop.[45]

The behaviour of John Burgess, the coachman, in saving up his salary for nine years (see p. 196) is probably to be explained by his desire to set up in business when he left Arley. This stored up salary was to be his capital. In a similar manner, John Allen, the farm foreman, drew four years salary, a total of £32, in December 1765 just before he left Arley. This was part of the capital he invested in his stock at Firtree Farm, Crowley, where he took over as Thomas Hough's tenant in early 1766. It was a large farm of 127 acres and he put 20 cows on the land.[46]

One of the Arley invoices helps provide an unusual view of this group of tenant farmers who were better off than the labourers. James Hulme was a tenant farmer who had a lease of the Firs in Crowley just beside Arley Hall, a farm of 19 acres for which he was probably paying a rack-rent of about £11 a year.[47] This farm was similar to Richard Latham's. In 1745, and probably for at least ten years earlier, he had rented another 68 acres of the Arley demesne for £28 p.a. giving him a total area of 87 acres which made a viable dairy farm.[48] He seems to have been one of the farmers who were badly affected by the cattle plague in 1749–50 when, like many others, he probably lost all his cattle and so lost much of his capital.[49] His rent to the Arley estate got in arrears and he had to give up the Arley demesne land. His farming business was so reduced that it did not provide him with a full-time occupation. He did some contract ploughing and other work for the estate, and no doubt for other farmers also, in the early 1750s. By November 1755 he and his wife had had 13 children whose names are set out in Table D below. In early 1756 Lady Betty must have noticed that the eight youngest children were all dressed

44 Foster, 1998, p. 76.
45 For John see *Garden History*, Vol. 24; for Elizabeth see Shipperbotham, 1997.
46 See Foster, 1992, and Foster, 1998, p. 69, for illustration of cow tithes in 1766 and Foster, 2003, Ch. 8 for Thomas Hough.
47 Foster, 1992, p. 76 lists the landlord John Haslehurst.
48 Foster, 1998, pp. 13–7.
49 WM Box 25, folder 2, Aston small tithes 1752.

Table D. *James Hulme's family, their ages in March 1756 and the clothes given to them*

Name	Age	Clothes
Mary	Died aged 10 in 1746	
Sarah	18.0	Not at home in Mar. 1756
John	14.8	Not at home in Mar. 1756
James	12.9	Not at home in Mar. 1756
Ellen	11.2	A gown and a petticoat; 'stays' and 'bodies' repaired
Alice	11.2	A gown and a petticoat; 'stays' and 'bodies' repaired
Thomas	9.10	Waistcoat and breeches
Martha	Thomas's twin,	Died aged 2 months
Jonathon	8.1	Waistcoat and breeches
Mary	5.11	Last gown
Vincent	4.0	Waistcoat and breeches
Joseph	2.3	Gown
Samuel	4 months	Gown

Source of children's ages: Great Budworth Parish Register

in rags, as she provided some cloth and told Peter Moores the tailor to make them new clothes. Some of the cloth may have been the 22 yards that Hannah Taylor sold on 26 January for £1 1s 6d. Peter Moores charged 12s 4d for his work in March.

Table D provides an illustration of how successful some tenant farmers were at raising large families in the country at this period. By 1756 James Hulme's three oldest children had left home to ease the burden on their parents. Sarah was a maid in Arley Hall, while her two brothers were presumably living and working with local farmers.

The family survived this difficult period with only the loss of baby Samuel at the age of four. The cow tithes of Crowley[50] show that they kept three or four cows every year between 1757 and 1766. James Hulme himself died in 1761 but his widow, Mary and their children kept up the farm and continued to pay the rent. In 1767 the second son James took over the farm when he married. His eldest son was born there in 1768. All this shows that it was possible to bring up a large family on a 20-acre farm paying a full rack-rent and underlines the privileged position of Richard Latham.

50 See Foster, 1998, illustration p. 69.

8. THE STRUCTURE OF ECONOMIC LIFE IN NORTH CHESHIRE ILLUSTRATED BY EXAMPLES DRAWN FROM THE BUILDING INDUSTRY, 1750-70

The Arley invoices illustrate many aspects of life in the 1750s and '60s. To describe more than a few would involve repetition because the same trends were apparent everywhere. I have selected the main examples from the building industry because construction was one of the principal activities of the estate. We have seen that at Smithills in the 1580s and '90s lime and lead were almost the only materials used in building that were not available in the immediate vicinity. By the 1750s the technology of building had been greatly developed and materials and components were drawn from a much wider area. The transport of these materials was a major part of the cost. A considerable number of businesses had come into existence to supply the materials and there was keen competition between them. The growing complexity of the technology and the competitive pressures were leading to the appearance of people with much wider skills than had existed earlier. These were the forerunners of the managerial and professional classes of the nineteenth century. The examples that follow will illustrate these trends.

The largest project Sir Peter Warburton undertook was the modernization of Arley Hall (see Figs. 48–50). The design of the improved mansion was worked out with William Lyon. He was probably the man who had built nearby Belmont Hall between 1752 and 1755, where he seems to have altered the designs of the London architect, James Gibbs, by adding semicircular bow windows to the main front. His design for Arley Hall (see Fig. 49) was similar. When Lyon first appears in Thomas Done's ledger in March 1750 he is styled 'Mr. Lyon, joiner'. Later, in 1758, when building work was under way, it appears that Lyon had provided an estimate for building the new south front and that stonemasons and bricklayers were at work under him. He was evidently more a builder than a joiner. Only in an invoice dated 12 June 1778 does it emerge that he had actually designed the new Arley Hall. It seems there had been a dispute between him and Sir Peter in 1758 over his estimates for the work and they had not parted as friends, so he had never sent in a bill for his design work. When Sir Peter's son, the 5th Baronet, heard this story in 1778, after his father's death, he insisted on paying. So it turns out that William Lyon was both architect and builder.

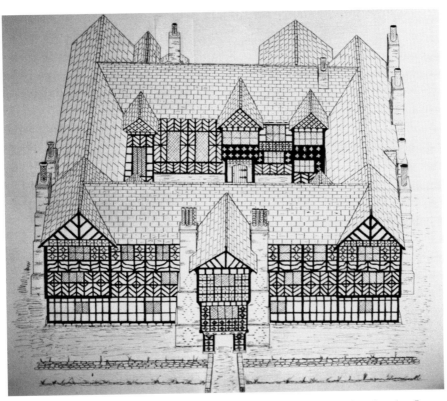

Fig. 48. The south front of Arley Hall, *c.* 1600–1750s. This drawing by James Barfoot is based on a reconstruction made by the author from a seventeenth-century plan and a sketch of the front elevation. The three-storey south front, with its great brick chimneys framing the entrance, was probably built in the last 30 years of the sixteenth century. Behind it, looking south over the courtyard, was the old Great Hall, built *c.* 1470 with the family wing to the west and the kitchen and servants' wings to the east. This original building was probably single-storey until the chimneys were built on the outside walls, enabling a first floor to be inserted in the wings. The Great Hall remained full height up to the roof timbers. Notice that, on all four sides of the courtyard, the old house was only one room thick. This can be contrasted with the new, more compact plan at Gawthorpe.

Two men replaced Lyon as supervisor of the building work. Matthew Glanham, who had experience of the erection of other large buildings (possibly for Lord Portland), came to live in the Hall at a salary of £50 p.a. He never seems to have been given a title except 'Mr'. The other man was John Hope who employed the bricklayers working first on the Hall and then on the Arley estate for the rest of the fourth baronet's life.

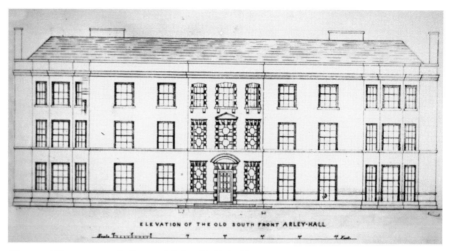

ELEVATION OF THE OLD SOUTH FRONT ARLEY·HALL

Fig. 49. The new south front of Arley Hall, built 1758–63. These new brick walls, with stone dressings to the windows and doors, enclosed the timber-framed structure of the old house which remained to support the roof. New walls created corridors around the courtyard, giving access to all the rooms without the need to go outside and up another staircase, as had been necessary in the old house. Nowadays almost the only survival of this old style of building is to be found in Oxbridge Colleges.

Accounting documents refer to him as either Mr Hope or John Hope, bricklayer. He did more than employ bricklayers. He supervised and 'measured' the work of bricklayers and stonemasons. Using the new techniques of 'quantity surveying' he priced their work and settled what they were paid for it. He designed new stone- and brickwork. In Mrs Raffald's *Directory of Manchester 1772*, he, or perhaps his son of the same name, appears as 'Surveyor and Builder of Alport Street'. Historians have to be wary of simple one-word job descriptions in this period.

The basic technology of building in brick and stone had been used at Arley since about 1600, as can be seen in the Tudor Barn, built in 1604, which still stands. The stone still came from the estate's own quarry in Appleton, worked by the Tilley family for several generations. In 1759, for instance, Thomas Tilley cut out 4,153 cubic feet of stone, which at 1½d a cubic foot cost £25 19s 1½d. It was transported to Arley in 101 wagon loads, which each carried 29 cu. ft (around two tons) and 72 cartloads of 17 cu. ft each. At 8s for a wagon and 4s for a cart, the transport cost £54 16s 0d.[51]

51 For illustrations of carts and wagons, see Foster, 1998, p. 58.

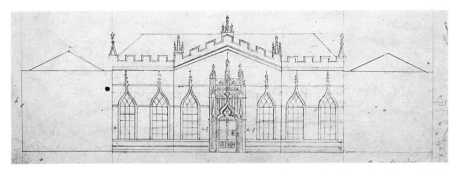

Fig. 50. Inside the courtyard of Arley Hall, the new Gothic façade to the Great Hall, built at the same time as the south front. The redecoration of the main rooms of the house incorporated quite elaborate plasterwork.

With the coal used to burn the bricks, the carriage also cost much more than the minerals. The coal used at Arley had always come from pits in south Lancashire about 15 miles to the north-west. In 1749 agreements were made with tenants to buy coal and transport it to Arley Hall for 9s 2d a ton. By 1754 this rate had risen to 10s a ton and from 1756 it was 11s 8d a ton. These increases seem to have been due to the growing demand for transport rather than a change in the price of coal at the pit. Sir Peter's building programme and his domestic consumption seem to have required at least 200 tons of coal in most years in the 1750s and '60s.

Humphrey Walker made most of the bricks used. He dug and worked the clay in the Marl Field behind the house, built the kilns and fired the bricks. He made two types: facing bricks, made in open fires with lump coal supplied by the estate, which cost 6s per 1,000, and ordinary bricks, fired in a kiln with 'slack' coal, which cost 5s per 1,000. Slack delivered to Arley from the pit cost 4d a measure. It seems that about 30 measures made a ton, so it may have cost about 10s a ton. The cost of open-fired bricks at Arley including the cost of coal was 11s per 1,000, so the coal was nearly half the total cost.

The opening of the Sankey Navigation in 1759 changed the estate's way of buying coal. The 'navigation' was really a canal linking the coal pits near the modern St Helens with the Mersey estuary at Sankey Bridges about 1½ miles west of Warrington. Its purpose was to reduce the cost of sea-borne coal in the Mersey Estuary. Peter Legh of Lyme, who owned the Haydock pit from which most of the coal used at Arley had traditionally come, cut his prices so as to hold on to his customers.

This pit was not on the canal. In 1760 he sold 185 tons at 2s 4d a ton directly to his old friend Sir Peter Warburton.[52] The price for carting it to Arley was fixed at 8s a ton, so the coal delivered there only cost 10s 4d in 1760, instead of the 11s 8d it had cost in 1759. As well as Peter Legh's coal, Arley bought from Edward Byrom and Company some 31 tons of slack that had come down the Sankey canal, at 3s 6d a ton. This probably came around to Wilderspool near Stockton Heath on a 'flat' from where it cost 4s a ton to cart it to Arley. At a total of 7s 6d a ton it was much cheaper than the 10s paid in 1759.

Much manœuvring over price and quality between rival suppliers went on in the next ten years. Peter Legh realized he had cut the price of Haydock's coal unnecessarily in 1760 and raised his prices by 9d a ton in 1761, then by another 9d a ton in 1762.[53] This brought the price to 3s 9d a ton at the pit. With 8s carriage to Arley, it made the price at Arley 11s 9d, which was almost the same as it had been in 1759. Edward Byrom offered coal at 5s 10d, and slack at 2s 4d in 1762, but was charging 6s 8d a ton in 1765 for coal, perhaps of a better quality. Sir Peter Warburton bought from them both and also from two new suppliers.

John Mackay had come to live at Bellfields in Appleton, as Sir Peter's tenant, in late 1762.[54] His father was a merchant in Inverness but he himself was living in London when he married in 1757, and was probably still there when, in 1761, he and Jonathon Greenall of Parr took out a patent for an improved method of refining salt. He evidently had capital as well as technical interests, and came to the Warrington area to investigate the possibility of investing in its new industries. He quickly got to work and was to play an important part in the development of the coal and glass industries.[55] In 1766 he sold Sir Peter 141 tons of coal that

---

52 Peter Legh's invoice, paid 25 February 1761, was for 3,464 baskets at 1½d a basket delivered in summer 1760. The date, the number of baskets, and the carter's name is given for each load. The carter's invoices (paid in October 1760) give the date, number of baskets, and the weight of each load at the Latchford weighing machine. These invoices show that baskets usually weighed more than 1 cwt each, so that 20 baskets usually weighed about 1 ton 2 cwt. The price of carting may have fallen slightly in 1760 because the canal had reduced the demand for horse transport.

53 Peter Legh's prices were 2d a basket in 1761, and 2½d a basket in 1762. See previous footnote.

54 He paid £100 p.a. for the house that Admiral Hore had built ten years earlier. The Admiral died in June 1762. Sir Peter was an executor and bought the property. Mackay paid for 6 tons of hay on 19 January 1763.

55 Barker, 1954, pp. 34–5.

had come down the Sankey at 6s 4d a ton and a further 191 tons in 1768.[56] By 1770 the Duke of Bridgewater's canal had opened to Stockton Heath. Sir Peter bought a boat-load there which weighed 6 ton 2 cwt, and cost 7s 6d a ton. It cost 4s a ton more to cart it to Arley.

The use of four different suppliers of coal in ten years seems not to have been at all unusual in this period. Competition was fierce and the pace of technical innovation was such that people evidently felt that something new or better or cheaper might be offered to them at any time. For example, the estate also used coke. Sir Peter Warburton had installed new kilns at his mills at Warburton and Arley when he modernized them in the early 1750s. These kilns dried oats to feed to horses, using coke as the fuel. The estate bought coke from six different suppliers in Lancashire and two in Staffordshire between 1757 and 1773.[57]

At Smithills in the 1590s, only lime from Clitheroe was used. At Arley in the 1750s, three grades were employed. The cheapest was burnt in kilns at or near Bankey (Bank Quay), Warrington.[58] The limestone probably came from north Wales, and the coal from one of the pits north of Warrington. The lime cost 6d a measure and carriage to Arley 4s 6d per cartload in carts carrying between 20 and 25 measures in 1750. The price had increased to 10s a wagon load of 40 measures by 1758. Between 1759 and 1761 Roger Gaskell sold 2,990 measures of lime at 6d to the estate. Including the cost of carriage, this lime cost about 9d a measure at Arley. It was probably only suitable for inside brickwork and plastering, as the mortar made from it would not resist rain.

The second grade of lime came from the Buxton area. A man called James Sutton, who appears to have been illiterate (as he did not sign his name), had a business in the Macclesfield area selling horse loads of this lime at 11d. It had evidently come on packhorses over the moors from Buxton, and James Sutton probably just warehoused it in an old barn.

56 The 1766 coal was 4 flat loads which Mackay charged as 121.5 Navigation tons at 4s 6d plus freight at 2s per ton, and river dues at 10d a ton. It actually weighed 141 tons at the weighing machine and cost 4s a ton to cart to Arley.

57 The Lancashire pits were Haydock, Atherton, Stone Pitt Green and Chaddock. John Mackay and an unnamed person supplied at Sankey. Richard Bell and James Taylor were the Staffordshire suppliers.

58 William Dumbell and Co. were the sellers in 1750. In the 1760s Dumbell and Barton appear, and so does Thomas Patten, who was the owner of Bankey. William Dumbell, Jnr, invoiced after 1768. Other invoices suggest that the Dumbells were partners or managers of the Pattens.

Some was carried to Arley every year in the 1750s by two tenant farmers, Jonathon Beswick and John Walton. They made journeys to Macclesfield with strings of 10 or 11 packhorses. They charged 7d a load in 1750. The price rose to 9d a load in the late 1750s when about 1,000 loads a year were carried to Arley. Some came by wagons that carried 40 measures for 15s. So we can see that a horseload was about two measures and that this lime cost about 10d a measure at Arley. This was probably the white semi-hydraulic lime that was used in mortar for external brickwork, because it would resist being washed out by the rain.

The third grade of lime came from a kiln at Damhouse, Astley, Lancashire, an estate that had earlier been owned by the Mort family. In this period, it passed through the female line to Thomas Sutton and then Thomas Frogatt. Both the coal and the limestone may have been quarried on the estate. It appears to have produced a fully hydraulic lime that could be used in brick- and stonework underground. It was used in foundations and drains where it would resist continual wet conditions. It was sold at the kiln at 8d a measure in the 1750s, and cost 6¾d a measure to cart to Arley, so it cost a total of 1s 2¾d a measure by the time it arrived there. Perhaps due to competition from the Duke of Bridgewater, who had similar limestone and coal on his estate at Worsley where his canal started, the Arley estate bought Damhouse lime at 6d a measure in 1765. The estate had it carried to Arley for only 4¾d a measure, so the total cost was only 10¾d a measure.

These examples of coal and lime show the complex problems of quality and price that existed in the 1750s and '60s. They show also that a large number of different suppliers were in the market-place and were competing vigorously with each other, trying to develop new and cheaper ways of supplying customers' requirements. The same picture can be seen in the supply of other building components.

Local supplies of timber had existed at Smithills in the 1590s. There was little fit for building on the Arley estate by the 1750s. Most of the timber used came from the Baltic or America. The estate sometimes bought from Gorell and Pownall in Liverpool. From there it was freighted up the Weaver Navigation to Northwich. Sometimes they bought at Bank Quay, Warrington, or in Northwich. Large structural timbers, say 1 x 1 x 25 feet long (priced at 15d a cu. ft), were conveyed on special timber carriages. Gorell and Pownall had sawing machinery, and sold ready-sawn lathes by the thousand for plastering and slating.

If the total weight of stone, coal, lime and timber transported by the estate each year is added together, there can have been few years in the 1750s or '60s when it was less than 500 tons. In addition to these materials, sand was quarried in Great Budworth and other pits on the estate. Sandstone 'slates' were bought at Moss Bank, Windle (now St Helens), and 'north country' (presumably Cumbrian) slates were bought in Liverpool. Flag stones of several grades were carted from various quarries up to 15 miles away. The grand total of building materials carried on the roads by the estate must have approached 1,000 tons in some years, and Sir Peter Warburton was only one of many people actively developing the economic life of the area. Some of the effects of all this movement of goods on the roads are described in the next section.

9. ROADS

In the sixteenth century, country roads in Cheshire had been wide green strips as shown in Fig.18 in Chapter 1 on page 47. These 'lanes' often linked wider open spaces known as Heaths and Greens. This land served the dual purpose of providing communal grazing and allowing movement from house to house. The lanes often ran through the middle of farm yards. The use of increasing numbers of carts and wagons churned the grass into muddy pools in low-lying places. By 1750 the obligation of each township to repair its own roads was well understood. Each householder acted in turn as Overseer of the Highways for a year and had to co-ordinate the work of his fellow householders to keep the roads in repair. Taxes were raised annually in each township to meet the expense. If anyone felt the roads were too dreadful they could appeal to the magistrates who had power to order the townships to repair them.

The thought of having to spend money on repairing roads used by other people led many people to try to find ways to avoid such a situation. One method was to keep roads 'private'. All the roads around Arley Hall were private because the estate, as the Lord of the Manor, owned the land and paid for all repairs. It only allowed people to drive carts down the roads it maintained with permission, though pedestrians and riders were normally allowed to use most lanes. The roads were usually gated and local people, who had permission to use the roads, knew where the key was kept. If people used the roads without permission, they were pursued, and under the threat of legal proceedings, were induced

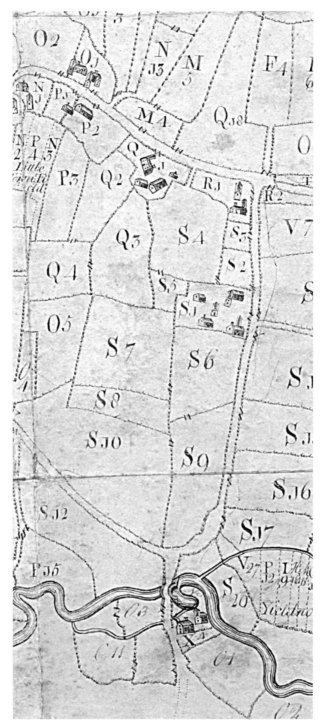

Fig. 51. The roads at Warburton Mill in an estate map of 1757. The mill is shown on the river beside the bridge. The Bent is at S1. The new road made by the Drinkwater family went from the Bent to the bridge beside S6 and S9. This allowed carts bound for Manchester to cross the bridge and go past the Bent to turn right at the junction by R1–2. Before this short-cut was opened carters had to turn left over the bridge, go through the village, then turn right to emerge by O2 – see the village centre in Fig. 52.

to sign 'acknowledgements' that they had used the road only with permission. Several of these documents survive.[59] At Arley these procedures were effective and the roads are still private.

In other cases the position was more complicated. The Arley estate had had a long lease of Crowley from the Crown between 1510 and 1656.[60] During that period the family at Arley had used the Crowley roads to reach their manor of Appleton and the market town of Warrington. After 1656 the land on which these roads ran was owned by a number of other people. The Warburtons had difficulties in the 1750s in getting Crowley residents to recognize that they had long-established rights of user over these roads. This problem was exacerbated by the large tonnage of stone, coal, lime and slates being carried from Warrington. To maintain good relations with his neighbours, Sir Peter Warburton had to pay for substantial repairs to the roads in Crowley.

The case of a section of road in Warburton was even more complicated. The Drinkwater family had had a three-life lease of the Bent, the largest farm in Warburton, from the estate since the sixteenth century. Sir George Warburton built a new mill on the Bollin in 1664. This river was the boundary between Lymm and Warburton townships. It seems that the Drinkwaters were the first leaseholders of the mill. In order to improve business they purchased a strip of land between the new mill and the old road in Warburton (see Fig. 51) and made it into a road for people using the mill. It was gated and they used to call on the people who used it who lived in both Lymm and Warburton townships to come and help repair it. This was done regularly until 1731. However, the use of the road increased so that Arnold Drinkwater complained in 1733 that only three out of 36 loads were from Warburton mill and that most of the rest were overseas goods. One Bredbury then appealed to the magistrates to declare the road a King's Highway and they did so in January 1735/6. Arnold Drinkwater then appealed to the courts in Chester and won the case in 1736. The road continued to be for the sole use of Lymm and Warburton farmers to take their oatmeal from the mills for sale in Manchester.[61] Keeping this road private was probably popular with Warburton householders because it discouraged carts travelling from Lymm to

---

59 WM Box 23, folder 6. The legal force of these documents was to show that these roads could only be used with permission, i.e., they were *not* public roads.
60 Foster, 2003, Ch. 2 (iii).
61 WM Box 23, folder 3.

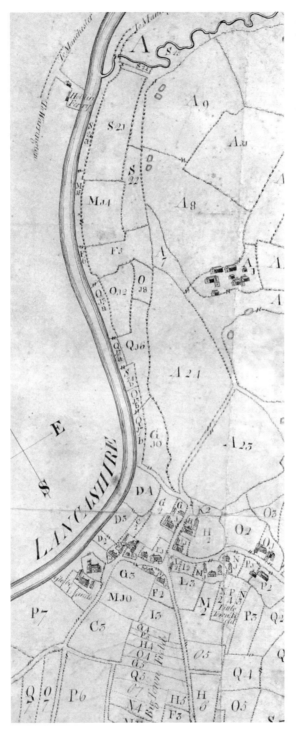

Fig. 52. The Hollin Ferry and the centre of Warburton village in 1757. The ferry is shown in the top left-hand corner at the end of the short lane leading from the Warrington–Manchester road. On the Cheshire side there was a grassy lane beside the river leading to the centre of the village by D4. Warburton Park, the home of the Warburton family *c.* 1300–1470, is A1. Notice the old Town Field to the left of the road at the bottom.

Manchester from using Warburton roads, thus keeping the repair bills low.

There was a greater controversy about another development at the Hollin Ford and Ferry, which might have led to much more traffic on the roads in Warburton. This dispute ended in a lawsuit. Fom time immemorial there had been a ford over the Mersey. In the summer Warburton tenants could drive their carts across to fetch coal from Lancashire pits (see Fig. 52). This was the only place to cross the Mersey between Warrington and the outskirts of Manchester. On the same site was Hollin Ferry, owned by the Rixton Estate. On the Lancashire side the ford and ferry were approached by a short lane off the main Warrington–Manchester road. Carts were charged tolls for the use of this lane and the ferry. On the Cheshire side, the ferry landed beside Warburton Park, where there was a long lane beside the river to the main roads in the centre of the village. No tolls were charged on this lane.

Two developments created the controversy. The Mersey and Irwell Navigation Co. found that the ford was so shallow in summer that it blocked the passage of boats. They drove in piles to narrow the river higher up and succeeded in scouring the ford away. Everyone then became dependent on the ferry. A blacksmith and shopkeeper in Dunham called Hodkinson developed a large business in goods that he ferried across. He began to use the Cheshire shore as a wharf and his carts caused much damage to the Warburton lanes.[62] Sir Peter Warburton wanted to build a bridge, the tolls on which would maintain both the bridge and the roads on each side. The Rixton Estate, who owned the ferry, would not agree so Sir Peter started and won a legal action which limited the traffic on the ferry.[63] A bridge was eventually built by R. E. E. Warburton in the middle of the nineteenth century. This was superseded by the present bridge when the Manchester Ship canal was constructed.

The main road from Lancashire to London crossed the Mersey by the bridge in Warrington and proceeded south through Stretton, Great Budworth and Allostock. The growing prosperity of Budworth after 1500 was partly based on the inns and other services it provided for travellers on the road. By the late 1750s, it was clear that the new turnpike that was being built northwards from Cranage Green to Knutsford might go on to Warrington as well as Manchester and so divert London traffic from the

62 WM Box 23, folder 6, 1 January 1764.
63 WM Box 23, folder 5.

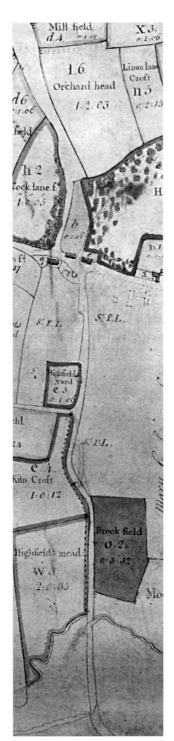

Fig. 53. The London road through Great Budworth as shown on the 1759 Arley estate map. Notice the bend by C4 and the even sharper and narrower twists at the crossroads.

old Great Budworth road. Sir Peter Warburton had a meeting with Sir Peter Leicester who had just bought the manor of Marston. With his property in Budworth, he had a significant interest in the prosperity of the villages through which the old road passed. Together they agreed to improve the road where it passed through their lands. They also jointly instructed the Knutsford lawyer, S. A. Wright, to apply appropriate legal pressure on the townships of Sevenoaks, Antrobus, Over Whitley (in the Whitley Lordship) and Stretton to make them widen the road to more than eight yards as it passed through their lands. It took eight years, from 1761 to 1769, to bring this legal work to a successful conclusion.[64] What the partners did in Great Budworth can be seen by comparing the two maps in Figs. 53 and 54. Unfortunately, Knutsford was a much more important place economically than Great Budworth and most of the traffic moved to the new turnpike, in spite of the efforts of the two Sir Peters.

10. THE DIVERSITY OF BUSINESS IN THE AREA

We should not leave Sir Peter's archive without noticing what it tells us about the variety of business that had developed in the area in the century between 1650 and 1750. I have described the Northwich salt industry and many of the business families in Warrington elsewhere.[65] Apart from these there was a surprising number of other enterprises in the area. The following brief tour through some of the less usual will, it is hoped, convey an impression of the breadth and scope of business in the Mersey basin.

Northwich was the site of a major timber business run by William Antrobus. This supplied timber for the mines and for the wharves and loading platforms which handled the salt and the coal. Nicholas Flynn had a business there specializing in chains and pulleys for similar reasons. John Jeffries played an active part not only in the salt business but also in the supply of ironwork for the pans and other equipment. A more unusual businessman in Northwich was William Stedman, who dealt in ground colours for paints. This was a part of his larger business which also supplied colours to the growing pottery industry in Stoke-on-Trent. Many of the raw materials used in the Potteries, as well as their finished products, travelled on the Weaver Navigation. These products were therefore on sale in Northwich. Mrs Catherine Yates supplied Arley with 68

64 A.R.I. 4/6/70.
65 Foster, 2003, Chs 7–10.

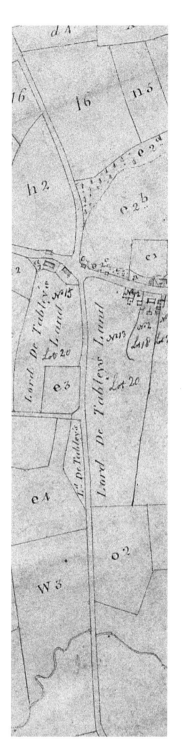

Fig. 54. The same road after 1769 seen in the 1833 map. The Leicester family's lands are marked 'Lord de Tabley' in this map and 'Sir P.L.' in the 1759 map.

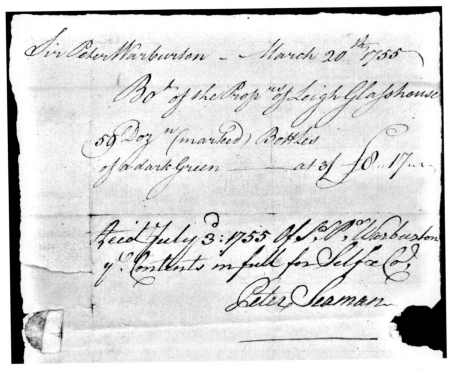

Fig. 55. An invoice for wine bottles from Leigh Glasshouses receipted by Peter Seaman, innkeeper of the *Eagle and Child* in Warrington and part-owner of the Glasshouses.

flint whiteware bowls, basins, dishes, chamber pots and such items from her shop there in 1768.

By contrast, Knutsford did not have these industrial businesses and was more consumer oriented. I have already mentioned the drapers' shops there and the butchers Sam Jeffrey and Thomas Gatley (above, p. 197). Thomas Poole seems to have been the main plumber and glazier in the area. Before he died in 1771 he had added many more lines: ground paint colours and linseed oil, pewter plates and pots, brass saucepans, lanterns, candlesticks and chamber pots to name just a few of the things he supplied to Arley. Henry Penney was certainly the apothecary whom all the gentry trusted. Pool Hurst ran a grocery shop that they patronized. John Frogatt was a soap boiler in the town, buying tallow and rendering it into candles and soap. John Harper and John Wilkinson had shops there which sold ironmongery. The latter was also described as a whitesmith, presumably because he would make or mend things of pewter, tin, brass and copper. In addition to all these shops there were many inns where the coach and horses could be put up while their owners enjoyed the town or the races.

These two towns and Warrington were not the only places where business existed. There were also businesses in the country. For example, most of the nails used in the reconstructed Arley Hall were bought in Great Budworth from Thomas Prescot, who also farmed in Aston by Budworth.[66] Tanners, like Thomas Knowles of Appleton, existed in several rural townships.[67] There were more technically complex businesses outside the towns. Cunliff and Stanton's Thelwall mills on the Mersey manufactured gunpowder. It was no doubt the source of some of the gunpowder exchanged for slaves in West Africa. Leigh Glasshouse on the coalfield in Lancashire supplied Sir Peter with 50 dozen dark green wine bottles marked with his crest, the Saracen's Head, at 3s a dozen in July 1755 (Fig. 55). How Sir Peter came to hear that the best flour-sieving machines were made by William Evers in Swillington, near Leeds, we do not know. Anyway, he acquired one as part of his improvements to Arley mills at a cost of 8 guineas in January 1762.

Very few of these businesses had existed in 1650. These notes give an indication of the huge changes that had occurred in the Mersey area between the end of the Civil War and the middle of the eighteenth century.

66 Foster, 1992, p. 28, 58.
67 Ibid., p. 73.

APPENDIX 7.1

*Warburton of Arley, two Dockwra families and Slaughter, 1641–1745**

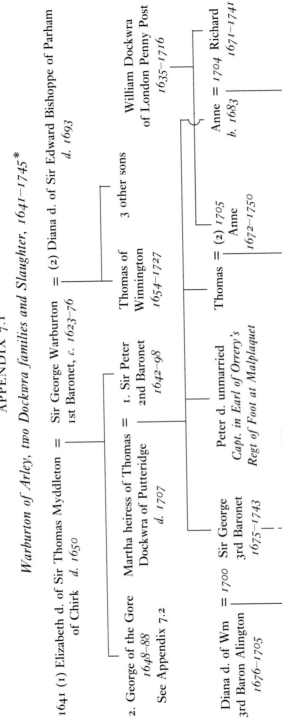

1641 (1) Elizabeth d. of Sir Thomas Myddleton of Chirk d. 1650 = Sir George Warburton 1st Baronet, c. 1623–76 = (2) Diana d. of Sir Edward Bishoppe of Parham d. 1693

William Dockwra of London Penny Post 1635–1716

3 other sons

Thomas of Winnington 1654–1727

Anne b. 1683 = 1704 Richard 1671–1741

George c. 1708–57

2. George of the Gore 1648–88 See Appendix 7.2

Martha heiress of Thomas Dockwra of Putteridge d. 1707 = 1. Sir Peter 2nd Baronet 1642–98

Thomas = (2) 1705 Anne 1672–1750

Peter d. unmarried Capt. in Earl of Orrery's Regt of Foot at Malplaquet

Sir Peter 4th Baronet 1708–74 = 1745 Elizabeth d. of 11th Earl of Derby d. 1780

Thomas Slaughter (natural son) = 1739 Anne 1706–1761

Diana d. of Wm 3rd Baron Alington 1676–1705 = 1700 Sir George 3rd Baronet 1675–1743

Dockwra (son) d. 1706

Diana 1702–30 = 1724 Sir Richard Grosvenor 4th Bt. d. 1732

Sources
1. Parish Registers: Great Budworth, Cheshire; Lilley, Herts; St Olave's Old Jewry, London.
2. WM Boxes 38, 39, 40 and 76, and Clutterbuck, 1827, p. 83.
3. C. Dalton, ed. *English Army Lists*, vol. 5, 1902, p. 263.
* *Many other children omitted for clarity.*

APPENDIX 7.2

The descendants of George Warburton of the Gore, 1648–88

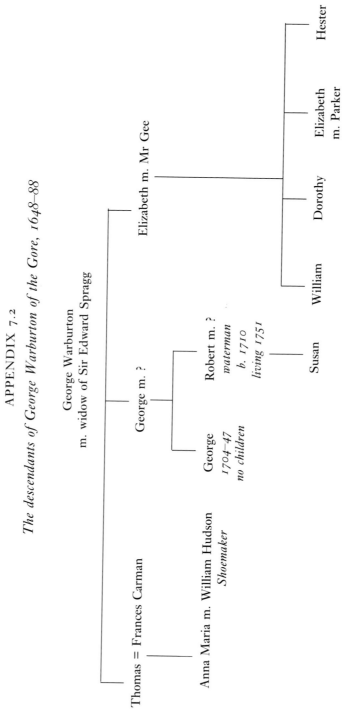

George Warburton
m. widow of Sir Edward Spragg

Thomas = Frances Carman

Elizabeth m. Mr Gee

George m. ?

Anna Maria m. William Hudson
Shoemaker

George
1704–47
no children

Robert m. ?
waterman
b. 1710
living 1751

Susan

William

Dorothy

Elizabeth
m. Parker

Hester

Sources
1. WM Box 24, Folder 9, subfile 4.
2. Arley Large Box 10, item 19.

VIII

Conclusion

The importance of these seven stories is that they provide much more detailed descriptions of the way of life of families in different positions in the social spectrum than are usually available to historians. The accounts of life in the two major gentry families are the least unusual as so much more information survives about the rich. To try to offset this distortion much of the material from their great archives that I have selected describes their contacts with less well-off groups – their employees and their suppliers. However, it is the mass of detail about families such as the Jacksons and the Lathams that is rare. When Thomas Jackson and Richard Latham inherited their three-life leaseholds of 15 and 20 acres respectively they were both about 26 or 27 years old and neither had much more capital than the value of their leasehold. For Jackson it was a springboard from which he was able to increase his wealth to over £1,000. For Latham it just provided enough to bring up his family without want. Both families are seen to have been surrounded by many others in similar circumstances. These stories therefore give us some idea of how the large number of families lived who are shown in rentals and surveys of the major gentry estates in Cheshire and Lancashire as part-owners of small farms.

Socially and economically midway between these three-life leaseholders and the major gentry were the copyholder/freeholders of whom our two examples have been the Shuttleworths and the Fells. In the 1670s the Fells with their 400-acre estate were around 20 times richer than Thomas Jackson, and the Warburtons with their 11,000-acre estate were of the order of 20 times richer than the Fells. The Shuttleworths seem to have owed their early rise to their acquisition of property rights around 1540 and their consequent ability to educate a child in the Law. The large fortune made by Sir Richard Shuttleworth and many other Elizabethan and Jacobean lawyers no doubt owed much to the chaotic position of English land law in the century from 1540 to 1640 when no man could be sure how much of 'his' land he really owned because so much depended on the interpretation of unwritten customs.[1] For example we have seen how Sir Richard had enough legal right to occupy the Smithills estate for 18 years, but he evidently felt his title was not strong enough to be passed to his nephew, so he gave the land back to the Bartons. His other early property investment at Forcett in Yorkshire was probably an example of the more common way in which lawyers became rich. No doubt he bought the land at a price that reflected the rental income of £30 p.a. he received in the 1580s. It will have been worth many times more by 1605 when it was bringing in £260 p.a., and the reasons for the increase are likely to have been connected with the tenure and customs of the tenants. How far such windfalls contributed to the creation of this estate we do not know, but it is interesting to note that it was the decision not to divide Sir Richard's property equally among his six nephews and nieces that allowed a major gentry-type estate to arise at Gawthorpe.

As well as these portraits of families in different economic groups these seven stories illuminate many details about how people in the two counties lived between 1582 and 1774. The information is too diverse to be summarized, but I will try to draw together two of the major aspects. First, all the stories illustrate how the market economy steadily developed over the two centuries. It did this in two ways: one was through technical innovation, the other was by trade which improved the variety, quality or price of the goods on offer. Three of the major technical innovations that have appeared in these stories are the introduction of coal burning in hearths with chimneys at Smithills in the 1590s, the appearance of framework knitting machines in Cheshire in the 1660s and 1670s and the building of the Sankey and Bridgewater canals in the 1750s and 1760s. These were not north-western innovations and inventions, but were introduced from elsewhere. For example, William Harrison tells us that chimneys were built on most of the houses in his Essex village in the 40 years before 1575,[2] but these major changes led to many others; for example, the building of chimneys promoted the use of bricks and mortar; the manufacture of these increased the demand for coal and so stimulated the development of larger and better designed coal mines which in turn encouraged coal-using manufactures like metalworking. We have glimpsed some of these changes in these households.

1 See Foster, 2003, Ch. 3 and Appendix 8.1 for some examples.
2 Edelen, 1968, pp. 200–1.

The other way in which the market economy increased wealth and the standard of living was by trade. At Smithills in the 1580s virtually all food and clothing was produced locally. The importing of cotton into Manchester from the eastern Mediterranean for the production of the fustian that the Shuttleworths bought in 1598 was an early improvement. The most important change after 1650 was probably the great expansion of coastal trading on the west coast, in which we have seen the Fells playing a part. Their sales in Liverpool and Bristol of grain grown in Furness were unusual as the main trade that grew up was in Cheshire cheese sold in London and the return into the Mersey, among many other things, of barley grown on the south coast. This import of a grain which didn't grow well in the north-west created wealth by allowing more land to be devoted to the dairy farming for which the area was climatically suited. The growing impact of trade on the occupations of north-westerners has appeared in many guises; the Latham daughters spun cotton imported from the West Indies and quite likely destined to be sold on the west coast of Africa, and Lady Betty Warburton bought textiles made in many other countries.

The second aspect to be highlighted is the different cultures of the seven households. Two of them, the Leicesters and the Warburtons, were old major gentry families and we have seen great similarities in their way of life. The head of the family lived in the big house and controlled the income of the estate. He was usually employed in Government either locally as a magistrate or nationally as a Member of Parliament. Sir Peter Warburton, 4th Bt, did his public service with the Weaver Navigation.[3] Daughters or sisters received a dowry on marriage which was put in a marriage settlement to provide property rights for their children and an annuity for themselves if they were left as widows. The owner's younger brothers or sons were given small allowances when they became adults and were encouraged to remain on the estate. The second son was often given some legal training at an Inn of Court in London so that he was not wholly unprepared to inherit the estate, but younger sons do not seem to have been encouraged to have any occupation except military service. Even the direct heir to an estate like Peter Warburton was not allowed by his uncle Sir George to play any part in managing the estate. He seems to have lived at Arley on a small allowance without an occupation for the ten

3 Described in Foster, 2003, Ch. 7.

years before he inherited. His way of life in this period was probably similar to that of his first cousin, George Dockwra, who seems to have lived his whole life on a small allowance without an occupation.

The four other families whose households have been described came from less high status and less opulent backgrounds. The Shuttleworth family's lands at Gawthorpe seem to have provided an income of about £1 a year in the early sixteenth century compared with the £94 a year the Leicesters' lands yielded or the £350 a year enjoyed by the Warburtons.[4] We know nothing about the possessions of the other three families at such an early period, but my examination of a 1545 tax return[5] suggests that most families then owned 'goods' of modest value. It is not surprising therefore that these four families had a different culture to that of the landed gentry. Although Sir Richard Shuttleworth was married to a lady who was both a daughter and a widow of major gentry families and they lived together on an old landed estate, he behaved differently. He himself worked at the Law. He bought a rectorship for his middle brother so that he had an occupation and he employed his youngest brother to manage his estate and keep the books. Like the Shuttleworths the members of all the other three families expected to work for their livings all their lives. We see most clearly in the Jackson household how these families divided their wealth fairly equally among all their children – male and female – and the Fells and the Lathams did much the same. Boys were trained in an occupation, and when they were qualified they were given their portions and expected to make their own way in the world.

Traditional English society was dominated by the landed gentry at whose head were the peers who owned the very largest estates. This society was buttressed by the Church and the Law whose leaders had a short period in the highest circles of government at the peak of their careers. The culture of lawyers and clerics was therefore close to that of the gentry. Richard Shuttleworth and Thomas Jackson were at ease in the gentry circles in which they spent much of their lives. When Thomas Jackson put his three sons into business as framework knitters he thought they would be protected from the harsh winds of competition by the ability of their City of London Company to restrict entry to the trade. His own career had flourished under the patronage of Sir Peter Leicester who had secured for him such well paid jobs as Steward of the Hundred Court at

4 See above, p. 56 and Foster, 2003, Chs 2 and 3.
5 Foster, 2003, Ch. 3.

Halton and of the Venables family's Manor Court at Kinderton. He must have thought that the patronage and protection of the Corporation of London were at least as strong, but the Framework Knitters' Company was unable to live up to his expectations and the sons' businesses were destroyed. They had not put their trust in their ability to understand and anticipate developments in the market or to innovate the technology, relying rather on a restrictive practice. It is interesting that their culture was not changed by their adversities. Charles, the brother who re-established himself best, entered the Government service in the Post Office where patronage was rife, and his clever son had a successful career in the Church. His elder brother Thomas's son recovered from poverty as an attorney in Knutsford.

The culture of the Fells and the Lathams was different. The Fells knew that Force Forge and their coastal trading ventures had to be fully competitive with anything that anyone else in Liverpool or Bristol was doing. Richard Latham knew that he could rely on nothing but his own knowledge and judgement when he bought and sold cattle and horses. The development of this 'business' culture was an important feature of North-Western life in the seventeenth and eighteenth centuries. It was much aided by the wide distribution of landed property in the region. In my earlier *Four Cheshire Townships* it is shown that about 194 freeholder and leaseholder families owned about 60% of the capital value of the land in the over 8,000 acres of the four townships around 1750.[6] The two counties were full of small property owners like this and some of them were the businessmen who had created the rich pattern of varied enterprises which were shown in the Warburton accounts to have existed in the Mersey Basin in the 1750s and 1760s. Despite the presence of this large number of small businessmen with their distinctive culture, the history of the descendants of George Warburton of the Gore show that it was difficult for children brought up in the gentry culture of Arley Hall to succeed in business. His two grandsons who were apprenticed to the respectable occupations of vintner and printer both failed to establish themselves and descended into poverty. This large subject of cultural differences and their economic consequences is examined more fully in the final volume of this series.

6 Foster, 1992, Tables 2, 3 and 4, pp. 11-3.

Bibliography

Armitage, G. J. and Rylands, J. P., *The Visitation of Cheshire 1613*, Harleian Soc., Vol. 59, 1909.

Awty, B. G., *Force Forge in the seventeenth century*, Cumberland and Westmoreland Antiquarian and Archaeological Society, Vol. 77, 1977.

Bagley, J. J., *M. Markland of Wigan*, L.C.A.S., Vol. 68, 1958.

Barker, T. C. and Harris, J. R., *A Merseyside Town in the Industrial Revolution: St Helens 1750–1900*, 1954.

Beckman, *Mercantile Papers*, New York Hist. Soc., 3 Vols, 1956.

Chapman, S. D., *The Genesis of the British Hosiery Industry 1660–1750*, Textile History III, pp. 7–50, 1972.

Clutterbuck, R., *History and Antiquities of the County of Hertfordshire*, 1827.

Cox, M., *History of Sir John Deane's Grammar School, Northwich 1557–1908*, 1975.

Crawford, W. H., *The Handloom Weavers and the Ulster Linen Industry*, Ulster Historical Foundation repr. 1994, 1972.

Crosfield, H. G., *Margaret Fox of Swarthmoor Hall*, 1913.

Durie, A. J., *The British Linen Company 1745–1775*, Scottish Hist. Soc., Fifth Series, Vol. 9, 1996.

Edelen, G. (ed.), *William Harrison Description of England*, Cornell Univ. Press, Ithaca, New York, USA, 1968.

Emmison, F. G., *Tudor Secretary. Sir William Petre at court and home*, 1961.

Farrer, W., *The Court Rolls of the Honour of Clitheroe*, Vols 2 and 3, 1912.

Fischer, D. H., *Albion's Seed*, 1989.

Fisher, F. J., *The Development of the London Food Market, 1540–1640*, Econ. Hist. Rev., Vol. 5, No. 2, pp. 46–64, 1935.

Foster, C. F., *Four Cheshire Townships in the 18th Century*, Arley Hall Press, 1992.

Foster, C. F., *Cheshire Cheese and Farming in the North West in the 17th & 18th centuries*, Arley Hall Press, 1998.

Foster, C. F., *Capital and Innovation*, Arley Hall Press, 2003.

Gilboy, Elizabeth W., *Wages in Eighteenth-century England*, Harvard Univ. Press, 1934.

Girouard, M., *Life in the English Country House*, 1979.

Hamilton, Henry, *The English Brass and Copper Industries to 1800*, 1926.

Harland, John (ed.), *The House and Farm Accounts of the Shuttleworths*, Chetham Soc., Vols 35, 41, 43, 46, 1856–8.

Harrison, C. J., *Grain Price Analysis and Harvest Qualities 1465–1634*, Ag. Hist. Rev., Vol. 19, pp. 135–55, 1971.

Horner, John, *Linen Trade of Europe*, Belfast, 1920.

Hoskins, W. G., *Harvest Fluctuations and English Economic History 1480–1619*, Ag. Hist. Rev., Vol. 12, pp. 28–46, 1964.

Hoyle, R. W., *The Estates of the English Crown 1558–1640*, 1992.

Ives, E. W. (ed.), *Letters and Accounts of William Brereton of Malpas*, Record Soc. of L.& C., Vol. cxvi, 1976.

Latham, R. and Matthews, W., *The Diary of Samuel Pepys*, Vol. 8, p. 182, 1971.

Lewis, P., *William Lee's Stocking Frame: Technical Evolution and Economic Viability 1589–1750*, Textile History, Vol. XVII, No. 2, p. 129, 1986.

Marshall J. D. (ed.), *Autobiography of William Stout of Lancaster 1665–1752*, Chetham Soc., Vol. 14, 1967.

Mason, S. A., *The History of the Worshipful Company of Framework Knitters*, Leicester, 2000.

McDonnell, Sir Michael, *The Registers of St Paul's School 1509–1748*, 1977.

Mendenhall, T. C., *Shrewsbury Drapers and the Welsh Wool Trade in the Sixteenth and Seventeenth Centuries*, 1953.

Montgomery, Florence M., *Textiles in America*, W. W. Norton, New York, 1984.

Ormerod, G., *Calendars of visitations of Lancashire* in *'Miscellanies'*, Chetham Soc., Vol. 25, 1851.

Ormerod, G., *The History of the County Palatine and City of Chester*, ed. T. Helsby, 3 Vols, 1882.

Palmer, A. N. and Owen, E., *A History of the Ancient Tenures of Lands in North Wales and the Marches*, pp. 204–11, 1910, 2nd edn.

Penney, N. (ed.), *Household Account Book of Sarah Fell*, 1920.

Pomfret, John E., *The Province of East New Jersey 1609–1702*, Princeton University Press, N.J., U.S.A., 1962.

Rogers, J. E. T., *A History of Agriculture and Prices in England*, Vols 2, 4, 5, 1882–7.

Ross, I., *Margaret Fell, mother of Quakerism*, 1949.

Raines, F. R., *Stanley Papers II*, Chetham Soc., Vol. 31, 1853.

Rylands, J. P., *Visitation of Cheshire 1580*, Harleian Soc., Vol. 18, 1882.

Shipperbotham, R., Introduction to Raffald, Elizabeth, *The Experienced English Housekeeper*, Southover Press, 1997.

Singleton, F. J., *The Flax Merchants of Kirkham*, H.S.L.&C., Vol. 126, pp. 73–108, 1977.

Stephenson, R., *Inquiry into the State and Progress of the Linen Manufacture*, Dublin, 1757.

Tait, J., *Taxation in Salford Hundred*, Chetham Soc., 2nd series, Vol. 83, 1924.

Thirsk, J. (ed.), *Agrarian History of England and Wales*, Vol. IV, 1967.

Todd, Thomas, *William Dockwra and the Rest of the Undertakers*, Edinburgh, 1952.

Weatherill, L. (ed.), *The Account Book of Richard Latham 1724–1767*, 1990.

Willan, T. S., *The Inland Trade: studies in English internal trade in the 16th & 17th centuries*, 1976.

Woodward, D. M., *The Trade of Elizabethan Chester*, 1970.

Wykes, D., *The Origins and Development of the Leicestershire Hosiery Trade*, Textile History, Vol. xxiii, No. 1, pp. 23–54, 1992.

Young, A., A. W. Hutton (ed.), *Arthur Young's Tour in Ireland*, 1776, Vol. 1, pp. 117–61, 1892.

Youngs, D., *Servants and Labourers on a late medieval demesne: the case of Newton, Cheshire 1498–1520*, Ag. Hist. Rev., Vol. 47, Pt. 11, 1999.

Index of names and places

This index also provides additional information about the peers and landed gentry whose names appear in the text.

Bent Farm, Warburton 216
Berry, Edmund, Margery, John 103
Beswick, Jonathon and Ann, of Lower
    Feldy Farm, Aston by Budworth
    175, 179, 214
Bickerstaffe, William 133
Birch, Samuel, of Whitborn,
    Hereforshire 73
    Elizabeth, his wife, b Leicester 73
Bishoppe, Sir Edward of Parham, Sx.
    225
Blackburn, Lancs. 2, 20, 54
Blackrod, township, Lancs. 2, 24–5, 61
Blawith, manor, Lancs. 124
Bolton, Lancs. 2, 24, 61
Bolton, Mr, coal-mine owner, 44–6
Bond, Elin 170
    Thomas 171
Bouteman, John 52
Bowden, Edmund 97
Bradley, Elizabeth, see Jackson
Bradwin, Mr, apothecary 112
Braithwaite, Edward 126
Brasenose College, Oxford, 65, 72
Bredbury, Mr 217
Brereton, Richard 89
    Sir William, of Malpas (d 1536) 19–20
Bridgewater's, Duke of, canal 213
Briggs, Elizabeth 130
Bristol 42, 134–7
Brittan, Edward 126
Brown, Lancelot (Capability) 202
Buckley, Charles 177
Bucklow, Hundred, Ches. 69, 72
Budworth, see Great Budworth
Burgess, Ann 200
    John 196, 204, 206
Burgoyne, John, General 195
    Lady Charlotte, his wife, b Stanley
    195
Burnley, Lancs. 2, 9, 20
Burrows Hall, Cogshall, in Whitley
    Lordship, Ches. 47, 69
Burrows, Tom 85

Bury, Lancs. 2, 20
Buttering, Henry 79
Buxton, Derby. 195, 213
Byfield, Thomas 190, 201
Byrom, Edward 212
Byron, John Byron, 1st Baron of
    Newstead, Notts. 68–70, 74, 87
    Eleanor, his wife, b Needham 69–70,
    87

Caldwell, John 155
    Mary, mantua-maker 200
Calow, Ann 130
Cann Lane Farm, Appleton 102–3
Cartell, Alexander 27
Chaddock, coal-mine, Lancs. 213
Chester 2, 42, 50–1, 65, 79, 102, 107,
    111
Chipping Campden, Glos. 111
Chorley, Lancs. 2, 177
Christ Church, Oxford 70, 84, 96
Clare, Mary 199
Clarkson, Alice 157
Clitheroe, Lancs. 2, 46, 50
Co(u)lthurst, Abraham 39, 55
Cockett, Margery 29
Colne, Lancs. 2, 20
Congleton, Ches. 104
Conishead Priory, Lancs. 122
Cook, Edward 139
    Hannah, his dau, see Fell
Coppock, family 100, 114
Coppoe, Joseph 170
Cornwall 135
Cottrell, Peter 177
Coward, Henry 133, 136
Cragge, John 85
    Will 85
Cramton, John 27
Cranage Green, Ches. 2, 219
Crofts, Francis 141
Croome Court, Worcs. 202
Cross Farm, Appleton 102–3
Crosse, Mrs 37

Christian, his dau, *see* Jackson
?, framework knitter 97, 105
Stedman, William 221
Steele, Lawrence 91–2
  Ned 85
Stockton Heath, Appleton 2, 212–13
Stoke-on-Trent, Staffs. 221–3
Stone Pit Green, coal-mine, Lancs. 213
Stones, John 21
  Peter 14
  Robert and his wife 18–19
  Richard 53
Stourbridge, Worcs. 42, 50
Strafford, Thomas Wentworth, 1st Earl,
    Ld.-Lieut. of Ireland (d 1641) 74
Strange, Ferdinand Stanley, Lord
    Strange, as heir of Earl of Derby
    55
  James Stanley, Lord Strange, as heir
    of Earl of Derby 195
Stretch, John 119
Stretton, township, Ches. 69, 219, 221
Sudlow, hamlet in Over Tabley, Ches.
    80
Sunner, James 157, 170
Sutton, James 213
  Thomas 214
  Sir Richard (d 1524) 65n
Swarthmoor Hall, Furness 120–8, 139–40
Swillington, Yorks. 224
Swinton, Peter, farmer 206
Swinton, Peter, stationer 82

Tabley Hall and Chapel, Ches. 2, 3,
    65, 69, 71–2, 74–80, 82–3, 85–6,
    91, 95–6, 107
Tarleton, Ralph 82
Tarvin, Ches. 2, 178
Taylor, William, of Aberdeen 132
  Elin 163
  James 213
  Hannah 207
Tilley, Thomas and family, of
    Appleton township 210

Tingreave Farm, Eccleston, Lancs. 2,
    14–21
Toft Hall 80
Tomson, Thomas 158
Tonge, Ann 38
Tootall, Bridget 199
Topping, Thomas 196
Townson, Henry 129
Trinity College, Cambridge 112
Trinity College, Oxford 186
Tubman, John 133
Turner, Adam 15
Twisse, Randle 103

Ulverston, Furness 120, 124, 127–8
Unsworth, Peter 27
Urmeston, Richard 42, 54

Valentine, Henry 145
Venables, John, of Agden, Ches. 74
  Byron, his wife, b Leicester 73–4, 110
  family, Barons of Kinderton, Ches.
    96
Vernon (Varnon), cousin of T. Jackson
    92

Walker, James, fuller 130–1
  Humphrey 211
  Ned 85
  Reginald 133
Walney, Isle of, Furness 134
Walnut Tree Farm, Appleton 102–3
Walton, John 214
**Warburton, Peter, of Arley (d 1626)
    34, 59
  part genealogy of family 225
  Peter, c. 1621–c. 1640, elder
    brother of 1st Bt, 70, 87
  Sir George, of Arley, 1st Bt, 71–2,
    186, 217, 225
  Elizabeth, his first wife, b
    Myddleton 186, 225
  George, of the Gore, their
    second son 181, 186, 226**

244

Subject index